Captain Marvel and the Art of Nostalgia

CAPTAIN MARVEL
and the Art of Nostalgia

Brian Cremins

UNIVERSITY PRESS OF MISSISSIPPI / JACKSON

www.upress.state.ms.us

The University Press of Mississippi is a member of the Association of American University Presses.

Cover design, frontispiece, and dedication page drawings by Keiler Roberts. © 2016 Keiler Roberts

∞

Library of Congress Cataloging-in-Publication Data

Names: Cremins, Brian, author.
Title: Captain Marvel and the art of nostalgia / Brian Cremins.
Description: Jackson : University Press of Mississippi, [2016] | Includes bibliographical references and index.
Identifiers: LCCN 2016024727 (print) | LCCN 2016025453 (ebook) | ISBN 9781496808769 (hardback) | ISBN 9781496808776 (epub single) | ISBN 9781496808783 (epub institutional) | ISBN 9781496808790 (pdf single) | ISBN 9781496808806 (pdf institutional)
Subjects: LCSH: Captain Marvel (Fictitious character) | Beck, C. C. (Charles Clarence), 1910–1989. | Binder, Otto O. (Otto Oscar), 1911–1975. | Comic books, strips, etc.—United States. | BISAC: LITERARY CRITICISM / Comics & Graphic Novels. | SOCIAL SCIENCE / Popular Culture. | BIOGRAPHY & AUTOBIOGRAPHY / Artists, Architects, Photographers.
Classification: LCC PN6728.C365 C74 2016 (print) | LCC PN6728.C365 (ebook) | DDC 741.5/973—dc23
LC record available at https://lccn.loc.gov/2016024727

British Library Cataloging-in-Publication Data available

For my grandmother, Patricia Budris Stango
(March 1, 1913–October 15, 1995)

CONTENTS

ACKNOWLEDGMENTS

Billy Batson was a heroic kid with plenty of magical powers, but he also had a lot of friends: his sister Mary, his buddy Freddy Freeman (also known as Captain Marvel, Jr.), Uncle Marvel, Mr. Tawny, and, of course, the mysterious wizard Shazam. In writing this book, I've followed Billy's example, as I've reached out to colleagues, friends, and strangers for help and insights. Any errors, of course, are mine. I'd like to welcome all the folks I list here as honorary members of the Captain Marvel Club. Without their generosity and support, the book you are now holding, about a little boy and his comic book daydreams, would not exist.

I like to think of Billy's subway tunnel, the place where he first meets Shazam, as a magical archive, one founded, of course, on the wisdom of Solomon. About fifteen years ago, I first got the idea for this book after discovering a batch of cheap *Shazam!* comics from the 1970s at one of Hal Kinney's comic book conventions at the Elks Hall in East Hartford, Connecticut. I started attending those conventions in the 1980s. Those shows, and my early experiences at Jim's Comic Book Shop on East Main Street in Waterbury, laid the foundation for the research that made this study possible.

I began more formal work on Captain Marvel at the Comic Art Collection curated by Randall Scott at Michigan State University. Thanks to Randy and his staff for tracking down obscure clippings and fanzines devoted to C. C. Beck (and thanks also to Randy for inviting me to play drums with him in his office after a long day of archival work).

A number of other librarians and archivists assisted me as I searched for material on Beck, Otto Binder, and Fawcett. I would like to thank Susan Kurzmann at the George T. Potter Library at Ramapo College of New Jersey; Greg Plunges, Trina Yeckley, and Kevin Reilly at the National Archives in lower Manhattan; April Pittman at the University of Illinois Chicago's Richard J. Daley Library; Jenny Reibenspies at Texas A&M University's Cushing Memorial Library; the archivists at the National Records and Archives Administration in Washington, DC, for their assistance in locating the Army War Show records from 1942; and Tim Philbin, our interlibrary loan wizard at the

Harper College Library. When I told Tim that I was working on a project about Billy Batson, he replied, "That's the kid who's friends with the talking tiger, right?" I knew I'd be in good hands.

Given the ephemeral nature of many of the texts that form the basis of my research, I must also thank the small bookstores and comic book shops that provided me with materials and expertise on all things Captain Marvel and Fawcett. Jack Delaney at My Mother Threw Mine Away in Torrington, Connecticut, always had a box of Fawcett comics waiting for me when I'd visit. Craig Ferguson at Legends of Superheros [*sic*] in Middlebury answered my questions about The Shadow and The Avenger. Many of the Otto/Eando Binder books listed in the Works Cited come from William Fiedler at the Gallery Bookstore on Clark and Belmont in Chicago. Alli Alleman at Graham Cracker Comics shared her memories of the character and located some essential but hard-to-find back issues.

My students and colleagues at Harper College have offered enthusiastic support for my research on comics and popular culture. Thank you to Jennifer Berne, Kurt Hemmer, Rich Johnson, Greg Herriges, Richard Middleton-Kaplan, Meg King, Brian Knetl, Lisa Larsen, Tara Mister, Judi Nitsch, Sue Borchek Smith, and Pearl Ratunil (who once pointed out a few similarities between Beck's Captain Marvel and Seth's *Palookaville* that got me thinking). Lisa Larsen put me in touch with Betty Hull, Emeritus Professor of English at Harper and a science fiction scholar. She and her late husband, Frederik Pohl, kindly answered my questions about Otto Binder.

The Sabbatical Committee and the Harper College Board of Trustees granted me the gift of time—more valuable, I think, than any magic word—in the summer and fall of 2015. Kurt Neumann, Chris Padgett, Jeff Przybylo, Dr. Judy Marwick, and Dr. Kenneth Ender all offered advice on my sabbatical application.

Along the way, several other writers and scholars generously took the time to speak with me about Captain Marvel, comics, memory, and nostalgia: Jake Austen, my cousin Patty Budris, Michael Chaney, John Cochran, Doug Ellis, Bob Ingersoll, Denis Kitchen, Laurie Lindeen, Alan Moore, Denny O'Neil, Enrico Riley, Bill Schelly, Kerry Soper, Tom Spurgeon, Carol Tilley, James Vance, and Dan Yezbick. Dr. Gloria Arfelis provided invaluable assistance and advice on the World War II chapter, as did the late Emil A. Petke, who once told me to write carefully about my surroundings and the history that had shaped them.

A superhero needs a dramatic origin story, but a writer needs a good editor. I've been lucky to work with John Lent at the *International Journal of Comic Art*; Anne Elizabeth Moore at the *Los Angeles Review of Books*; Frank Bramlett, Roy T. Cook, and Aaron Meskin from *The Routledge Companion to Comics*; Roy Thomas and P. C. Hamerlinck at *Alter Ego/Fawcett Collectors of America*; and Ed Piacentino, Judith Yaross Lee, and John Bird at *Studies in American Humor*. An earlier version of a portion of Chapter 3 appeared as "'What Manner of Man Is He?': Humor and Masculine Identity in Captain Marvel's World War II Adventures" in *Studies in American Humor*, New Series 3, no. 27 (2013), 33–62.

I'd like to single out Roy and Paul for special mention here. Both have encouraged me to find my voice in the numerous essays I've written for them over the last few years. My articles in *Fawcett Collectors of America* provided a starting point for ideas I develop throughout the book, especially in Chapters 2 and 3. Paul has generously shared memories of his friend C. C. Beck and copies of the essays he's written about Captain Marvel and the history of Fawcett. As you will find in reading this book, Roy and Paul's work, which has kept the memories of Captain Marvel, Otto Binder, and C. C. Beck alive, is a cornerstone of my research.

If reading this book inspires you to learn more about Billy Batson and those who created him, you'll find a treasure of other texts waiting for you. My study builds on the scholarly example set by Bill Schelly, Richard Lupoff, John G. Pierce, and Trina Robbins. Captain Marvel's story, like Billy's subway tunnel, has many corridors, each filled with fascinating articles, essays, and books about the character and his long history.

At the 2012 Louisiana Book Festival, Steve Yates asked if I had anything I'd like to pitch. Working with the University Press of Mississippi has been a pleasure. Thank you to Walter Biggins, Kristi Ezernack, Katie Keene, John Langston, Courtney McCreary, and my excellent and supportive editor, Craig Gill. The anonymous readers at *Studies in American Humor* and at the Press responded to the early drafts of what you are now holding and made suggestions that have shaped its final form. I would also like to thank copyeditor (and fellow Orson Welles fan) Peter Tonguette for his meticulous and thoughtful copyedits.

I wouldn't have been at the Louisiana Book Festival in 2012 talking about Walt Kelly if it weren't for Brannon Costello, who got me writing again when he and Qiana Whitted asked for a contribution to *Comics and the U.S. South*. Brannon, Gina, Nora, and Josie always make us feel welcome when we visit Baton Rouge. When I put another band together, I'm calling on Brannon and Qiana to get in the van with me. Randy Scott can bring his guitar. Be ready for it.

In my second year of grad school at the University of Connecticut, I met two fellow students whose writing and comradeship changed the course of my academic life. Thank you to Charles Hatfield and to Gene Kannenberg, Jr., for their continued friendship and support. At UConn, I studied with Clare

Eby, who continues to support my work and kindly offered suggestions on this book when it was still in the proposal stage. Two of my former University of Connecticut office mates, Richard Hodge and Barbara Campbell, also deserve thanks for the (typewritten) letters, phone calls, holiday zines, and texts about prog rock and doom metal. As an undergraduate at Dartmouth, I was privileged to study with Melissa Zeiger, Peter A. Bien, and William W. Cook, all of whom encouraged me to keep writing even when I was turning in messy, off-topic papers about punk rock and comic books. At Dartmouth, I also met Shiamin Kwa, my friend and fellow comics scholar, who has been encouraging me as a writer since our first-year undergrad seminar course.

In early 2014, Harlan Ellison and I talked for an hour about Beck, Binder, and Captain Marvel. He then carefully edited the transcript of that interview, later published in *Alter Ego*. That experience was a miniature seminar in creative writing. Thank you, Mr. Ellison, for those phone calls, for your writing, and for your kindness. Thanks also to Jason Davis at Harlan Ellison Books and to Susan Ellison for facilitating that interview.

At a conference in St. Louis, Trina Robbins reminded me that, although the magic word *Shazam*, as Jules Feiffer once put it, only seems to work for Billy, we each have one of our own. We just need to search for it. I'd like to thank Trina for sharing her memories of and correspondence with her friend C. C. Beck. She's been a champion of this research from the start.

I often joke that, while I like comics a lot, I *love* music, and I've been blessed with bandmates who've taken an interest in my academic work. As any musician will tell you, it's tough to find a good rhythm section, but I've been lucky, and without the love and friendship of my late drummer and friend Andy Cayon, I wouldn't have made it through grad school or developed the confidence I needed to tackle this project. Meanwhile, Tris Carpenter and I still trade secrets about old Sunn amps and slide guitars. Poet, drummer, and teacher Tony Trigilio keeps weekly tabs on my progress and, at every stage of this project, has offered his help and his advice (as well as his incandescent Jaki Liebezeit-like beats). Wayne Sefton, Rich Hay, and Jack Mohr at Midwest Buy & Sell have kept me supplied with Fenders, Gretsches, Guilds, and Rickenbackers, while never failing to ask, "How's the book going? Aren't you done yet?"

Keiler Roberts drew and designed this book's beautiful cover, an image that introduces many of the themes I explore in the following pages. She also contributed the pencil sketch that appears as the frontispiece and the drawing of my grandmother on the dedication page. I can't thank Keiler enough for her comics, her art, and her friendship.

My father, the Honorable William T. Cremins, has been my research assistant on this comic book adventure for four decades now. When writing about a complex case like the *National v. Fawcett* battle, it helps to have an attorney and a judge in the family. But he was there long before that trip to the National Archives in the summer of 2014. Loving and steadfast, he's been with me from those walks to the spinner-rack at the 7–11 on Davis Street in Oakville to the Illustration, Comics, and Animation Conference at Dartmouth ("Comics are pretty big now, aren't they?" he asked). When I was a kid, my mom, Nancy Cremins, wrote and drew little stories that I'd try to copy. I learned to love reading and writing from her, especially when she'd play Cat Stevens, Crosby, Stills, & Nash, or Donna Summer records and insist that I listen carefully to the *words*. She and my sister Alison are the other scholars in the family, the keepers of our history, the oracles. Chapter 3, as I mention later, is a conversation of sorts with my maternal grandparents, Nunzio Stango and Patricia Stango, and with other members of my family who lived through World War II, especially my great uncle, Vincent J. Budris, and my great aunts, Annie Grigoraitis and Julia Budris.

Allison Felus read and edited every word of this book before I even knew it was a book. She also made sure that I ate, wrote songs, and went to the record store after I'd been staring at the computer screen too long. Her love, and her magic, are at the heart of what I do.

And what would a day of writing and listening to Brian Eno be without my two furry friends, Rocky and Rosie, and their silent companionship? (Well, they're mostly silent, except when they're hungry.)

I wrote this book because of my admiration and affection for the comics of Otto Binder and C. C. Beck. I hope that, after reading it, you seek out their work, and that you find it as wonderfully strange, compelling, and complex as I do.

And that magic word? Well, as Trina Robbins has said, you'll have to discover that for yourself.

A NOTE ON AUTHORSHIP

Like other publishers in the 1940s and early 1950s, Fawcett rarely included credits for their writers and artists in their comic books. C. C. Beck was a notable exception, as he sometimes received a byline as "Chief Artist" on the comics he drew with his assistants. Otto Binder, writing under his pseudonym *Eando Binder*, also received credit for the Jon Jarl text pieces that appeared in *Captain Marvel Adventures*, but he did not receive billing as one of Captain Marvel's writers. In Chapter 1, I focus on two stories that Beck, as he noted in later essays and interviews, wrote and drew on his own. In order to discuss how Beck applied his theories of comic art, I felt it necessary to focus on narratives where he was responsible for the *complete* work of bringing a script to life—that is, providing the layouts, pencils, inks, and, often, even the letters. Chapter 2 includes an analysis of Otto Binder's Mr. Tawny stories, a series that he discusses in his letter to *Alter Ego* in 1964 ("Special!" 111). According to Beck's 1977 interview with Chris Padovano, he provided the art for the majority of those stories, most likely with his longtime collaborator Pete Costanza. In Chapters 3 and 4, I shift my focus from Beck and Binder and the personal touches in their work to an analysis of the themes and the cultural impact of Captain Marvel's wartime adventures. In order to meet the demand for the character, Fawcett, as I discuss in Chapter 1, employed art studios like the one founded by Beck and Costanza. Read Beck's "Shop Talk" interview with Will Eisner or "What's Behind That Comic Cover?" in Don Maris's "best of" collection for information on the assembly-line-like system used to produce those comics. Where possible, I have included footnotes with information on the writers and artists that might have worked on those comics from the early 1940s. For more information on story credits for those issues, visit the Grand Comics Database online. DC's *Shazam! Archives,* and the company's various reprint collections of Fawcett's stories, also include credits for some of Captain Marvel's early adventures.

A NOTE ON CITATIONS AND IMAGE SCANS

Fawcett was inconsistent in their use of page numbers in their comics. Where possible, I have included citations with page numbers from the stories I analyze. Stories from the late 1940s and into the 1950s, however, like the Mr. Tawny ones, are not paginated. Meanwhile, some of the scans, especially those for hard-to-find (or prohibitively expensive) comics from the early 1940s, come from various reprint editions and collections. Unless otherwise noted, however, I have scanned all of the images in this book from the original comics. Now several decades old, these books are often delicate and brittle, so you may notice flaws in some of those images, including rips and tears, marks left by those who read and enjoyed these comics in the first place.

Captain Marvel and the Art of Nostalgia

"TINY FLASHES OF LIGHT"

Comic Books, Nostalgia, and Billy Batson's America

It all starts with a kid and his books.

On March 18, 1948, Wallace H. Martin, an attorney for Fawcett Publications, asked editor and writer Bill Parker to recall the steps leading to the creation of a character who, after a few revisions, would capture the imagination of young readers in the 1940s as Captain Marvel. Parker was testifying on behalf of Fawcett, which had been sued by National Comics Publications, Inc., for copyright infringement. Captain Marvel looked and behaved, they claimed, especially in his early appearances, a little too much like Jerry Siegel and Joe Shuster's Superman, that heroic alien being from another world.[1] The character, Parker maintained, was not inspired by Superman, but by another set of popular myths. "Where did you get the idea of someone being a leader of men?" Martin asked. And what about the boy hero with a secret past? The old wizard? Magic spells, mysterious villains? No, not Superman. Parker replied, "Specifically I got it from the Stories of King Arthur and the Knights of the Round Table, stories with which I had been familiar and had read as a child" (Parker 692).[2]

After a few more questions about Parker's background and his duties at Fawcett, Martin asked again about the writer's love of King Arthur. "Is this a book of yours?" The attorney passed a copy of *Stories of the King* to the witness.[3] "Yes, it is," Parker replied. "When did you get that book?" Martin asked. "When I was a small boy" (Parker 737). It's a startling and poignant image: a man in his forties, testifying in a copyright infringement case between two of the largest and most influential comic book publishers of the day, holding a relic from his childhood. "We do not have to have that in evidence," the judge assured Parker (738).

Other writers have told the story of Captain Marvel's origin, his popular success, and his gradual decline.[4] The narrative of the lawsuit and the eventual settlement between Fawcett and National would fill a book all its own. There are many tales to tell about the original Captain Marvel, the one created by Parker and artist C. C. Beck with guidance from Fawcett Editorial Director Ralph Daigh and suggestions from artist Pete Costanza. The one in this book is about the relationship between the medium of comics, the lure of nostalgia, and the art of memory. "The real secret of the success of Captain Marvel," Beck wrote in 1988, "which few people recognized, was that Billy Batson *told* about Captain Marvel's exploits over his radio and television programs" (Beck, "Real Facts"). Although his magic word enables him to become a superhero, Billy is also a not-so-distant relative of other daydreamers of twentieth-century American literature: Jay Gatsby, Walter Mitty, even Willy Loman—although Billy, of course, is a far less tragic figure than any of them. He is, after all, a boy in a comic book, a wizard's apprentice, with a talking tiger as a friend. "As far as anyone ever knew," Beck noted, "Billy may have made up every story he ever told over the air" ("Real Facts"). Billy's America is a landscape of nostalgia, one filled with a longing for the hidden, the vanished, and the forgotten. It is strange, then, that some of the best and most detailed accounts of the character's origin appear in the court records of the *National v. Fawcett* case. Billy may have lived the daydreams he shared with his readers, but he was not immune to poverty, war, racism, and lawsuits.

For some comic book readers who came of age in the 1940s and 1950s, the legal dispute that ended Captain Marvel's career is a marker of lost innocence, another sign, along with Fredric Wertham's *Seduction of the Innocent*, that the Golden Age of comic books in the United States had come to an abrupt and unfortunate end. "It would have done me no good to discover two of my idols," writes Jules Feiffer in *The Great Comic Book Heroes*, "staunch believers in direct action, bent over, hands cupped to lips, whispering in the ears of their lawyers. No one should have to grow up that fast" (Feiffer 25). Although Superman's publisher first sued Fawcett in 1941, a decision in the case did not come until 1950, when Judge Alfred Conkling Coxe, Jr., summarized a decade's worth of depositions, evidence, and testimony (Steranko 17, Ingersoll 21). Portions of that decision read like an article in a comic book fanzine, as Coxe lists the names and attributes of characters that remain familiar icons in American popular culture. Although Superman and Captain Marvel would not meet in the pages of a comic book until the 1970s,[5] they'd already shared space in Coxe's ruling. Both heroes, he noted, have "clean-cut faces" and "wear the conventional regalia of the gymnast or circus acrobat" as they exhibit "marvelous strength and speed" in their adventures.[6] Captain Marvel, however, lacked the "romantic element" of the Superman stories. There was no Lois Lane in Billy's universe, but he made up for that absence with "an ever-present evil enemy," the mad scientist Dr. Thaddeus Bodog Sivana.[7] At times,

Coxe sounds (inadvertently) like a dedicated comic book fanboy. Who's got the better villains? The sharper costume? Who'd win in a fight?

At other times, the judge writes like a comics scholar. What is a comic book, anyway? How do we read it? Why are they so appealing? Coxe explains that "panels are not used merely to illustrate the text," but work "together with the explanatory text" and therefore "constitute the literary work—the story intended to be depicted." The depositions and courtroom testimony in the case, typed on fragile onionskin paper, fill ten boxes at the National Archives in lower Manhattan. Those papers include other statements and observations like these—what comics are, how writers and artists worked in collaboration to produce them, the sorts of effects made possible when combining words and pictures. But the attorneys for National and Fawcett were not conducting a seminar on comic art or researching a treatise on the state of the medium. They wanted an answer to what appeared to be a simple question: had Fawcett infringed on National's copyright?

Yes and no. Despite the pages and pages of testimony—the "claimed similarities and dissimilarities between the portrayals of the two characters, their facial appearances, costumes, etc."—Coxe was "satisfied from all the evidence that there was actual copying." Although it appeared that National might win, the judge had his doubts about the legitimacy of the company's copyright on Superman. Because of questions related to the Superman newspaper comic strip, National lost the case. Although they would soon appeal Coxe's decision, Captain Marvel was safe, at least for now.

What happened? The answer to that question involves National's relationship with the McClure Newspaper Syndicate. From Coxe's perspective, the two companies had embarked on a "joint venture," that is, "an association of two or more persons to carry out a single business enterprise for profit"[8]—in this case, to create and distribute comic strips based on Siegel and Shuster's popular hero. McClure failed again and again to include copyright notices on the Superman strips. Some strips included those notices, but others did not. McClure's lack of consistency would cost National dearly. As far as Coxe was concerned, "the publication of the McClure syndicated newspaper strips resulted in the abandonment by plaintiff of the copyrights on the 'Action Comics' stories." In other words, Superman was now in the public domain. Suddenly, whether or not Fawcett had copied Superman was beside the point. As Bob Ingersoll points out in his article about the lawsuit, Coxe's decision had potentially devastating consequences: "Literally anyone could publish Superman stories" if the ruling were allowed to stand "and there wouldn't be a thing that National could do about it" (Ingersoll 22). If National, because of their relationship with McClure, "had abandoned its copyright on Superman" (Ingersoll 22), the company had no grounds to sue Fawcett. A year later, the

Second Circuit Court of Appeals reversed Coxe's ruling. National must have been relieved, but their attorneys were still looking for an answer to the question of Fawcett's alleged infringement. Judge Learned Hand wrote the appellate decision in August 1951.

Hand and the two other judges who heard the case were skeptical of Coxe's logic. If National had intended to abandon its copyright on Superman, why would they have included copyright symbols on comic books featuring the character? For that matter, only *some* of the McClure strips lacked the proper copyright symbols. McClure "had no conceivable purpose in allowing its rights to lapse."[9] Besides, a "'joint venture,'" Hand noted, is "incidentally one of the most obscure and unsatisfactory of legal concepts."[10] Although the appellate decision saved Superman from the public domain—a fate far worse than anything dreamed up by Lex Luthor, at least from National's point of view—the question of whether or not Fawcett would have to pay damages was left unanswered. Like a good comic book serial, the case moved from one cliffhanger to the next.

National's legal team, headed by attorney Louis Nizer, filed a petition asking the Second Circuit Court to clarify its decision. Judge Hand did so, on September 5, 1952, but the results were not what National or even Fawcett had hoped. In order to pursue further action, National would have to provide *specific* examples of infringement. "Each such comparison really involves the decision of a separate claim; there is no escape from it," Hand wrote in his clarification: "The plaintiff may put in suit as many strips as it pleases, but it must prove infringement of each, or it will lose as to that strip."[11] While National was ready to continue the fight, Fawcett no longer saw any financial incentive in defending their star hero for another decade or more. "Further than the foregoing we refuse to go," Hand wrote in the conclusion of his clarification. Fawcett seemed to agree. The company settled with National for, according to Michael Uslan's and Ingersoll's accounts, about $400,000 (Uslan, "When Titans" 10; Ingersoll 23; see also Steranko 21). It would no longer publish Captain Marvel comic books. Later, Captain Marvel writer Otto Binder described this decision as "canny business" on Fawcett's part because it ended up "saving enormous court costs" in what appeared to be "a dying cause" (Binder qtd. in Steranko 21).

My version of the Captain Marvel story begins here at the end of his otherwise successful career as one of the best-selling comic book heroes of the 1940s. It's easy to imagine Captain Marvel, like Charles Foster Kane or Richard Harris's King Arthur, looking over the ruins of his once-prosperous kingdom, puzzled and alone, wondering what to make of this "dying cause." Captain Marvel's creators and his fans felt this sense of loss, too. Billy's adventures, most of them written by Binder, were, as Jim Steranko once described them,

0.1 Billy witnesses his past thanks to Shazam's Historama, "a super-television screen capable of depicting past, present and future events," from *Whiz Comics* no. 2 (February 1940). Script by Bill Parker and art by C. C. Beck. Reprinted in *The Shazam! Archives* volume 1 (23). Captain Marvel and related characters © 2016 DC Comics.

"once-upon-a-timers," the kind of "folksy, low-key adventures" that appealed so strongly to readers in the 1940s (Steranko 15). As a character rooted in the myth of King Arthur, perhaps Captain Marvel's demise was both inevitable and fitting. No fairy tale, no matter how magical, ought to last forever.

In his book *Supergods*, Grant Morrison argues that Billy Batson's "power came from a spell. He was a magician" (Morrison 32). Billy's "power," as Beck himself once described it, is a result of "fun magic," abilities made possible "by a benevolent old wizard with a long beard" who resembled "a cross between Moses and Santa Claus" (Beck, "Real Facts"). But Billy's "magic," like that of the comics medium itself, also lies in its uncanny ability to document and interrogate memory itself. Before Shazam gives Billy the word that activates the young orphan's powers, the two watch Billy's past unfold on "a super-television screen" called a Historama. That machine is like a comic book in miniature, a device "capable of depicting past, present and future events," often simultaneously (fig. 0.1).

In each of these two panels, we are looking over Billy's shoulder. Like the protagonist in Delmore Schwartz's "In Dreams Begin Responsibilities," Billy watches his tragic origin, but he is unable to lift a hand to stop it. He, and the reader, can only observe each panel-within-a-panel. As a visual medium, comic books demand that we open our eyes, that we see with greater clarity. That clarity can only come as a result, in this case, of an understanding of the demands that history makes on us. Reading is a form of magic, of time travel. The past, no longer fixed, appears to be infinite in meaning. None of this would be possible, however, without an ending of some sort. For Billy, it's the loss of his parents and his uncle's cruelty. For readers, it's Captain Marvel's disappearance from newsstands and drugstores. That end point inspires feelings of nostalgia as we seek to recover the lost, the neglected, and the seemingly impossible.

While the original Captain Marvel—at least the one written by Otto Binder and drawn by C. C. Beck—would never return, the writers and artists who worked on his adventures and the readers who enjoyed them remembered him long after he was gone.[12] Writer and editor Richard Lupoff, one of those fans, has described Captain Marvel as a kind of phantom still "making ghostly guest appearances" in the pages of DC Comics, formerly National Comics Publications, which now, along with its parent company Time Warner, owns the rights to the character and to Fawcett's other heroes (Lupoff, "Introduction" 9). In that same essay, an introduction to Bill Schelly's comprehensive biography of Otto Binder, Lupoff echoes the sentiment of other Captain Marvel fans when he admits that he has "doubt that we will ever again see anything to match those grand adventures" of the 1940s, stories which he calls "treasures all their own" (9), an archive of work that, despite its tremendous popularity seventy years ago, has generated only a small body of scholarship and criticism. That body of work begins with Lupoff's groundbreaking essay "The Big Red Cheese," first published in 1960 in the science fiction fanzine *Xero* and later included in the collection *All in Color for a Dime*, edited by Lupoff and Don Thompson in 1970. A significant figure in the history of comic books in the United States, Captain Marvel also plays a central role in several histories of the medium, from Les Daniels's *Comix: A History of Comic Books in America* and *The Steranko History of Comics* to Bradford W. Wright's *Comic Book Nation* and Gerard Jones's *Men of Tomorrow*. It is my hope that this book will inspire other scholars and critics to investigate Fawcett's rich legacy.

I have divided this study into three sections, each devoted to a different aspect of Captain Marvel, his creators, and his impact on popular culture in the United States. The first two chapters focus on C. C. Beck and Otto Binder. As the co-creator of one of the best-selling characters of the 1940s, Beck is a fascinating figure who wrote extensively on the theory and practice of comic book art. While his career as a cartoonist was not as lengthy as that of peers such as Will Eisner and Jack Kirby, Beck remained active in comics fandom until his death in 1989. Although Beck often worked with assistants in the 1940s, most frequently with Pete Costanza, I have focused my analysis on two stories that Beck composed, penciled, and inked on his own. I write in detail about Billy's first appearance in *Whiz Comics* no. 2 (1940) and the first issue of *Fatman, the Human Flying Saucer* (1967), a later collaboration with Binder, to explore how Beck applied his theories in his visual storytelling. In the first chapter, I also discuss Beck's Critical Circle, the group of writers, artists, and fans with whom he corresponded in the two years before his death. A prolific writer, often cantankerous but good-humored, Beck, like Eisner, was an important, if unheralded, artist and critic whose body of work remains one of the great achievements in twentieth century comics in the United States.

Beck's friend and colleague Otto Binder began his career in the early 1930s, writing for science fiction pulps including *Amazing Stories*. Readers might also recognize Binder's name because of his work on Superman in the 1950s and early 1960s, the post-Fawcett phase of his long career chronicled in Schelly's *Words of Wonder* (2003). In Chapter 2, I focus attention on the autobiographical elements in Binder and Beck's Mr. Tawny stories. Tawny, the talking tiger, enabled Binder to reflect on his struggles as a freelance writer making a living in comics and science fiction in the early 1950s. Those tales are among the most delightful in the entire Captain Marvel canon, a mixture of slapstick comedy, animal fable, and first-person confession. Some of Beck and Binder's most enduring work, Tawny's adventures are also a lot of fun— silly, sentimental, and touching all at once.

In Chapters 3 and 4, I consider Beck's theories of comic book art in the context of Billy's World War II adventures and in relation to Steamboat, Billy's other friend, a stereotypical blackface character who appeared as a sidekick until 1945. These two chapters consider the limitations of the "magic" that Beck described ("Real Facts"). In that same Critical Circle essay, Beck asserted that writers like Binder "knew that children, and for that matter most adults, are far more interested in fantasy and magic and outrageous fiction than in facts, which are dull and stupid things" ("Real Facts"). I put Beck's theory to the test in these two chapters as I examine how Fawcett's editors, writers, and artists imagined the violence and terror of World War II. What role did a fantastic hero like Captain Marvel have to play in battles against the Axis? Billy's America, the one revealed in these comic books, is a bleak one: as Satanic forces sweep across Europe, North Africa, and the Pacific, the United States struggles with issues of race and class. The landscape I describe in these two chapters is an ugly one, filled with racist stereotypes of Asian and African Americans, images that also raise significant questions about comics and representation. How did cartoonists of this era imagine the war as the United States entered the conflict? Why were these artists and writers, often progressive in their politics, unable or seemingly unwilling to draw African American characters in as ideal and heroic a form as Billy Batson? These questions remain significant in contemporary discussions of comic art as the form continues to attract increased scholarly and popular interest.

I leave other speculations on the art of comics for the third and final section of the book, in which I draw on contemporary theories of nostalgia from the fields of literary theory and psychology to examine Captain Marvel's impact on the comic book fanzines of the 1960s and early 1970s. While Fawcett's popular hero, at least in his original form as conceived by Parker and Beck and later refined by Otto Binder, ceased to exist after Fawcett settled with National in 1953,[13] Billy inspired numerous fans to write about their memories of their favorite comics and adventures. Essays such as Lupoff's "The Big Red Cheese" are foundational texts for comics studies in the United States, a discipline that, like the growing field of memory studies, has expanded tremendously in the last two decades. My fifth chapter, then, suggests parallels between these two modes of inquiry. A study of the relationship between comics and theories of nostalgia promises to be fruitful not only for other scholars but also for cartoonists fascinated with the history of the medium and its gradual emergence from the drugstores and newsstands of the 1940s to the comic book shops, online debates, and academic archives of today. To understand why comic books or graphic novels are so ideal as a medium for memory and nostalgia, it is also necessary to study the ways in which early innovators like Beck and Binder grappled with questions of identity, autobiography, and mortality. In the final chapter, I map Captain Marvel's history in the fanzines of the 1960s and 1970s, which included numerous first-person accounts of the 1940s and 1950s from Beck, Binder, and their colleagues.

Binder once described the Golden Age of comics in the United States—a convenient if flawed name for an era that begins roughly with the first appearance of Superman in 1938 and ends with *Seduction of the Innocent,* Wertham's study of the alleged links between comic books and juvenile delinquency, in 1954[14]—as a kind of Camelot. In a letter published in the early and influential comics fanzine *Alter Ego* in 1964, Binder, who spent so much of his career imagining the future, offers a warning to those who study the past. As he recalls "those days of yore," Binder describes that "Golden Age" as if it were Arthur's lost kingdom:

> To attempt any sweeping, definitive picture is madness. Only in the tiny flashes of light given by individual anecdotes and recollections of those of us in the field as pros at the time can come any rational picture of what to me is still an incomprehensible rise-and-fall of a great empire—the world of picture-story heroes whose peers will never again be seen. (Binder, "Special!" 112)

Billy Batson's journey is the story of comic books in the United States in miniature, a pop-culture allegory. The character begins as a colorful and intriguing, if derivative, variation on King Arthur and Superman, with hints of Edgar Rice Burroughs's Tarzan and John Carter of Mars (the orphan whose only way out is a life of adventure; the man who dreams himself into another, impossible reality). Slowly, he reaches commercial and aesthetic heights, only to disappear, slowly but inevitably, into relative obscurity after Fawcett's settlement with National. Then, less than a decade later, writers and editors, those who remembered Captain Marvel from their childhoods, begin researching the history of these comics. His story was now theirs as well, one strand in the larger fabric of a personal narrative to be shared with other nostalgic fans and budding comics professionals. There's a danger, of course, in identifying one's point of origin with that of an imaginary character.

In *Times Square Red, Times Square Blue*, Samuel R. Delany, like Binder, warns of the limits of nostalgia, which "presupposes an uncritical confusion between the first, the best, and the youthful gaze (through which we view the first and the best) with which we create origins" (Delany 16). Maybe that confusion is inevitable, even necessary, especially for writers and artists. This uncertainty, that tension between "the first" and "the best," lies at the heart of many studies of nostalgia, even in Johannes Hofer's 1688 dissertation, the text that gave this condition its name.

COMIC BOOKS AND NOSTALGIA

The relationship between nostalgia and the study of comics has long been of interest to critics and scholars. In the introduction to *All in Color for a Dime*, Lupoff and his co-editor, Don Thompson, describe the writer who embarks on an analysis of Golden Age comics as "a three-headed monster" who embodies the qualities of "a misty-eyed nostalgic," "a bibliographically inclined research scholar," and "a social-literary-artistic critic" (Lupoff and Thompson 14–15).[15] As Bart Beaty points out in *Comics Versus Art*, this "second wave" of comic book fans in the US included those "born in the 1930s and 1940s who wrote nostalgically about the comic books that they had read in their formative years" (Beaty 154). Beaty also notes the influence these men and women had "on the general development of organized comics fandom" in the United States, which provided a foundation for the North American comics scholars, including Beaty, Charles Hatfield, Gene Kannenberg, Jr., and Amy Kiste Nyberg—to name just a few—who came of age in the 1990s. What these "second wave" writers of the 1960s often had in common was affection for Captain Marvel and at times even a reverence for Billy's creators. Lupoff and Thompson, for example, dedicated *All in Color for a Dime* to Binder. To write about Captain Marvel, then, it is also necessary to write about the nostalgia these fans had for the character and for the comic books in which he appeared.

Lupoff and Thompson's "three-headed monster" metaphor raises other important questions: Where does nostalgia end and inquiry begin? Are the two distinct? Should they be? How might one inform the other? These questions remain relevant for scholars and critics as a new generation shapes comics studies in books, journal articles, online magazines, blogs, Tumblr accounts, and Twitter feeds. Taking the lead from Billy and his Historama, we might find answers to these questions in the past. As the late film critic Roger Ebert, a frequent contributor to *Xero*, observed, "fanzines were Web pages before there was a Web," just as letter columns "were message threads and bulletin boards before there was cyberspace" (Ebert 10). Given the recent body of work on nostalgia, it is important to define this term carefully and to investigate its legacy in medicine, psychology, and literary history/aesthetics. When we assert that writers like Lupoff or Roy Thomas were *nostalgic* for the past— for childhood memories inextricably tied to comic book heroes like Captain Marvel—what do we mean?

Svetlana Boym's work has shaped my thinking on nostalgia's role in the creation and the study of comic books and other graphic narratives. Boym argues that nostalgia cannot be reduced to any single, satisfactory definition. Drawing on Hofer's 1688 dissertation, she describes this desire as "a sentiment of loss and displacement," one which sometimes leads to "a romance with one's own fantasy" (*Future* xiii). Later in the introduction to her 2001 book, Boym describes nostalgia as a

> rebellion against the modern idea of time, the time of history and progress. The nostalgic desires to obliterate history and turn it into private or collective mythology, to revisit time like space, refusing to surrender to the irreversibility of time that plagues the human condition. (*Future* xv)

Understood from this perspective, nostalgia enables one to imagine other possible realities, ways of being, what Boym refers to as "third-way" thinking in her 2008 book *Architecture of the Off-Modern* (4).

For Boym, that "third-way" or "off-modern" ideology is one whose transformative potential lies partly in its emphasis on *adventure* (Boym, *Architecture* 6). Otto Binder would no doubt have agreed. In his professional correspondence from the 1950s and in his letters to the fan press in the 1960s, Binder emphasized the significance of swashbuckling fantasy in the lives of young readers. Binder's comments, when read through Boym's theoretical lens, might explain why Billy's origin story remains so compelling in its simplicity. "I always stoutly maintained, to all and sundry in those days who sometimes quite viciously attacked the comics (even neighbors and friends) that red-blooded adventure (which comics were) was almost a *necessity* for the young," Binder wrote in 1964 ("Special!" 112). While Binder no doubt had in mind Edgar Rice Burroughs, Rudyard Kipling, and the other writers that first inspired him and his brother Earl to try their hand at science fiction in the 1930s, Boym's thoughts on adventure are based on her reading of sociologist and philosopher Georg Simmel: "Literature and philosophy provide many models of potential spaces—not utopias," she writes, "but an imaginary topography that can offer models for the future" (6). These "potential spaces," Boym suggests, are not possible without passionate acts of the imagination. "Adventure provides a possibility for reverse mimesis" because, Boym explains, "instead of imitating nature" it "offers an architecture of the future" (6).

Although Boym is writing specifically here about the work of Vladimir Tatlin, she notes that both "[l]iterature and philosophy" might be understood as "forms of 'paper architecture'"—that is, they are examples of the "potential spaces" central to her thinking (Boym, *Off-Modern* 6). I would argue that comic books are archives or records of these "spaces," in which protagonists like Billy Batson go in search of a fixed point of origin—perhaps like the one Delany describes in *Times Square Red, Times Square Blue*—that can be accessed only through a willing act of "adventure," which, like nostalgia, "is time out of time; while bounded by its beginning and ending, [adventure] reveals the limitless force and potential of life" (Boym, *Future* 7). The joy that Boym alludes to here is an essential component of Captain Marvel's appeal. For writers like Lupoff, the real magic of Captain Marvel had nothing to do with the wizard Shazam, bolts of lightning, or talking tigers. While a child sees Billy as a peer, a guide, and possibly as a protector, the adult understands Billy and Captain Marvel as doorkeepers who grant access to forgotten or neglected memories.

The late editor and comics critic Kim Thompson recognized the significance of these childhood artifacts in a 1986 essay on the art and appeal of funny animal comics. By "re-reading, re-viewing," and "re-experiencing" books, films, and comics from childhood, Thompson argued, we "*become* [our] former selves, all experiencing the marvels at once" (Thompson n.p.). Consider, for example, the concrete details in recollections of those "second wave" fans, such as Lupoff's memory of a "balmy winter's day nearly 30 years ago, in the sunbaked village of Venice, Florida," where he and his brother ate ice cream and discovered *Whiz Comics* for the first time (Lupoff, "Big Red" 67). In an essay written shortly after Beck's death, Trina Robbins honored her friend and mentor by recalling her "childhood discovery" of Billy Batson's alter ego and, more meaningfully, of his sister Mary, "a *girl*, not a *woman*, with super powers," the star of comic books that proved to be "a pretty major inspiration" on her career as a cartoonist (Robbins, "An Appreciation"). There are many stories like these in fanzines, letter columns, essays, and comic book memoirs: *I remember Captain Marvel*, they say again and again, and, more important, *I remember* who I was *when I first discovered him*. Those memories are often tied to specific places (*nostalgia*, after all, is a form of *homesickness*)—Lupoff's

Florida, *Fawcett Collectors of America* editor P. C. Hamerlinck's memory of a spinner rack at a drugstore (Hamerlinck, "Introduction" 6), Harlan Ellison's "magazine and cigar shop" in Painesville, Ohio (Ellison, "Nay, Never Will I"). Just as Robbins found in Mary Marvel a possible future for herself, Ellison saw in Billy a reflection, a mirror of his fears and of his dreams: "So I was able to identify with Billy's world because I was a small, lone boy in a small town in Ohio" (Ellison, "Nay, Never Will I"). These memories are all strands in what Kim Thompson called "a golden thread strung through the decades," one that leads from a memory of "these works of the imagination" (Thompson n.p.) to the lived reality of the present.

National was right. Captain Marvel's beginnings weren't terribly original. It's an old story, one with parallels to narratives from around the world. Billy's life, that work of comic book fiction, is, like that of his readers, a mystery, a series of accidents, consisting of one unexpected encounter after another. Billy gains his powers after he investigates the corridors and secret passages of his city. Like all great heroes of myth and legend, from Odysseus to King Arthur to Superman, Billy just wants to go home. But, as Boym suggests, often that "home" either "no longer exists or has never existed" (*Future* xiii).

All superhero stories, like all books of memory, have to start somewhere. The records from the lawsuit, and the articles written by fans and collectors, tell only a small part of Billy's history. His America began in Fawcett's New York offices, where, in the fall of 1939, Ralph Daigh approached Bill Parker with a new assignment.

THE ORIGIN OF CAPTAIN MARVEL

By the late 1930s, Bill Parker, a Princeton graduate, had worked as a reporter, writer, and editor for almost a decade. After spending time at the *New York Herald-Tribune* and at *Literary Digest*, he took a position at Fawcett in 1937, where he served as coordinating editor for *Movie Story Magazine*.[16] With Fawcett about to enter the comic book market, Daigh needed someone to come up with ideas for a new line of titles. By late 1939, comics featuring characters like Superman and Batman were a hit with readers. Although he had only a passing interest in comic strips and virtually no knowledge of comic books, Parker accepted the challenge. "It gave me an opportunity which I had wanted to have for a long time," he testified in the *National v. Fawcett* case in 1948, "of being an editor of a magazine" (Parker 686).

First, Parker came up with a hero who would be "a leader of a group of men." Like Arthur's knights, each member of the team would embody a different strength or virtue. Daigh was concerned that a team of characters might "cause too many difficulties" and suggested that Parker combine those "characteristics" into one hero (693). In his 1948 testimony, Parker recalled that Daigh believed a large cast of characters "would be unwieldy, hard to draw, hard for the reader to distinguish one from the other" (695). As Parker revised the concept, Al Allard, Fawcett's art director, asked Charles Clarence Beck, a staff artist, to come up with character designs (Steranko 11). Beck enjoyed comic strips and was an avid reader of Edgar Rice Burroughs and other science fiction and fantasy. In the second volume of Steranko's *History of Comics*, the artist remarked, "I never read comic books because most of them were tasteless. I considered my magazines to be illustrated boy's adventures and handled the art accordingly" (Beck qtd. in Steranko 11). With actor Fred MacMurray as the real-life model for the hero, Beck designed a character who looked more like a military officer in a colorful dress uniform than a tough guy in circus tights (Steranko 11). Captain Thunder's name eventually changed, too, thanks to Pete Costanza, who suggested *Captain Marvelous* (Bridwell 9). By the time the hero finally appeared on newsstands, after a black-and-white "ashcan" edition was published to interest distributors and for copyright purposes, he was Captain Marvel.[17]

Featured as the lead story of *Whiz Comics* no. 2, Billy's origin story is a variation on the King Arthur myth, with elements of James Hilton's *Lost Horizon*.[18] Billy Batson, a young orphan who sells newspapers and makes his home in a subway station, meets a stranger who leads him to the old wizard Shazam. The wizard selects Billy as his successor. By saying the wizard's name, the boy becomes Captain Marvel. Billy gains his powers just in time, as a "maniac scientist" named Dr. Sivana has been terrorizing the city and threatening to silence all radio broadcasts. After the meeting with Shazam, Billy tracks down Sivana's thugs and destroys the madman's "radio-silencer." At the end of the story, Billy manages to land a job with Mr. Morris's Amalgamated Broadcasting Company. Although there's no sword in a marble stone for Billy, traces of Parker's original idea remained in Billy Batson's magic word *Shazam*, which enables the young man to call upon the wisdom of Solomon, the strength of Hercules, the stamina of Atlas, the power of Zeus, the courage of Achilles, and the speed of Mercury.[19]

Although he played a significant role in the creation of the character, Parker entered the military in the fall of 1940 and would not return to Fawcett until late 1945 (Parker 681). Otto Binder began writing for the company in 1941.[20] Like Parker before him, Binder brought a literary sensibility to Billy's adventures. Slowly, Captain Marvel's stories became the comic book equivalent of the "boy's adventures" that Beck admired. Recalling his work with Binder in an essay he wrote not long before his death in 1989, Beck noted "a good deal of the Frankenstein and Faust legends in our comic stories of the golden age; our scientists were all mad and evil, our heroines were all blonde and pure, and our heroes were all brave and strong but with the hearts of simple peasants beating in their breasts" (Beck, "Racial Inheritance"). Shazam also plays the role of Billy's Merlin, a father figure who leads the young man to his destiny.

What made Captain Marvel so popular, as admired as Superman and Batman? Billy enabled young readers, as scholars Bradford Wright and Christopher Murray argue, to imagine what it might be like to possess magical powers (Wright 18–19; Murray 28–29). As a stand-in for the reader, Murray notes, Billy is the hero's "secret weapon" (28), although some writers, including Jules Feiffer, recall their disappointment when they discovered that Billy's magic word only works in the pages of a comic book (Feiffer 25).[21] Once the United States entered World War II, Murray writes, comic book heroes like Captain Marvel provided psychological comfort to children who felt helpless in the face of overwhelming historical change brought about by modern, mechanized warfare. The "transformations" central to the origin stories of Captain Marvel and Joe Simon and Jack Kirby's Captain America served "as inspirational fantasies for children," especially for "young boys" during wartime hoping "to participate in a more direct way than buying war bonds" (Murray 156). Those "fantasies," as we have seen, persisted long after Captain Marvel had disappeared. The concept of a character who possesses two distinct bodies inspired such later heroes as Roy Thomas's 3-D Man and Alan Moore's version of Mick Anglo's Marvelman, the Captain Marvel look-alike created for the British market in the wake of Fawcett's settlement.[22]

As Judge Coxe and Judge Hand both noticed, Superman and Captain Marvel had a number of similarities. Like Siegel and Shuster's hero, Captain Marvel had a tendency to trash automobiles and elevators in his mission to protect the world from evil. Aside from the basics of their origin stories, however, the two also had some key differences, as Binder noted to Jim Steranko. While Billy's alter ego was "human to the core," Superman and "most of the other super-characters" popular in the 1940s tended to be "alien, almost austere, infallible, haughty—doing a machine-like job of nabbing crooks and crushing evil, without once taking off a moment to lounge around and relax" (Binder qtd. in Steranko 14). Binder and Beck agreed that Billy was the true hero of their stories. In later essays and interviews, both men attributed Captain Marvel's success to his alter ego. As the narrator of Captain Marvel's adventures, Billy is quite different from Superman's Clark Kent, Batman's Bruce Wayne, or Captain America's Steve Rogers. If we take Beck at his word, and believe that Billy *imagined* all of these stories, the character is a relative of George Marcoux's Supersnipe, another popular if now neglected Golden Age hero, the little boy who loves comics so much that he dreams of what it would be like to have powers of his own.[23]

As he grew in popularity, Captain Marvel, now also the star of a 1941 serial from Republic Pictures, gained a large cast of popular supporting characters, including his friend Captain Marvel, Jr., his sister Mary Marvel, the Lieutenant Marvels, Uncle Marvel, and Hoppy the Marvel Bunny, who appeared in *Fawcett's Funny Animals*, which featured Chad Grothkopf's striking and innovative artwork. Fawcett employed some of the best freelancers in the business. Binder and Manly Wade Wellman, for example, already had years of experience as writers for the science fiction pulps. Other artists who worked for Fawcett, including Mac Raboy and Kurt Schaffenberger, were, like Beck, among the finest comic book illustrators of the 1940s. The late Marc Swayze, whose style blended Beck's simplicity with Raboy's realism, also made significant contributions to the Marvel Family. Joe Simon and Jack Kirby even played a role in the first issue of the title that became *Captain Marvel Adventures*.[24] Eventually, Fawcett gave creative control to Beck, who, with Costanza, opened an art studio that employed an assembly-line system to meet the public's demand for the character. Binder's brother Jack and his studio also produced comics for Fawcett, prompting Jim Steranko to joke that the brothers "might be called the first family of comics" (Steranko 37).

Almost two decades after Captain Marvel's final appearance, Larry Ivie, at the close of a long article in his fanzine *Monsters and Heroes: The Magazine of Pictorial Imagination*, lamented the loss of "the moral values within these well-written stories," narratives "that were so influential upon the children who followed them" in the 1940s (Ivie 28). Writing in 1969, Ivie believed that, because of Fawcett's settlement, "the entire field has suffered" (28). John G. Pierce, who for the last three decades has written prolifically on Captain Marvel's legacy, echoed Ivie in a 1982 article published in Don and Maggie Thompson's magazine *The Golden Age of Comics*. Fawcett's writers and artists, Pierce argued, "made some very powerful and positive statements about life," including, later in the series, stories about tolerance and nonconformity (Pierce, "Levity" 78). These laments for lost innocence are rooted in a nostalgic ideology borrowed not only from Victorian notions of King Arthur's chivalry but also from a key figure in American folklore.

Scott Reynolds Nelson reads Superman, and the characters who followed him, as the descendants of John Henry, that "balloon-muscled strongman, so much like the Communist symbol of workers' strength," a figure "who became many men: Superman, Captain America, Wonder Man, and Captain Marvel" (Nelson 161). John Henry, the "steel driving man" who sets out to defeat a machine with nothing more than his strength, determination, and a simple hammer, is a hero who, as his legend grew, came to represent everything from "the position of black men during Jim Crow" and "the dangers of mining" to "the coming of the machine age" and a "nostalgia for the past" (Nelson 40).

If Nelson is correct, if Superman and Captain Marvel have inherited John Henry's mantle, then we can see some of this nostalgia for a pastoral, pre-industrial age—another Camelot—on the covers of *Action Comics* no. 1 and *Whiz Comics* no. 2, both of which feature a brightly colored hero demolishing an automobile. These images, strikingly similar and now iconic, also resonate with discourses on the automobile in numerous novels and short stories of the early twentieth century. Both covers represent nostalgia as a form of active resistance to technology and its promise of a dazzling but uncertain future.

NOSTALGIA IN ACTION: SUPERMAN AND CAPTAIN MARVEL VS. THE AUTOMOBILE

At trial, Louis Nizer asked Parker about the covers of *Action Comics* no. 1 and *Whiz Comics* no. 2. The first one, from 1938, shows a man in a blue, yellow, and red costume smashing a green automobile against a rock.[25] A headlight hovers over the hood as shards of glass fall from the windshield. Superman moves effortlessly. He stands in what appears to be a desert landscape, with a hill behind him. Two men run away in terror, while another, on his knees, appears stunned and confused. In his recent history of the Man of Steel, Larry Tye notes the ambiguity contained in this dramatic image (fig. 0.2). What is the man in blue, yellow, and red "fuming at" (Tye 30)? "Hopefully he was on our side," writes Tye (30). The absence of any background details, aside from the yellow-and-orange halo that circles the automobile, places the reader's attention squarely on this powerful figure. Despite what Tye describes as "the rage of a being who could single-handedly lift a car into the air" (30), Siegel and Shuster's hero looks calm and determined. Look again at his face: this is not an act of desperation, of blind fury, but of certainty. The fate of the automobile, like that of the three other men, is inevitable and, as we learn in the pages of Superman's origin story, justified, as he saves Lois Lane from Butch's gang of thugs.

Louis Nizer wanted answers. Did Parker "consider those two similar?" The writer responded that, yes, "both have an automobile in them," but he also noted a few differences. "Well," he testified, "the characters in the *Whiz Comics* are obviously evil characters, but the others [the figures from *Action Comics*] you cannot tell whether they are evil characters or not" (820–21). Why? The *Whiz* cover includes, according to Parker, such "conventional symbols" as "the machine gun coming out of the car, which indicates those are gangsters" (821). Captain Marvel stands beneath a wall of skyscrapers, a bank of clouds overhead (fig. 0.3). Perhaps sensing that Parker's testimony might not be convincing, Fawcett's attorney also asked C. C. Beck to discuss the two drawings.

0.2 Superman takes issue with an automobile on Joe Shuster's cover for *Action Comics* no. 1 (June 1938). Reprinted in *The Superman Chronicles* vol. 1 (3). Superman © 2016 DC Comics.

Beck denied that he had copied *Action Comics*, calling the images "two entirely different pictures" (Beck, trial tr. 873). Beck testified that he based his design on the climactic scene from Billy's origin story, the panel in which Captain Marvel destroys Sivana's radio-silencer (figure 0.4). Sivana's machines, like the automobile, are no match for Captain Marvel. The first panel on page ten of the story is a clutter of vacuum tubes, coils, wires, and transformers. Captain Marvel violently dismantles this wall of glass, iron, and steel.

During his testimony, Beck offered a lesson on how to read a page of comics. That image of Captain Marvel destroying the automobile, he said, was

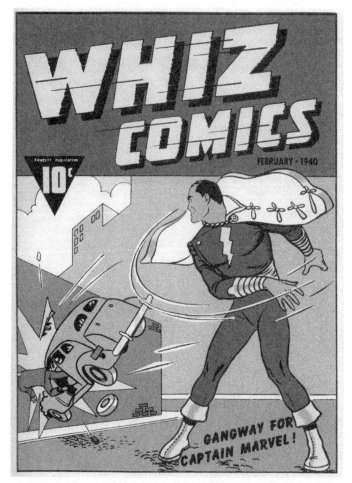

0.3 C. C. Beck's explosive cover for *Whiz Comics* no. 2 (February 1940). Reprinted in *The Shazam! Archives* vol. 1 (19). Captain Marvel and related characters © 2016 DC Comics.

"the same picture" as this explosive panel only "reversed" for dramatic effect. In a comic strip or a comic book, Beck explained, "the action always moves to the right, with the result that in the story he came out lefthanded, because if he was righthanded we would have had his back. When I took that as a cover idea to make him righthanded I reversed the picture" (Beck, trial tr. 875).[26] The depositions and court records provide ample material for scholars interested in weighing the merits of Parker and Beck's statements about the cover. While what Judge Coxe described as "conflicting testimony" offers legal scholars a fascinating case study in the history of copyright law in the United States, I remain interested in the *content* of these images. Why do Superman and Captain Marvel hate the automobile so much?

0.4 Captain Marvel takes action against one of Dr. Sivana's thugs in a panel from *Whiz Comics* no. 2 (February 1940). Script by Bill Parker and art by C. C. Beck. Reprinted in *The Shazam! Archives* vol. 1 (29). Captain Marvel and related characters © 2016 DC Comics.

The two heroes, like comic strip funny animals, embody a preindustrial era, one in which technology is no match for brute strength. Les Daniels argues that "dumb animals"—characters like Mickey Mouse and Donald Duck and Pogo—"provided a link with a vision of America" characterized by "small towns and barnyards," that fantasy of a "collective past" that some cartoonists "had left behind" (Daniels 53).[27] Heroes like Superman and Captain Marvel serve a similar purpose, with one key difference: their power enables them to fight these rapid and unsettling social and historical changes.

The automobile as a harbinger of a sometimes ominous, inhuman future is a fixture in American literature published in the first quarter of the twentieth century.[28] George Minafer Amberson, the spoiled and nostalgic protagonist of Booth Tarkington's 1918 novel *The Magnificent Ambersons*, boldly states that "all automobiles are a nuisance" and "had no business to be invented" (Tarkington 274). They are diabolical symbols of the larger social and economic changes taking place in his "Midland town" (10). Later in the novel, George barely survives his encounter with one of these machines as it, moving slowly, still manages to strike him with "gigantic violence" and a "roaring and jolting" (490) that leaves his body shattered. F. Scott Fitzgerald's Myrtle Wilson, like one of the doomed characters in David H. Keller's 1928 science fiction story "The Revolt of the Pedestrians," is not so lucky, as, after being accidentally struck by Daisy Buchanan, she "knelt in the road and mingled her thick dark blood with the dust" (Fitzgerald 137). The road that leads through the Valley of Ashes in *The Great Gatsby* resembles the dark, empty, almost infinite space that surrounds Superman's city in *Action Comics* no. 1.[29] Lacking Superman's power, Gatsby has no choice but to lie in order to save Daisy and what little is left of boyhood dreams pieced together from Ben Franklin broadsides and countless dime novels. What Gatsby and Amberson fail to understand is that, as Tarkington's inventor Eugene Morgan explains, "automobiles have come, and they bring a greater change in our life than most of us suspect. They are here, and almost all outward things are going to be different because of what they bring" (Tarkington 275). Amberson and Gatsby are unwilling to accept the fact that these changes "are here," but Superman and Captain Marvel, in the four-color fantasy realms they inhabit, possess the power to resist the passage of time and its inevitable end. Perhaps the "rage" that Larry Tye senses on the cover of *Action Comics* no. 1 is the same anger that fuels Tarkington's protagonist, who, only after his accident, begins to accept his fate and that of his family: "Nothing stays or holds or keeps where there is growth, he somehow perceived vaguely but truly" (Tarkington 498). For Tarkington's and Fitzgerald's heroes, clinging to the past, or to what Boym calls that "romance with one's own fantasy" (*The Future* xiii), has devastating consequences.

Paul Gilroy argues that automobiles and "the curved, reflexive surfaces they provide can show us our distorted selves" (30). The same might be said of these two covers, as they reveal a desire—like the one expressed in Tarkington and, to some extent, in Fitzgerald—for a paradise that existed before these machines, as Eugene Morgan notes, brought with them a "spiritual alteration" (275) whose consequences, at least in 1918, could not yet be fully imagined or understood.

What did readers in 1938 and 1940 see as they stared at these two covers? It is important to distinguish between our perspective and that of those who first bought these comics on newsstands and at drugstores. This is the process of nostalgia itself: as we gaze at the past, we try, often without success, to distinguish the *real*—historical fact, documentary evidence—from the imagined. Each of these covers is an exercise in nostalgia, an active, violent attempt to move time backwards. Myrtle Wilson's brutal death in *Gatsby* proves that flesh and blood are no match for the machine, with its disregard for love, beauty, and stillness. In destroying these automobiles, Superman and Captain Marvel assert their dominance over these mad symbols of human progress.

A "CENTER OF UNUSED OBJECTS AND UNWANTED OBJECTS"

In 1978, underground filmmaker and performance artist Jack Smith, an influence on contemporary comics maker Edie Fake, indulged in nostalgia for the future. Smith also starred in and, by some accounts, helped to direct Andy Warhol's unfinished, albeit strange and alluring, version of Batman.[30]

What would Smith's ideal society look like? How would it function? What role might the artist play in creating it? "I can think of billions of ways for the world to be completely different," he said (Smith 115). For example, "in the middle of the city should be a repository of objects that people don't want anymore, which they would take to this giant junkyard." For Smith, that junkyard might include stills from Maria Montez's films, bits of costume jewelry, snippets from old 78s, pastel-colored scarves, and glitter. He imagines a space that is a museum and a playground, a "center of unused objects and unwanted objects" that might "become a center of intellectual activity" (Smith 115). Smith's junkyard is a variation on Walter Benjamin's magical arcades, where abandoned bits and pieces of consumer culture promise moments of sudden revelation.[31]

The study of old comic books is like a tour of this junkyard, as these once meaningful but now "unused objects" take on new life for writers, artists, and scholars. I read Smith's description of utopia as a profound insight into nostalgia itself. That "center" is a living archive of ideas and thwarted desires. Any writer who sets out to study comic books, memory, and nostalgia should heed Binder's and Delany's warnings while at the same time embracing the possibility that Boym and Smith celebrate in their work.[32] In comics studies, nostalgia always plays a role, even for those writers and scholars who have no direct personal connection to the work they study.

Comics theorist and scholar Thierry Groensteen assures us that we need not fear this obsession with the past, either our own or one we inherit from those who came before us. "Yes, why not admit it?" Groensteen writes. Often, as we go about "delivering our clever papers," those of us who think and write about comics "are probably doing nothing more than holding out our hands to the kids we used to be" (Groensteen, "Why Are" 11). Comics studies, of course, must not be a closed system, open only to those who as children first discovered and enjoyed comics. Nostalgia is no prerequisite for academic inquiry or for other creative pursuits. The only price of admission to Smith's utopia is a visionary compassion that recognizes a pattern of meaning in the "unwanted objects" ignored and neglected by the culture that produced and adored them in the first place.

I do not have an origin story like those of Richard Lupoff, Bill Schelly, P. C. Hamerlinck, Trina Robbins, Harlan Ellison, Roy Thomas, John G. Pierce, or the other writers and scholars whose work serves as the foundation for this book. I have only vague childhood memories of Captain Marvel, most of them associated with the live-action Saturday morning TV series from the 1970s. I discovered Binder and Beck's work two decades later, not in its original form, but as reprints in quarter bin issues of DC's *Shazam!* series from the

1970s. My single distinct memory of the TV show is one of total boredom: as a child, I preferred cartoon heroes, not grown men in tights. Where were Flash Gordon and Spider-Man when I needed them?

Captain Marvel, Beck once pointed out, starred in comic books filled with "fantasy and imagination and goodnatured hokum, never intended to be taken seriously!" (Beck, "Real Facts"). In that same essay, Beck insisted that what set Captain Marvel apart from other heroes of the era was his personality. He was, after all, "funny, not sobersided and stuffy" ("Real Facts"). Beck would no doubt consider aspects of this book "stuffy," but I hope he would be amused to discover that, on my first meeting with Captain Marvel, I dismissed the hero—played on Saturday morning TV by Jackson Bostwick and later by John Davey—as too *realistic*, not a superhero but a long-haired man in an ill-fitting suit. Only later, as an adult, would I discover the appeal of the "goodnatured hokum" in those Fawcett comics.

I fear that, were I to follow Thierry Groensteen's advice and speak to that "kid" who resigned himself to watching *Shazam!* on WFSB Channel 3 in Hartford, Connecticut, sometime in the 1970s, he would ask, "Why Captain Marvel?" I don't know if my answer would satisfy him, as the only response I know is this: "Look more carefully." This is the lesson offered in *Whiz Comics* no. 2, and by comic books and graphic novels in general, especially the ones obsessed with recovering a vanished past. As Binder warned, there is no guarantee that these "tiny flashes of light" will reveal that world to us, but they do provide an outline of what Billy's America—real and imagined—looked like in the 1940s and 1950s. What follows, then, is not the definitive history of Captain Marvel, which even Binder, it seems, believed would be impossible to tell. It is, rather, a series of "tiny flashes," and a record, like the comic books themselves, of possibility and, I hope, of wonder.

Chapter 1

"A FABRIC OF ILLUSION"

The Art of C. C. Beck

In a 1974 "capsule autobiography," C. C. Beck—the illustrator, cartoonist, comic book artist, writer, musician, and critic—claimed that he was neither "an editor" nor "an idea man" (Beck qtd. in Hamilton). Just a few years before his death in 1989, however, he wrote to his friend and fellow cartoonist Trina Robbins about a plan to share his theories of comic book art with other fans and professionals. Since the early 1970s, Beck had published essays in numerous fanzines, newsletters, and magazines. In a letter dated March 7, 1988, Beck wrote, "I have just given birth to a new idea (parthenogenetically): How about my lining up a dozen or more people like yourself with whom I correspond and sending them one of my unpublished articles every so often?"[1] Beck spent the next year mailing rough drafts of articles—some of which would eventually be published in *The Comics Journal* or, posthumously, in *Fawcett Collectors of America*—to what came to be known as his Critical Circle. After receiving replies from the members of the Circle, he would compile and summarize those responses, then share them in mailings with the rest of the group. That body of criticism remains a rich, if little known, resource for contemporary comics scholars, readers, and cartoonists. Beck's enthusiasm for the project also proves that, despite what he'd claimed in that 1974 interview, he was never short on inventive new ideas.

In a detailed obituary published in the *Comics Buyer's Guide* after Beck's death on November 22, 1989, John G. Pierce concluded that Captain Marvel's co-creator would be remembered not only for his work at Fawcett but also for "his oft-repeated viewpoints on the need for simplicity in art" (Pierce, "C. C. Beck" 32), theories Beck first developed in his role as the Chief Artist for Captain Marvel in the 1940s and later refined in his essays for the fan press. The Critical Circle enabled Beck to express his ideas on art, literature, politics, memory, and nostalgia with the same concision, wit, openness, and joy on display in his comics.[2] Although he enjoyed his reputation as a "crusty curmudgeon"—also the name for his column published in the 1980s in *The Comics Journal*—Trina Robbins has insisted that Beck's "crustiness was an act. He was a [believer] in and a practitioner of the gentle and humorous in life and comics" (Robbins, "An Appreciation"). Despite his role in creating one of the most popular and best-selling characters in American popular culture of the 1940s, Beck remains a somewhat underrated figure in the history of comic art in the United States. The scope of Beck's achievement as an artist cannot be understood without a close analysis and consideration of the body of theory he produced in the last two decades of his life. Like his friend and colleague Will Eisner, Beck is significant as both a cartoonist and as a critic.

Often remembered for his unadorned, clean-line style of cartooning, Beck, in that 1974 interview, proudly declared himself "an illustrator" (Beck qtd. in Hamilton). His comics, he explained time and time again, drew inspiration from theatre, film, and comic strips. Describing himself in the third person, Beck wrote, "Give him a set of blueprints of a building you have in mind and he'll make you a fine 'artist's rendering' of what it will look like when finished" (Beck qtd. in Hamilton). Although Beck's friend Otto Binder attended college with the hope of one day becoming a scientist, Beck was the technician in their collaboration, the builder who understood his task in clear and logical terms. The comic book artist, as he once explained to Eisner, is the "extension of the writer" (Beck qtd. in Eisner, "Shop Talk" 73). More significant than Beck's simplicity is his compositional sense. In Captain Marvel's origin in *Whiz Comics* no. 2, Beck's expressive use of perspective in realistically rendered, if sometimes fanciful, backgrounds is remarkable for its economy and restraint. "There was seldom, in Captain Marvel stories especially, any 'beautiful artwork,'" Beck claimed in an essay for *Inside Comics* in the early 1970s (Beck, "May We" 24). Just as Beck was more of an "idea man" than he gave himself credit for, his best work—produced alone or, during his days at Fawcett, with assistants—can be described, despite his objections, as beautiful, always humorous, and often moving.

In his final essays and letters, Beck wrote frequently about his childhood in Minnesota, as well as his early years in Chicago and later in New York. Just a few months before his death, he compiled a booklet of autobiographies written by the members of the Critical Circle. That Beck would be so fascinated with the forces that shaped his life and those of his friends should come as no surprise. Having spent most of his career as a comic book artist supervising and drawing stories about a boy and his search for an identity and a stable home, Beck, like Otto Binder, understood fantasy not as a form of escapism but as a necessary counterpoint to lived reality (however that might be defined). If all of Billy's stories, as Beck once implied, are daydreams ("Real Facts"), then his style is the perfect accompaniment to these fantasies. Already visionary and strange, Billy's tales need no embellishment. Like nostalgic memories, they persist because they are so simple and logical that they appear to be true.

THE LIFE AND TIMES OF C. C. BECK

Just as his most famous character had a magical origin story, Beck often remarked, with his characteristic impishness, on the cosmic circumstances of his birth. In the spring of 1988, after asking the other members of the Critical Circle to write about their childhoods, he replied to Trina Robbins and thanked her for sharing her memories. In the letter, he writes, "I always figured I was dropped off Halley's comet in 1910 when it picked up Mark Twain."[3] In the third essay that he wrote for the Critical Circle, Beck described his childhood in Zumbrota, Minnesota:

> No matter when or where we're born, I believe that we're all pretty much alike as children. I was born in a small town in Minnesota in 1910. Both the place and the time were in many ways different from anything to be found today, but I don't think that I was much different as a child from children born in other places or times either earlier or later. (Beck, "Childhood Habits")[4]

The son of a Lutheran minister and a schoolteacher (Pierce 27), Beck was a good student but disliked sports, which he found "childish and silly" (Beck, "Is the Wagon . . . ?"). In high school, he found himself "popular with the members of the debating club, the literary and art society, and at Sunday School and Junior League affairs," activities that, he jokes, nearly transformed him into "a bespectacled, bow tie-wearing, completely ridiculous nerd" until he took up smoking, drinking, and swearing ("Is the Wagon . . . ?"). "I even took dancing lessons and learned to play cards and to bowl," he remembered, "although I was never any good at such things" (Beck, "Is the Wagon . . . ?").

Proud of his upbringing, Beck nonetheless remained skeptical of Christianity, as he explained in another 1989 letter to Robbins. "I'm not a Christian either," he wrote, "although my father was a Lutheran minister and I have taught Sunday School, sung in choirs, and fed collection plates for many years."[5] Although he did not consider himself a Christian, Beck's Lutheran background is often evident in his criticism, which is sometimes highly moralistic. Beck's occasional rigidity, however, should not obscure the spirituality that informed his theories. Despite his doubts about organized religion, there is often a mystical quality to Beck's writing, especially some of his later, unpublished work, in which he reflects on the relationship between art and reality. His drawing style also owes a debt to the training he received after he completed high school and left Minnesota for Chicago.

In a 1983 interview with Will Eisner, Beck recalled the year in the late 1920s he spent at the Chicago Academy of Fine Arts (Eisner, "Shop Talk" 55). "Everything was booming," Beck told Eisner. "I got a real good job in a lampshade factory drawing comic characters. Smitty was one and Orphan Annie was another. Handpainted lampshades" (Eisner, "Shop Talk" 55). Despite his conservative upbringing, and his self-described "nerdy" tendencies, in his Critical Circle autobiography Beck remembered "the flappers and shieks and bootleg gin and ukuleles" of the era, which ended with the crash of 1929 (Beck, "Racial Inheritance"). Beck returned to Minnesota, but the year spent in Chicago had a tremendous impact on his budding career. In his conversation with Eisner, Beck recalled some advice from one of his instructors at the academy. The young Beck, his teacher was certain, had the potential to "be a fine children's illustrator" (Eisner, "Shop Talk" 55). After moving back home, Beck continued his studies at the University of Minnesota before he landed a job as staff illustrator at Fawcett (Beck, "Preacher's Son" 60; and Eisner, "Shop Talk" 55). After the company moved its main editorial offices to New York, Beck and his wife, Hildur, relocated to the East Coast in 1936 (Pierce, "C. C. Beck" 27; Beck "Racial Inheritance").

Beck's career gained momentum after he and his family arrived in Connecticut in order for him to be closer to Fawcett's offices ("Racial Inheritance"). Following the success of Siegel and Shuster's Superman, Fawcett decided to enter the comic book market. Editorial Director Ralph Daigh assigned writer Bill Parker the task of coming up with a character or characters that would follow in Superman's alien footsteps. Beck came up with the character designs that would bring Parker's ideas to life.

Beck's novella *The World's Mightiest Fat Head,* published posthumously in *The Comics Journal* in the early 2000s, is a fictionalized but thinly veiled autobiographical account of these early years. Wally Baker, the story's protagonist, is "an unimpressive little man with thick glasses and a big head of hair," an illustrator who slowly learns the ins and outs of cartooning. Baker has doubts that he has the right skills for the job. "I'm no cartoonist, Mr. Drake," Baker admits. His boss reassures him: "'You don't have to be, Bake,' Drake said. 'Comics strips today aren't funny, you know'" (Beck, "Fat Head" part 1, 38).[6]

In this autobiographical novella, Beck repeats an assertion that he made at several points over the course of his career, from his deposition and his courtroom testimony in the 1940s to his later essays and articles. Despite what his publisher might have asked of him, he denied copying any of Siegel and Shuster's early Superman stories. In the fictionalized account of Captain Marvel's origin, Drake, the art director, provides Baker with samples of other comic books for the illustrator to imitate. "By the way," Drake asks, "where are all the clippings I gave you to follow?" Baker explains that his "wife accidentally threw them out with the garbage. She thought they were some of our kid's drawings, she said. Julie doesn't know much about artwork" (Beck, "Fat Head" part 1, 41). In the first essay Beck wrote for the Critical Circle, dated March 17, 1988, Beck again insisted that Billy's alter ego was not an imitation of Superman: "Where the Man of Steel was an alien from another universe, Captain Marvel was the World's Mightiest Mortal" (Beck, "What Really Killed Captain Marvel?"). Fawcett's "Mightiest Mortal" proved to be just as popular with readers and as a result became one of the best-selling characters in comics in the 1940s.

While fans who remember reading Captain Marvel's adventures in the 1940s and 1950s often attribute the character's success to Binder's well-written scripts and Beck and his assistants' simple, often elegant art, the appeal of these stories can also be attributed to the lively, collaborative atmosphere at Fawcett during the height of Captain Marvel's popularity. Like others who worked for the company in the 1940s, Beck enjoyed working with his writers and editors (see De Fuccio A-80–A-84; Beck, "Preacher's Son" 60–61). "The parties we had during the forties are my fondest memories," Beck remembered in his 1977 interview with *Fan*. "We had no pot or rock music, but plenty of booze and old-time [accordion] and guitar music" (Beck qtd. in Padovano).

Several Fawcett staff members were, like Beck, musicians. Artist Marc Swayze recalled that when Beck overheard the other Fawcett staffers playing, the co-creator of Captain Marvel joined in on guitar and later learned upright bass. "We jammed to our hearts' delight in the late afternoons and eventually decided we'd like to hear how we sounded," Swayze wrote in one of his columns for *Fawcett Collectors of America*.[7] Swayze remembered that the group, which also included artists Irwin Weill and Vic Capalupo, enjoyed their jam sessions and called themselves The Famous Fawcett Four (Swayze 76). Despite his conservative reputation in comics circles in the 1980s, Beck—minister's son, avid reader, artist, and guitarist—insisted that he "was something of a trendsetter back in the '40s," and therefore resented in his later years being "lumped with the Joe McCarthys and other old conservative Republican bigots of my time" (Beck, "Is the Wagon . . . ?").

As Captain Marvel's popularity and sales increased, Fawcett began to hire other artists to produce enough material to meet the demand. In his conversation with Eisner, Beck explains that the publisher, unhappy with the uneven quality of the work produced at some of these shops, decided instead to grant Beck more creative control (Eisner, "Shop Talk" 61). With Pete Costanza, Beck established a studio in Englewood, New Jersey, and began recruiting from "all the art schools to try to get the brightest students" (Beck qtd. in Eisner, "Shop Talk" 62). Unlike many of his contemporaries, Beck eventually received billing as the "Chief Artist" of *Captain Marvel Adventures*, sharing a byline with editors Will Lieberson and Wendell Crowley.

As the artist in charge of the Fawcett's flagship title, Beck had the opportunity to develop and refine the ideas on comic art that he would later share in his letters and essays. In his conversation with Eisner, he remembered creating "a little book of how to cartoon and how not to." The handbook included "samples in there drawn by some of the different artists," including, Beck recalled, examples from Harold Gray's *Little Orphan Annie*, one of his favorite strips (Beck qtd. in Eisner, "Shop Talk" 63).

Meanwhile, a small community of comics writers and artists began to take shape in Englewood. Otto and Ione Binder also made their home there, and it became a place for discussions about the medium and its potential (Schelly, *Words* 107). This festive, collaborative atmosphere—where "sing-alongs," Bill Schelly writes, would often be followed by "late night bull sessions" about the business and the art of comic books (Schelly 107; Steranko 17; Beck, "Preacher's Son" 61)—no doubt played a role in Beck's desire to create the Critical Circle in the late 1980s. Just as he remembered with fondness his youth in Minnesota, Beck in his later essays affectionately recalled his collaborations with Binder ("Real Facts," "Name Calling"). "All of us lived, ate, and dreamed comics in the Golden Era," Binder explained to Jim Steranko. Topics of conversation, Binder remembered, included "which characters were best," amazement at "Jack Kirby's layouts," and gossip on how many pages Jack Binder's studio could produce in a month (Binder qtd. in Steranko 17). In addition to his early work with Parker and his long-standing relationship with Binder, Beck worked closely with Constanza. "Pete was my partner all the way through," Beck told Eisner (Beck qtd. in Eisner, "Shop Talk" 62).

Following the end of World War II, characters like Captain Marvel declined in popularity as readers turned their attention to romance, crime, and horror comics. Beck attributed this change of fortune to Fawcett's mishandling of the character. "Eventually he became just what Superman's publisher had claimed at the start—a poor imitation of the Man from Krypton, who now looked just like the overweight, sadly altered Big Red Cheese" (Beck, "What Really"). In 1953, after years of legal battles with National, Fawcett canceled all of its Captain Marvel titles and most of its line of other comics. Many of the company's writers and artists, including Binder and artist Kurt Schaffenberger, found work at National. As a result, they brought the Fawcett style and sensibility to the company's Superman titles in the 1950s and early 1960s.[8] Meanwhile, Beck drifted away from the world of comic books and relocated with his wife and children to Florida. Before returning to a career as a commercial artist, Beck owned The Ukulele Café, where, as he recalled in "Preacher's Son," he found himself "washing dishes, waiting on customers, cooking, and cleaning toilets," although he also found time to entertain his patrons by singing and playing guitar (Beck, "Preacher's Son" 65; see also Brown, "C. C. Beck" 7).[9] After closing the restaurant, Beck worked for other commercial art agencies before he eventually struck out on his own with the C. C. Beck Studio of Art and Design (Brown, "C. C. Beck" 7).

Beck returned to comics in the mid-1960s, when, as the nostalgia for the comics of the 1940s and 1950s began to grow, former Fawcett editors Lieberson and Crowley reunited Beck and Binder for *Fatman, the Human Flying Saucer* ("Preacher's Son," 65–66; Schelly 193–95). Beck had hoped for the kind of storytelling the team had excelled at in the 1940s, but Binder insisted that they work in a style closer to the one popularized by Marvel Comics in the early 1960s. Binder advised Beck that readers in the 1960s expected "action packed scenes" filled with "wisecracks and insults. This, he said, was the modern way to write comics" (Beck qtd. in Padovano). Beck disagreed, and while he maintained a friendly correspondence with Binder until the writer's death in 1974, they did not continue working together. When DC Comics revived Captain Marvel in the early 1970s, Beck returned as the artist, but, unhappy with the results, he drew Captain Marvel for only the first ten issues in new adventures written by Denny O'Neil, Elliot S. Maggin, and E. Nelson Bridwell.

Beck was vocal in the comics press of the early 1970s about his contempt for most of DC's new Captain Marvel stories. Already unhappy that the company would not allow him to employ artist Don Newton as his assistant on the series, Beck also took issue with the quality of the scripts.[10] What I suspect was also missing for Beck, as it was during the failed *Fatman* experiment, was the camaraderie and energy of Fawcett in the 1940s. Beck publicly expressed his disappointment in "May We Have the Next Slide Please?" published in the magazine *Inside Comics* in 1975, not long after "The Prize Catch of the Year," his last original work for DC, was published in *Shazam!* no. 10.[11] "I worked on the drawings, for a while. Somehow, things weren't right." Finally, he admits, "I gave up. As an illustrator I could, in the old days, make a good story better by 'bringing it to life' with drawings. But I couldn't bring the new stories to life no matter how hard I tried" (Beck, "May We" 26).

The Fawcett community of editors, writers, and artists was long gone, so Beck turned his attention to commissions, producing paintings for Captain Marvel fans.[12] In a letter to Trina Robbins from the summer of 1989, he notes that he "retired at age 73," following "a stroke" that affected his "right eye."[13] As an essayist and a prolific letter writer, he remained vocal in comics fandom. In the early 1980s, Beck served as an editor for Bernie McCarthy's *Fawcett*

Collectors of America newsletter and added the subtitle *SOB*, or *Some Opinionated Bastards*. In a review of *FCA/SOB* for *The Comics Journal* no. 64 (July 1981), Dwight Decker praised the newsletter as "an excellent buy," despite being possibly "hazardous to the health of fans whose blood pressure is already too high" (107). By the mid-1980s, Beck was a regular contributor to *The Comics Journal*. In addition to his work as a critic, he continued to write comic book scripts, and at the time of a debilitating stroke in 1989, was looking forward to a new hardcover edition of the popular Monster Society of Evil serial first published in the 1940s in *Captain Marvel Adventures*.[14] Although, in the last two years of his life, he was critical of the depictions of extreme violence and graphic sexuality that characterized the "mature" comics that followed in the wake of titles like Alan Moore and Dave Gibbons's *Watchmen*, Howard Chaykin's *American Flagg!* and Frank Miller's *The Dark Knight Returns*,[15] Beck nonetheless had faith in the medium. He often encouraged those creators whose work he enjoyed, including Robbins, as well as Wendy and Richard Pini, whose series *Elfquest* was one of his favorites of the 1980s.[16]

In a Critical Circle essay from January 1989, Beck warns of the dangers of that realistic trend in comics. He frames this argument in the form of a paradox: "When a culture reaches a point where its writing and art are too realistic its members start to lose touch with reality" (Beck, "What Kind"). After making this seemingly contradictory claim, Beck offers an apocalyptic vision of a society too reliant on realism:

> Soon they can't tell the artificial from the real and their buildings fall down, their vehicles crash and kill people, their very food and water kill them. Hideous wars break out and eventually destroy the culture that has lost touch with reality. (Beck, "What Kind")

Beck spent most of his career creating the kind of art inspired by "impossible stories," by "jokes," and "flights of fancy," all of which, he believed, were "good for one's health," narratives that "take the human mind away from this dreary world and to the farthest reaches of the universe" (Beck, "What Kind"). For Captain Marvel's co-creator, these fantastic tales, like the ones Billy told in his role as a broadcaster and later as a TV host, are "the purest kinds of art and literature" ("What Kind"). But, as he did so often in his letters and in his critical essays, Beck ended "What Kind of Writing and Art Do You Prefer?" with a question: "What do you think?"[17] Beck always enjoyed a good debate.

Although the world Beck created for Billy Batson was one filled with strange figures, shadowy tunnels, and ancient magic, it was surrounded by the realities Beck refers to: war, poverty, greed, and violence. It is worth remembering that Billy—whom Beck referred to indirectly as "poor but honest," like one of the "disinherited princelings" from a German folk tale (Beck, "Racial Inheritance")—is an orphan whose uncle steals his fortune. He sells newspapers to survive and, as he tells the stranger on the first page of *Whiz Comics* no. 2, makes his home "in the subway station. It's warm there." Realism in art, at best, is an illusion, and at worst, a deception, because, from Beck's perspective, it needlessly reveals what already exists, and does so without a consideration of what is possible. The world of "dragons, magic swords and charms and mighty spells" (Beck, "Racial Inheritance")? Not only is it more fun, but it also promises relief from, as Beck put it, that "dreary world" (Beck, "What Kind") with which all of us are already too familiar.

"NEVER DRAW ANY MORE THAN NECESSARY"

While Beck wrote extensively, in both his letters and his articles, about his theories, he also occasionally wrote fiction and comic book scripts. "Vanishing Point," published in the July 1959 issue of *Astounding Science Fiction*, is one of the most concise summaries of his thoughts on the intersection between art and "real life." In the narrative, an artist named Carter invents a "perspective machine" that he believes might reveal the secrets of reality itself. Beck's work of speculative fiction is a meditation on how art shapes our sense of the world around us. Carter explains his ambition: "We are so well-trained that we see everything just as we are taught to see it by generations of artists, writers, and other symbol-makers" (Beck, "Vanishing Point" 138). Is reality nothing more than a gallery of these mediated symbols? At the end of the story, Carter has his answer, but it terrifies him. The machine threatens to destroy the universe, or at least our *perception* of it, which Carter discovers are one and the same: "The artists were right all the time . . . there *is* no reality!" he exclaims. "It's all a fabric of illusion we've created ourselves!" (139). If reality is a mutually agreed-upon fiction, one recorded by "symbol-makers" interpreting what they see, then realism is just another kind of fiction, one masquerading as truth.

Beck's obsession with the relationship between reality and fantasy might explain some of his compositional choices in Billy's origin story. Like "Vanishing Point," Billy's first appearance in *Whiz Comics* can be read in the context of his theories. Although he often warned against the use of unnecessary details, Beck fills Captain Marvel's debut with simple drawings—from the dark sidewalk outside of Billy's subway tunnel to the offices and penthouses of impossibly tall buildings—that evoke a sense of place. Billy's city, which looks like a mixture of Chicago and New York, is sometimes ominous and threatening, but it also promises salvation because of the literal magic that exists beneath its surface. That salvation, however, is only possible because of

1.1 Billy meets the stranger who will lead him to Shazam on the first page of *Whiz Comics* no. 2 (February 1940). Script by Bill Parker and art by C. C. Beck. Reprinted in *The Shazam! Archives* vol. 1 (20). Captain Marvel and related characters © 2016 DC Comics.

Billy's willingness to explore those spaces and, like Carter, to observe carefully those who inhabit them. Over the course of the story, Beck illustrates Billy's gradual transformation by drawing a series of doorways, windows, and television screens. Captain Marvel's origin is a study of setting and the expressive role it plays in visual narratives.

In an undated letter Beck mailed to Trina Robbins in 1988, not long after the Critical Circle was up and running, Beck offered "a few pointers," a summary of his theory of good comic art. First, he advises, "never draw any more than necessary."[18] And backgrounds? The simpler they are, the better. In his interview with Eisner, Beck praises *Beetle Bailey* cartoonist Mort Walker for his skill at communicating with readers while still drawing as simply as possible: "You don't throw in anything," Beck told Eisner. "You cut your backgrounds down to just symbols" (Beck qtd. in Eisner 72). When readers meet Billy on the first page of *Whiz Comics* no. 2, the newsboy stands, as he often does throughout the story, before one of the many portals that will lead him to a new life and new adventures (figure 1.1). Beck fills that first panel with various "symbols": a silhouette of the city's skyline, a clock tower, and two pedestrians. It is almost midnight. Billy stands alone, dwarfed by the entrance to the station. Over the course of the next three panels, Beck slowly eliminates these backgrounds as he focuses instead on the two figures, Billy and the mysterious stranger. In the

1.2 Billy follows the stranger and discovers the magic that lives beneath the city on the second page of *Whiz Comics* no. 2 (February 1940). Script by Bill Parker and art by C. C. Beck. Reprinted in *The Shazam! Archives* vol. 1 (21). Captain Marvel and related characters © 2016 DC Comics.

second narrative panel, the reader gets a better look at the subway entrance. Billy and the reader now have no choice but to follow that stranger, cloaked in shadow, only his eyes and his right hand visible.

That subway entrance leads to a stairway on page two, which sits above another passage, one crowned with a blue lintel (figure 1.2). The second panel of this page echoes the design of the first one. Billy and the stranger, in the lower right-hand corner of the image, now stand on a platform. A torch lights the entrance to Shazam's great hall. In the left-hand corner of this final panel, Beck includes what appear to be two reptilian figures—are these statues?

1.3 Billy stands before another doorway, this time the one for the Skytower Apartments from
Whiz Comics no. 2 (February 1940). Script by Bill Parker and art by C. C. Beck. Reprinted in
The Shazam! Archives vol. 1 (26). Captain Marvel and related characters © 2016 DC Comics.

Rock formations? Eyes stare from the darkness, like the headlights of the train
itself, which looks like a grinning skull. The caption in the middle of the page
describes the train "with headlights gleaming like a dragon's eyes," a mechanical creature that lives beneath the city. Next, Billy and the reader encounter a
series of strange objects throughout this "weird, subterranean cavern."

These doorways and passages suggest the multiple identities and destinies
that are now open to Billy. Beck often positions our point of view just behind
that of the protagonist, so that, as we read, we become his companions, following him from one impossible revelation to the next. On the bottom of
page four, for example, Billy watches his childhood with the help of the Historama, a machine that has enabled the wizard to monitor the young man (see
fig. 0.1). Later in the story, the evil Sivana will also use a TV screen to communicate with his thugs, but Shazam's device has a different purpose. Billy
and the reader watch as the boy's "wicked uncle" steals his fortune. His uncle
has cast the boy out of paradise, that sunny, tree-lined street. In the next panel,
Beck draws the back of Billy's head in the lower right-hand corner. For the
first time, he sees his uncle counting the inheritance that is rightfully his, "the
money and bonds" left by his father (see fig. 0.1).

The other doorways Billy enters over the course of the story are less mysterious but just as detailed as the ones Beck includes on these first few pages. On
page seven, after overhearing two of Sivana's men, Billy "watches them enter

1.4 Captain Marvel shatters the window of the penthouse in a climactic scene from *Whiz Comics* no. 2 (February 1940). Script by Bill Parker and art by C. C. Beck. Reprinted in *The Shazam! Archives* vol. 1 (28). Captain Marvel and related characters © 2016 DC Comics.

the swanky Skytower Apartments" (figure 1.3). Trees and shrubs surround the building's entrance. Two red columns and tiny panes of glass frame the doors.

The last three panels on page eight show Billy, his hands clasped behind his back, looking upward at two towers, one of which, the Skytower building, houses Sivana's machine. "How am I going to get into the apartment house without being seen?" Billy wonders. From Billy's point of view in the fourth panel, Beck shifts, somewhat abruptly, in the fifth panel to a shot of the building next to Skytower. A caption informs the reader that Billy has taken the elevator to the adjacent skyscraper's "observation tower." A word balloon reveals Billy's location—he's now looking down upon Sivana's penthouse. "This is a job for Captain Marvel!" he says. This is another of Billy's secrets: as he explores the city, maps its perimeter, he learns to use the power Shazam has granted him. Beck illustrates this sudden change on page nine of the story.

1.5 Billy asks Shazam a question after their first meeting in *Whiz Comics* no. 2 (February 1940). Script by Bill Parker and art by C. C. Beck. Reprinted in *The Shazam! Archives* vol. 1 (22). Captain Marvel and related characters © 2016 DC Comics.

Having studied his past, Billy is now ready to act in the present. Until now, he's spent too much time on the *outside* of things, staring at what he's lost or at what he cannot have. The violence on page nine of the story illustrates this final step in Billy's journey to become a hero. After a three-panel sequence in which Captain Marvel jumps from the other skyscraper to the penthouse, the hero looks through a window and discovers Sivana's thugs. In the next image, one of those men—slim, with a double-breasted suit and a cigarette—stares at the TV screen he uses to communicate with the mad scientist. In the sixth panel, the reader sees a close-up of Sivana, an image within an image, a panel that doubles as the TV screen itself. Beck then inserts a drawing of a ticking clock, its hands, like those of the clock tower on the first page, almost at midnight. The hero has only "a few seconds" to destroy the "fiendish radio-silencer" that will remove the Amalgamated Broadcasting Co. and other stations from the airwaves. (Without the radio, after all, how will Billy tell his stories?) In the eighth and final panel of the page, Captain Marvel finally breaks the window (fig. 1.4). In doing so, he also breaks the frame of the narrative that has contained the newsboy up to this point. No longer peering around corners, down long passageways, or staring at television screens, Billy is now, at last, the hero, the wizard's true successor.[19] Intelligent, courageous, and honest, he is also curious, not only about himself and his history but about his city and the various characters who inhabit it.

While the conclusion of Billy's origin includes plenty of action, violence, and spectacle, the single most affecting image of the seventy-three panels that make up the story appears on the third page.[20] Compared to Beck's other drawings—the train, that hall of statues, Shazam's majestic throne—it might appear insignificant, simply a way of getting from one plot point to the next. But look again, first at Billy's eyes, and then, at the bottom of the drawing, his left hand (figure 1.5). For the first time in the story, Billy looks directly at the reader and asks a simple question: "H-how did you know my name?" Billy stands before a blue background. The action is all in his eyes, those two dots, and in that hand, just barely visible.

In his 1988 letter of advice to Robbins, Beck wrote that figures like this should be treated in the same way as panel backgrounds. "The characters must move, roll their eyes, shrug, wave their arms, sweat, frown, glower, smile, laugh, cry."[21] If a figure has no expressive purpose, if it fails to move a story forward in a significant way, it should be erased: "Any character who is not doing anything should not be shown." In this single panel, Beck compresses the emotion of the entire story into a single gesture. The only clutter here is the speech balloon. This single, solitary figure, raising his hand like a student in a classroom, is a fitting emblem for Beck's entire body of work. If reality is "a fabric of illusion," one must carefully observe its shape and dimension. At the center of that illusion, like this portrait of Billy, is the figure, dynamic and always in motion, asking questions of itself and of the world that surrounds it.

"THERE'S TOO MUCH ARTWORK!"

In the lower right-hand corner of the cover of *Fatman, the Human Flying Saucer* no. 1, published by Milson Publishing and dated April 1967, Tinman, Binder and Beck's "teen-age hero," holds a sign that celebrates the duo's new collaboration. This comic, the sign announces, was "Written & Drawn by the creators of the original Captain Marvel" (there's no mention of Bill Parker). A text page included in the issue describes Beck and Binder's working relationship on the new series. In interviews and essays Beck often described his role as being secondary to that of the writer, but this page points out that the artist "makes changes in the story-line and dialog at times that the writer, Binder, always finds an improvement. That was how they worked together in the old Fawcett days, with a close meeting of minds and 'compatible' approach to comics" ("Fan-Man"). This last statement was no doubt wishful thinking on the part of Lieberson and Crowley, the other Fawcett veterans involved with

1.6 Beck contrasts the art of Charles Schulz and Barry Windsor-Smith in an illustration from his article "May We Have the Next Slide Please?" (25). Illustration © 1975 C. C. Beck.

the ill-fated series (Brown 7; see also Schelly, *Words* 194–95). Although Binder and Beck remained popular and respected by comic book fans and collectors, *Fatman* only lasted three issues, a victim of poor distribution (Schelly, *Words* 195). In one of his columns for *The Comics Journal*, Beck wrote in detail about his disagreement with Binder on what direction the series should take. "While our differences of opinion didn't result in a nasty fight between us," he remembered, "it demonstrated that our old cooperative way of working, which had served us so well in the '40s, was no longer possible" ("Name Calling" 109). By the third issue, Beck admits, he and Binder had reached "an impasse."

The comic energy of the first issue, however, is undeniable. *Fatman*, like Billy's first appearance in *Whiz Comics*, provides another example of Beck working without assistants as he brings a writer's vision to life. As Gary Brown points out in a profile of Beck published in 1973, the artist was responsible for all of the work on *Fatman*, including "pencilling, inking, lettering and about one-third of the coloring" (7). These comics, then, like the *Shazam!* stories Beck would later draw for DC, enabled him to put his theories into practice. While Billy's first appearance is a case study in composition and perspective, with Beck's simple backgrounds adding depth and atmosphere to Parker's script, Tinman's origin, included in *Fatman* no. 1, is a master class in cartoon figure drawing.

In his 1988 letter to Robbins, Beck, as he did often in his later criticism, took issue with realistic depictions of the human figure in comic books. Beck disliked "shadows," he explained, because "they break up the figures."[22] In his article for *Inside Comics* from 1975, he drew a parody of Barry Windsor-Smith's work on the first issue of *Conan the Barbarian*, published by Marvel in 1970 (fig. 1.6). For Beck, examples of "true comic strip illustration" can be found in Charles Schulz's *Peanuts*, not in the pages of Marvel Comics. The samples from *Conan* are, Beck explains, "'action packed' . . . but each panel is a separate bit of eye-catching art" (Beck, "May We" 25). Although Beck admires the technique necessary to draw comics in this style, he admits that "the tricky page layouts and the startling displays of anatomy" cause "museum fatigue" that distract him from the story being told. "There's too much artwork!" he concludes (25).

Smith's early style, especially the Jack Kirby-like work he produced for *Conan*, is no more realistic than Beck's drawings of Captain Marvel or Tinman. By "too much artwork," Beck seems concerned with a lack of dynamics and motion in these figures. He raised a related concern in his conversation with Eisner in 1983, in which he lamented the lack of "variety" of character types in superhero comics. "The world has all kinds of things in it," Beck noted, so why should comic books be limited to "one little narrow form," especially given the range of characters on display in comic strips (Eisner, "Shop Talk" 74)? For Beck, figures are at their most expressive when the artist has rendered them as simply as possible.

Lucius Pindle, Tinman's alter ego, as Gary Brown notes, looks like a thinner, less tragic version of Billy Batson (Brown 7). Although he dresses like Billy, Pindle also resembles Stan Lee and Steve Ditko's Spider-Man. Like Peter Parker, Pindle is "the butt of many jokes," but, unlike Billy and Peter, no ancient wizard or radioactive spider will come to his rescue. After enduring another round of insults from his classmates—"Hey, the skeleton has escaped from biology class!"—Pindle is determined to become "the strongest man in the world!"[23] He has a lot of work to do. Pindle's exercise routine allows Beck to experiment once again with the relationship between figures and the backgrounds they inhabit.

The story begins, as Beck's Fawcett stories often do, with a large splash panel that introduces Fatman and Tinman, followed by narrative panels in which Lucius suffers the ridicule of his peers. On the next page, Pindle's posture communicates his frustration as well as his resolve: in the first panel, for example, notice the balled fists, the purposeful step, the four brushstrokes to the right of his face (fig. 1.7).

Lucius is the focus of each of the four panels on this page as he struggles with a barbell, a punching bag, and lastly with a trampoline. By the fifth panel, his shoulders slumped and his arms hanging at his side, Lucius, looking defeated, stands on a bathroom scale. While Beck eliminates the backgrounds in panels three and four (except for the floor beneath the trampoline in the

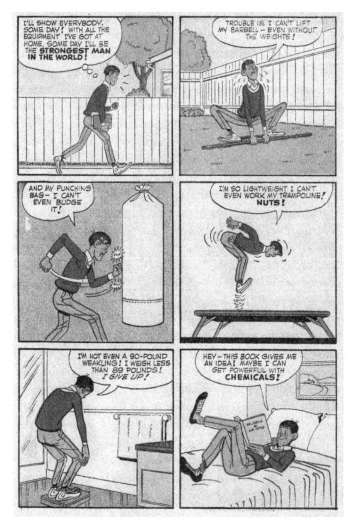

1.7 Lacking a magic word, Lucius Pindle searches for other ways to transform himself. From *Fatman, the Human Flying Saucer* no. 1. Script by Otto Binder and art by C. C. Beck. Fatman and Tinman © 1966 Milson Publishing Company, Inc.

fourth panel), the details of setting in panels one, two, five, and six include symbols of the character's life in the suburbs. White picket fences shield impeccably cut green lawns. Trees shade the window of a yellow house with a white gutter (the lines of the house and of the gutter run parallel with those of the fence and of the panel border). The details Beck includes in the fifth panel are equally clean, precise, and suburban. Standing on a scale, Lucius faces a white wall with a white towel hanging beside an orange countertop. To his left is what appears to be a door, maybe to the shower or to a linen closet (figure 1.7). We're a long way from the magic and splendor of Billy's subway tunnel.

1.8 Beck provides an example of the relationship between figures and simple backgrounds in Tinman's origin story from *Fatman, the Human Flying Saucer* no. 1. Script by Otto Binder and art by C. C. Beck. Fatman and Tinman © 1966 Milson Publishing Company, Inc.

Lucius's clothing also tells his story. He wears Billy's familiar red-and-gold sweater, a white shirt, and Chuck Taylors. "The purpose of illustrations is to show the actions and emotions of the characters," Beck explained to Robbins, "not the details of their costumes and anatomy."[24] Like Billy, he's an ordinary kid, although Lucius doesn't have an evil uncle hoping to steal his fortune, and he doesn't have to sell newspapers to survive. In the last panel on the page, finally at ease, he studies a copy of Stevenson's *Dr. Jekyll and Mr. Hyde.* "Hey—this book gives me an idea!" he exclaims. "Maybe I can get powerful with chemicals!" The details in this last panel are as quotidian as the ones that preceded it. Now looking more like Alfalfa from *Our Gang* than like Billy, Lucius lies on a bedspread the same color as the punching bag in panel three and the house in panel one. He's removed his sneakers and lies with his legs crossed and the book propped against his left knee. No longer frustrated, struggling, or defeated, he now appears elated, resting his head on a white pillow and scratching his chin (figure 1.7). This final panel establishes the context for the next page, in which Beck draws Pindle in a series of different postures. Despite his failures, Pindle is determined to keep working towards his goal.

Beck increases the rate of action on the page that follows by employing a simple nine-panel grid, with the final two combined into a single rectangular panel to emphasize the sound effect "Baroom!"—that clap of thunder that will transform Lucius into Tinman (fig. 1.8). Just as he and Pete Costanza did in the popular Mr. Tawny stories, Beck fills the backgrounds on this page with in-jokes, including a childlike sketch on Lucius's bookshelf and Otto Oscar Binder's initials printed on a pennant hanging on the wall in the first panel. On the previous page, Beck also included one of his favorite touches, a picture-within-a-picture—not a doorway or a window like the ones in Billy's origin story, but a painting hanging above Lucius's bed. That painting, like the bookshelf, test tubes, dresser (hairbrush included), and mirror, adds to the depth of these simple drawings.

After drinking the "chemicals" that be believes might transform him, Lucius purses his lips and closes his eyes. The formula is nothing more than "common salt," which fails to turn him into a powerful beast of a man like Mr. Hyde. In the next four panels, he studies *Old Formulas and Charms*, a book from his shelf. Although it's filled with "a lot of old supernatural junk," he finds one charm that might transform him into a "Shynyng Knight." First he looks with great anticipation at the book. Only two panels later, however, he looks as disappointed and frustrated as he did on the first page of the story. Lucius's worst fear is coming true, and the background details Beck includes only confirm it: he's as ordinary as the mirror on the wall, the brush on the dresser, the doorway to his left. What Lucius lacks most of all, of course, is patience. Standing in silhouette in panels seven and eight, his wish finally begins to come true.

Over the next two pages, Beck reverses the action, as Pindle, now in his armor, dismantles, piece by piece, the objects and obstacles that once stood in his way. First, he looks at himself in the mirror. He doesn't have the muscles of Captain Marvel—or of Barry Windsor-Smith's Conan the Barbarian, for that matter. Even though he's a "shining knight," his body hasn't changed: "But I'm so long and thin I'm more like a tin man!" he notes as he stares at himself. He tears the door of his room off its hinges, demolishes the punching bag, and finally jumps from the trampoline "100 miles up" into space. When he reaches his "apogee," Beck includes a drawing of the surface of the Earth.

Although he varies his page designs, Beck often employs simple and familiar grids of six or nine panels. His use of repetition, notably in the Tinman story, enables the reader easily to identify the characters and to follow that left-to-right action he mentioned in his 1948 testimony. Beck's characters, like the heroes in the "illustrated boy's adventures" he so admired (qtd. in Steranko 11), exist in spaces that offer opportunities for escape. "Vanishing Point" again offers a clue to Beck's philosophy: that "fabric of illusion," like Lucius Pindle's suburban home, or Billy's tunnel, is vexing *because* of its simplicity. It's all too real, too solid. "Is the world a thing by itself, and all we know illusion?" asks Carter before he switches on the machine in "Vanishing Point" (138). In order to answer that question, he, like Billy and Lucius, must study that reality with focus and determination. It won't reveal its secrets so easily.

"A SPIRITUAL PROCESS"

For Beck, drawing was a technical feat with a spiritual dimension and ethical obligations. First, the illustrator or cartoonist has an obligation to the writer. The artist's responsibility is to bring the writer's concepts to life, to animate the words of a script with a series of images. Beck once referred to this as a process of translation: "The illustrator of a story is an interpreter who puts written words into the language of pictures" (Beck, "Apples and Oranges"). The artist also has an important obligation to the reader. These images, faithful reproductions of the writer's vision, must inspire and shape the reader's imagination. A form of visual analysis, drawing is also an act of faith. As Beck describes it, the artist's intention is always utopian. In "Good Art," an essay published in *The Comics Journal* in the spring of 1986, he writes, "The true purpose of art is this: it is an attempt to make some kind of order out of the world by putting down in pictorial form a version of the world as it *might* appear, not as it actually appears" ("Good Art" 8–9).[25] Working in collaboration with an editor, a writer, and sometimes fellow artists, the illustrator, having studied carefully what already exists, draws what is possible. If the artist does so with discipline and with love, the reader will, in the moment it takes to read a page of comics, believe that these daydreams, like Billy's fantastic adventures, are true.

In their conversation, Eisner prodded Beck to explain what role an artist's subjectivity plays in the creative process. Do these theories make any room for self-expression? Beck responded by describing himself as an actor. He

1.9 Billy recalls his past in a flashback scene from *Shazam!* no. 1 (Feb. 1973). Script by Denny O'Neil and art by C. C. Beck. Captain Marvel and related characters © 2016 DC Comics.

used Peter Sellers as an example: "Every personality he had was a playwright's creation" (Beck qtd. in Eisner, "Shop Talk" 73). Although Peter Sellers, like a comic version of Lon Chaney, often submerged himself in his characters, his style of acting would hardly be described as naturalistic. While Sellers's "personality" ("Shop Talk" 73) might be hidden beneath Dr. Strangelove's sunglasses or Inspector Clouseau's fedora, his presence is undeniable. No matter what character he is playing, the audience has no doubt that they are watching Peter Sellers as he brings his manic energy to the screen. Beck's style is also instantly identifiable, even in the many Captain Marvel stories on which he worked with Pete Costanza. While Beck's simplicity is a hallmark of his art, even more remarkable is the relationship between his figures and his backgrounds. The pleasures and the beauty of Beck's art can be summed up in one panel, the final image on the second page of *Shazam!* no. 1 from 1973 (fig. 1.9).

In a script by Denny O'Neil, Billy meets a cartoon version of Otto Binder. Why hasn't Billy aged a day since the 1950s? "I don't blame him for wondering," Billy remarks. "I almost can't believe what's happened myself!" (2).[26] The page is a six-panel grid with the last two panels combined into a single rectangular box. Beck makes room for Billy's memories. Figures appear to emerge from a cloud of shadows. It's another familiar story: the rain, the buildings, the stranger. Beck invites us to look through one doorway after another. The panel's border frames the portrait of Billy, then the memory itself. His wide eyes stare into the past.

This is Beck's story, too. It's in the lines: first, the right ear, nothing more than four semicircles. Or the two small, curved eyebrows. The mess of hair, now looking a little longer. His chin casts a shadow on his left shoulder. Billy's nose, just three brushstrokes and a circle. In a 1960 essay, art historian and critic Otto Benesch describes Rembrandt's "*spiritual* process": "Drawing in its deepest sense is handwriting, an immediate emanation of personality, of its rhythm of life and its creative faculty" (Benesch 30; emphasis in the original). Benesch notes that, later in his life, Rembrandt reduced that process to its minimum, scratches from a reed pen on a sheet of paper. An experienced artist, Benesch writes, "avoids the roundabout methods of complicated and refined technical processes. The simplest ones," he notes, "which give direct expression of personality, are just the right ones" (Benesch 30–31). That simplicity is also an admission: even after decades of careful observation, reality remains more elusive than ever. Beck was perhaps being modest or coy with Eisner when he suggested that he didn't "believe in the artist expressing himself at all" (Beck qtd. in Eisner, "Shop Talk" 72), as his style is a reflection, by his own admission, of the world he knew as a child.

As he looked back on his boyhood in Minnesota, Beck noted the "Pennsylvania Dutch" influence on his sensibility. He describes them—and, by extension, himself—as a "plain people" who "admire hand-crafted furniture and simple tools and have little use for the latest gadgets and styles, being by nature conservative and oldfashioned [*sic*]," he explains, "even when we are laughed at by our neighbors, who call us narrowminded [*sic*] and out of touch with the real world" (Beck, "Racial Inheritance"). Then again, why bother so much with that "real world" when there are so many other possibilities, almost infinite, to observe and explore? This is Beck's "handwriting," his signature: drawings of a universe so complex that its beauty must be communicated with simplicity, elegance, and grace.

Chapter 2

OTTO BINDER AND THE SECRET LIFE OF MR. TAWNY, THE TALKING TIGER

Even a talking tiger gets writer's block sometimes. For Mr. Tawny, Billy Batson's good friend, it happened at the worst possible moment, just as *Captain Marvel Adventures* was celebrating its 100th issue in 1949. In "Captain Marvel Battles the Plot Against the Universe," Mr. Tawny, who first appeared in *Captain Marvel Adventures* in 1947, is hard at work on his autobiography. Sitting at a writing desk in his "modest home," dressed in a green sports coat, Mr. Tawny stumbles as he writes about his "great friend," Captain Marvel.[1] Startled, Tawny, holding his pen in his right paw, exclaims, "Dear me! I can't finish!" Billy has never told Mr. Tawny of that first meeting with Shazam—the mysterious stranger, the subway tunnel, the gallery of statues. When Billy comes to visit, Tawny asks for help: "I'm stuck, Billy! Tell me, when, where, and how did Captain Marvel come into existence?" Mr. Tawny at his side, Billy returns to the tunnel, where Shazam is waiting to provide the details the tiger needs to finish his memoir. Later, Dr. Sivana shows up with a spider gun and a time ship, but that's another story.

Mr. Tawny, a character Martin Williams once described as "a sports-jacketed American suburbanite" (Williams 79), was a favorite of Beck and Binder's.[2] Although Mary Marvel, Billy's sister, was Binder's "pride and joy" (Binder qtd. in Lage 60), Mr. Tawny was no doubt a close second. But not all of Captain Marvel's readers shared this fondness for Billy's furry friend. What was a talking tiger doing in a superhero comic book?[3] With a touch of self-deprecating humor, Richard Lupoff, in "The Big Red Cheese," writes that he "never warmed to Mr. Tawny" perhaps "because he seemed unrealistic" (91). Jokes aside, Lupoff is right—Mr. Tawny does seem out of place in Billy's dreamworld. The tiger is too ordinary, too flawed, too dull. He's more of an adult than Captain Marvel and spends most of his time fretting about his job or worrying about his legacy. Most of all, he's afraid of getting old, a concern that never enters Billy's mind. For John G. Pierce, the well-dressed and sophisticated tiger, whom he compares to Carl Barks's Uncle Scrooge, "was one of the most real characters ever to appear in comic books" (Pierce, "'One of the Most'" 31).

The "realness" of Mr. Tawny was no accident. As Bill Schelly, Binder's biographer, and Beck have noted, Billy's melancholy friend was a comic book version of the writer himself. Mr. Tawny was no idealized version of Binder, however. Tawny did not possess a magic word that would make him stronger, smarter, or invulnerable. Tawny's adventures, among the most appealing of those produced by Binder, Beck, and Costanza in the late 1940s and early 1950s, are the writer's cartoon diary, a record of his hopes and his frustrations as a freelancer working anonymously in a popular medium which prized action, thrills, and spectacle over emotional honesty, directness, and intimacy. The Tawny stories should be read not as superhero narratives but instead as cartoon fables in the same tradition as Walt Kelly's *Pogo*.[4] The autobiographical traces in Tawny's adventures also mark them as early, indirect precursors of contemporary graphic narratives that employ talking animals as vehicles of expression and truth-telling.

Schelly describes the twenty-three Tawny stories, which appeared between 1947 and the end of *Captain Marvel Adventures* in 1953, as "burlesques of Binder himself," narratives whose themes the writer first explored in his science fiction work of the 1930s (Schelly, *Words* 99–100). Binder and Beck had such faith in Tawny that they hoped he might star in his own comic strip, but the samples they produced did not attract the interest of any of the syndicates (Binder, "Special" 111; Schelly, *Words* 100–101).[5]

The Tawny stories published in *Captain Marvel Adventures* reveal the nature of Binder and Beck's working relationship. Beck, the trained illustrator, was the theorist, the technician, working with what he called a "blueprint" (Hamilton n.p.) to bring narratives to life. Beck understood, as he once wrote, that Binder "had a lot of fun laughing at himself in the Mr. Tawny stories" (Beck, "The Human Quality" 29). This fact might explain why he took such care with the character, as he noted in the 1977 interview with Chris Padovano: "I always tried to draw Tawny's adventures myself, as nobody else managed to make him believable" (Beck qtd. in Padovano). Tawny's "believable" qualities, which so endeared him to some readers, are the direct result of the experiment in autobiography that Binder was conducting with these scripts.

Tawny even dressed like Binder. "Otto in Binderland," a feature included in the fanzine *Alter Ego* from the summer of 1965, includes a photograph from 1944 of the writer in his home office. In the photo, he is leaning against a bookshelf filled with what appear to be pulp magazines. To Binder's left is a drawing of Captain Marvel and a skull. "Pajamas and a robe represent

2.1 Mr. Tawny works diligently on his book in a panel from "Mr. Tawny's Fight for Fame" from *Captain Marvel Adventures* no. 126 (Nov. 1951). Reprinted in *Shazam!* no. 14 (September–October 1974): 54. Captain Marvel and related characters © 2016 DC Comics.

'working clothes,'" Binder explains in the caption that accompanies the photo (qtd. in Thomas and Schelly 142). In "Mr. Tawny's Fight for Fame" from *Captain Marvel Adventures* no. 126 (November 1951),[6] Tawny wears these same "working clothes" as he writes his "dry old book!" (fig. 2.1).[7] The tiger is now writing a scientific dissertation called *Homing Habits of Hibernating Animals*. But he's had no more luck with this project than he did with his tale of Billy's first meeting with Shazam. "I live in obscurity. Like a hermit! Nobody ever hears of me," he complains.

Comics scholar Michael Chaney has argued that "the animal referenced in comics is" often "a ludic cipher of otherness" whose "appearance almost always accompanies the strategic and parodic veiling of the human" (Chaney 130). For Binder, the animal enabled and inspired an openness and emotional honesty, one not available to him in his other writing for comics or for the science fiction market. "He always had his great dreams," Binder explained to Matt Lage, "with unfortunate results" (Binder qtd. in Lage 64). Mr. Tawny's failed dreams reflect Binder's own uneasiness and anxiety, especially as he wrote his way through what Bill Schelly has described as one of the lowest points of his career in comic books. By the late 1940s, as he set his sights again on writing science fiction, Binder "was both physically and creatively burned out" (Schelly, *Words* 118). That sense of fatigue permeates many of the Tawny stories.

In his interviews with Jim Steranko and with Matt Lage, Binder often spoke about the literary figures that inspired his work on Captain Marvel, including Jonathan Swift and Lewis Carroll: "I always felt I was exploring and exploiting human nature too, digging out its zany aspects to show that much of life was a joke and full of craziness" (Binder qtd. in Lage 64). Locked into his daily routines, Tawny again and again attempts to dream his way out of loneliness and boredom. Although Captain Marvel often comes to his rescue, Billy's alter ego, as Binder explained to Lage, "was really just a minor character" in Tawny's narratives, a "sidekick" (Binder qtd. in Lage 64). While most of the Tawny stories, as Pierce has pointed out, convey a moral or lesson to Captain Marvel's readers (Pierce, "'One of the Most'" 31), the character never finds peace and happiness.

Mr. Tawny also inspired Binder to reflect on the act of writing itself. Aside from his letters to fans in the 1960s and "Memoirs of a Nobody," written in 1948 but not published until recently in *Fawcett Collectors of America*, the Mr. Tawny stories are as close as Binder got to writing an autobiography. "Mr. Tawny's Fight for Fame" (1951) and "Captain Marvel and Mr. Tawny's Quest for Youth" (1952), for example, both reflect Binder's struggle to change direction and to return to the science fiction market where he had begun his career in the 1930s under the pen name Eando Binder (initially in collaboration with Earl, his older brother, the *E* of "E and O" Binder). Perhaps Tawny "just didn't fit," as Lupoff puts it ("Big Red" 91), because Binder, an early and influential innovator in comic book storytelling, was entering a largely unexplored territory.

The autobiographical elements in the Tawny narratives make them strong candidates for the kind of analysis that comics scholars have provided in their studies of talking and funny animal comics. Aside from their historical interest, this "non-serial succession of sequels," as Binder described the Tawny narratives (Binder, "Special" 111), will no doubt attract contemporary readers, young and old, because of the quality of the artwork and the self-referential humor of the scripts. Just as Captain Marvel is Billy's dream self, Mr. Tawny plays the same role for Binder, but, rather than "veiling" (to borrow Michael Chaney's phrase) Binder's flaws and anxieties, Tawny highlights them. As a result, the Tawny stories are a counter-narrative to Billy's. At the end of a Tawny adventure, there is often a lingering sense of doubt, even dread, especially in "Captain Marvel and Mr. Tawny's Quest for Youth." Like other talking animal narratives, the Tawny stories lend themselves to complex readings, but they also posses a quality that even the most sophisticated literary theory would be at a loss to explain: filled with meditations on friendship, compassion, and mortality, Tawny's adventures are a lot of fun.

FUNNY ANIMALS AND AUTOBIOGRAPHY

When I teach Franz Kafka's *The Metamorphosis*, often with Peter Kuper's black-and-white comic book adaptation, I can anticipate the questions students will ask: Is he *really* a bug? What kind? What happened? *Is it all a dream*? The animal as a figure that expresses a shadow self, one hidden from the world, has its roots in traditions much older than Kafka's short stories and his moles, mice, apes, insects, and other unclassifiable creatures. Nevertheless, Kafka is an important figure to consider when thinking about talking animals because of his indirect influence on Art Spiegelman's *Maus*.[8]

Over the course of his interview with Hillary Chute in *MetaMaus*, Spiegelman identifies the various sources that shaped the telling of his father's story. Kafka's "Josephine the Singer, or the Mouse Folk" was part of the mix, but, Spiegelman explains, "I don't think I'd even focused on it specifically as a metaphor for the Jewish people back then. It was just one more Kafka fable I'd absorbed" (Spiegelman 113–14). Just as meaningful for Spiegelman were the comics he'd read as a child, including the work of Carl Barks. "Whatever the funny animal surface was," Spiegelman remembered, "I could climb way further behind that surface than I could when trying to identify with, say, Peter Parker's problems" (Spiegelman 193). That "surface" has long fascinated both cartoonists and comics scholars and critics. In studies of talking animals, many scholars describe the strange and compelling hold characters like Mickey Mouse, Donald Duck, or Pogo, to name just a few examples, have had on the imagination of readers. The act that Spiegelman describes, that of a bottomless search for meaning, is one of the qualities Kim Thompson once identified as a key component of the funny animal genre. "The inherent irreality of the concept gives them an instant fantastical quality," Thompson argued in a 1986 essay, "and, paradoxically, a *reality* that far exceeds the dulled naturalism of 'realistic' comics" (Thompson 32).

In his assessment of Spiegelman's use of cats and mice (and dogs and frogs and other creatures) in *Maus*, Joseph Witek echoes Thompson's sentiments as he describes the "magical, or at least mysterious" characteristics of these creatures and their ability "to open a generic space into a precivilized innocence" (Witek 111) that has fascinated cartoonists from George Herriman and Walt Kelly to Spiegelman and, more recently, Sam Sharpe and Edie Fake. In his analysis of talking animals in animation, comic strips, and comic books, Les Daniels argues that characters like Donald Duck and Pogo enabled their creators to imagine or recall a lost innocence, a kind of preindustrial wonderland (like the one Superman and Captain Marvel defended, perhaps, on the covers of *Action Comics* no. 1 and *Whiz Comics* no. 2, respectively). These "dumb animals," as Daniels calls them, "were echoes of the collective past" that some cartoonists "had left behind" (Daniels 53). More recently, in "Animal Subjects of the Graphic Novel," Chaney writes that a "process of defamiliarization" is at work in these comics, as readers laugh at the antics of these all-too-human beasts while reflecting on questions of identity and mortality (Chaney 130). But the use of animals as embodiments of human fears and anxieties is not unique to comics. As Lorraine Daston and Gregg Mitman point out in their

2.2 Captain Marvel and Mr. Tawny take a stroll on the cover of *Captain Marvel Adventures* no. 82 (March 1948). Captain Marvel and related characters © 2016 DC Comics.

introduction to the 2005 collection *Thinking with Animals*, "humans past and present, hither and yon, think they know how animals think, and they habitually use animals to help them do their thinking about themselves" (1–2). Mr. Tawny's first appearance on the cover of *Captain Marvel Adventures*, from issue no. 82 (dated March 1948, just a few months after his debut in 1947),[9] provides a telling example of that "defamiliarization," as the tiger, arm-in-arm with Captain Marvel, walks past a group of startled onlookers (fig. 2.2).

"It's good to see you again, Mr. Tawny!" says Captain Marvel, who, as always, looks cheerful and welcoming. The tiger is dressed elegantly, a green fedora perched between his ears. The yellow-and-orange pattern of his sports coat matches the color of his fur. Walking stick in hand, Mr. Tawny enjoys a cigar. To the tiger's left is a newsstand with copies of *Captain Marvel Adventures* no. 82. There's the cover image again, repeated three times in miniature. The vendor, like the pedestrians who stare in amazement, looks terrified. Even cartoon people don't know what to make of a tiger who walks, talks, and dresses like a man (Tawny, however, never wears shoes). What distinguished Captain Marvel from Superman, Binder once pointed out, was that Clark Kent's alter ego never took the time "to lounge around and relax" (Binder qtd. in Steranko 14). This cover is an example of Captain Marvel's more "relaxed," casual persona. Unlike Superman, Batman, or Captain America, Captain Marvel is always up for a stroll.

The cover, which advertises an issue that will at last reveal how the tiger first learned to speak, also signals the difference between Tawny's stories and Captain Marvel's typical adventures. There are no time ships here, no evil scientists, no spider guns or Historamas. This image exhibits one of the qualities critic Jeet Heer attributes to children's comics. Comics for children, like the bulk of the stories Binder and Beck produced for Fawcett, "tend to be quieter, more relaxed and funnier," Heer points out, than "teenage comics" which are often "more frantic[,] detailed, and earnest" (Heer, "A Colloquy" 244).[10] "Captain Marvel and the Return of Mr. Tawny," in which the tiger defends his friend Tom Todd against a charge of murder, is a story with hints of Kipling's *The Jungle Book* and Burroughs's Tarzan novels (the tiger gains his ability to speak thanks to a serum provided by a hermit who looks a little like C. C. Beck himself). At the end of the story, once he's cleared Todd's name, the tiger embraces his friend and, behaving like a house cat, licks his face. In that final frame of the story, Tawny is wearing Binder's "working clothes" again: a robe and polka-dot pajamas. Even while lounging at home, the tiger is impeccably dressed. Despite these human characteristics, Tawny has an uncanny presence. He might dress and behave like a human being, but he is still a tiger, and his friend is still a Fred MacMurray look-alike wearing a bright red costume. These images, then, are uncanny in the Freudian sense—that is, they are familiar but reveal what otherwise might "remain secret" or "hidden away" (Freud 132), those fears and anxieties we recognize even as the unconscious attempts to suppress them.

Svetlana Boym's reading of Russian formalist Viktor Shklovsky's concept of *ostranenie* is useful in a discussion of the uncanny aspects of funny animals. The "defamiliarization" that Michael Chaney refers to suggests a connection to Shklovsky's theories as defined in the groundbreaking essay "Art as Technique." In her analysis of Shklovsky's ideas on art and literature, Boym writes that he employs the term *ostranenie* "to suggest both distancing" as well as "making strange" (*Architecture* 18). For Binder, that "making strange" involves introducing ordinary, often unremarkable daily setbacks or challenges into

2.3 Mr. Tawny leads another group of visitors through the museum in an opening scene from "Mr. Tawny's Fight for Fame" in *Captain Marvel Adventures* no. 126 (November 1951). Reprinted in *Shazam!* no. 14 (September–October 1974): 53. Captain Marvel and related characters © 2016 DC Comics.

an otherwise fantastic narrative of super-beings and talking jungle cats. "Estrangement is what makes art artistic; but by the same token," Boym writes of Shklovsky's theory, "it makes life lively, or worth living" (Boym, *Architecture* 18–19). Mr. Tawny, as the fictional stand-in for Otto Binder, takes part in the adventures that the writer himself, sitting in his "working clothes" at his manual typewriter day after day, will never experience. As Boym points out, the "making strange" at the heart of artistic expression is often playful and joyous (*Architecture* 18–19).

Given his ability to guide readers through the struggles and setbacks of day-to-day life, Tawny's job should come as no surprise. When he is not at home, Kafka-like, spending sleepless nights working on his writing, he is a docent in a natural history museum (fig. 2.3).

One of the more bizarre images in "Mr. Tawny's Fight for Fame" from 1951 appears on the first page of the story. "We all have disgruntled moods at times," declares the caption in the upper left-hand corner of the story's first panel, "and Mr. Tawny is no exception!" The skeleton of a dinosaur looms as a glass display case obscures its legs and torso. Tawny thinks to himself, "Day after day I conduct these museum tours! I know my spiel by heart! I've given it 999 times!" An animal stares back at him from the display, and in that moment an otherwise familiar image—a museum filled with visitors and a guide leading them from one exhibit to the next—is also "made strange": a talking animal lectures cartoon human beings about other "wild animals" and "their natural habitats!" There's a joke here, too—a wink at the reader. What else would a talking tiger be *qualified to do?* In the next panel, as he walks home, the sun setting behind him, the tiger thinks, "Time after time I plod my weary way home to my quiet cottage and unlock the door!" Tawny, like his creator, is successful but not content with his lack of fame. The details in these panels are commonplace: museumgoers with tweed suits and glasses; a two-storey suburban home surrounded by tall trees and a well-kept lawn. What hope do the rest of us have if Mr. Tawny—that time traveler, crime buster, cat of letters—can't find happiness?

Although Binder did not identify Franz Kafka's work as an influence on his science fiction or on his comics, the parallels between Mr. Tawny's literary ambitions and the academic standing of the narrator in "A Report to an Academy" are difficult to ignore. Walter Benjamin's commentary on the relationship between historical memory and Kafka's animal characters is also worth considering in a study of comic books and nostalgia. Just as Billy Batson represents a kind of absence—a fiction of lost innocence, a marker of the idealized notions of boyhood and masculinity in American in the 1940s—Mr. Tawny might be read as a character that embodies a form of amnesia that Benjamin describes in his analysis of stories like "The Burrow." For Kafka, Benjamin explains, "animals are the receptacles of the forgotten" (*Illuminations* 132). In reading about an animal, we are invited to consider our own animal nature.[11] Benjamin points out that if "the most forgotten alien land is one's own body, one can understand why Kafka called the cough that erupted from within him 'the animal'" (Benjamin, *Illuminations* 132). Like the cartoonists described by Les Daniels—those who looked back with a sense of longing at an inaccessible "collective past"—Kafka, writes Benjamin, sought to locate a history that was beyond his reach, a "prehistoric world" that could be imagined but was almost impossible to describe (*Illuminations* 131). Understood in this light, "making strange" becomes a strategy to locate these "prehistoric" spaces, ones that can only be reclaimed through imagination but not with memory.[12] Our animal past is too distant and obscure. This private, intimate history, one that will lead us back to a point of origin, is something that we carry with us, like the body itself, that "heavy bear" of Delmore Schwartz's poem (74).[13] Given that "the most forgotten alien land is one's own body," as Benjamin argues in his notes on Kafka, it is no wonder that Mr. Tawny held so much appeal for Binder, the one-time science fiction writer who had explored so many "alien" territories in his fiction. Even as he found ways to address private concerns in the Mr. Tawny stories, however, Binder never lost sight of his audience and their desires. As Beck argued, young readers don't have much time for "soul-searching" ("Man of Steel" 7), let alone philosophy and metaphysics.

Tawny's adventures, light comedies written for an audience of young readers, do not have the same emotional heft as Spiegelman's harrowing *Maus* or Sam Sharpe's recent, critically acclaimed short story "Mom." What the Binder and Beck stories share with those two examples of comics autobiography is an attempt to invent another self, a storyteller, one whose status as a "ludic cipher of otherness," as Chaney describes these talking animals (130), grants the writer, the artist, and the reader the ability to observe human behavior with a detachment that encourages self-reflection. In Sharpe's recent narrative, he tells the story of his mother's mental illness with a cast of dogs, rabbits, elephants, ducks, and even a giraffe. Towards the end of the story, as his mother grows more unstable and delusional, the narrator, in a caption, describes his inability to *see* as his mother does, to enter the world of shadows and paranoia she inhabits due to her condition: "Our realities had finally drifted so far apart that we could no longer understand each other" (Sharpe n.p.).[14] While Tawny is not a tragic figure like the title character in "Mom," he remains a startling creature, especially as he strolls about with Captain Marvel or guides tourists through the museum. Despite his anxieties, he remains poised and elegant. We sympathize with him because, unlike Billy, he is at the mercy of time just as we are. The tiger understands how it feels to age and to remember (and to long for) the past.

Writing these stories almost two decades before Justin Green published *Binky Brown Meets the Holy Virgin Mary*—the comic that inspired other artists, like Spiegelman, to tell their own life stories—Binder did not inaugurate a tradition of autobiographical comics. Readers in the early 1950s had no idea that the tiger was Binder's alter ego. The Tawny stories, however, though long neglected or dismissed as simple children's fables, provide an example of the value and the flexibility of the funny animal genre. A brief detour into Binder's life and times will help to explain why the writer felt the need to express himself more directly in these stories. While Binder was a gracious, witty, and playful figure, he also took his craft seriously, and found in comics a new medium that was at times frustrating but also exciting and filled with promise (Steranko 17; Schelly, *Words* 77–78).

"I KNOW A WRITER WHEN I SEE ONE. YOU HAVE IT IN YOU."

Born to Austro-Hungarian immigrants in Bessemer, Michigan, in 1911, Binder and his family lived in Randolph, Nebraska, before relocating to Chicago in 1922 (Schelly, *Words* 23–27).[15] The young Binder, like Beck, adored the fiction of Edgar Rice Burroughs and later discovered the work of H. P. Lovecraft and Robert E. Howard in the pages of *Weird Tales* (*Words* 29). Although he began college with the hope of becoming a scientist, his life took a different and unexpected direction when he and his older brother Earl wrote and submitted "The First Martian" to *Amazing Stories* (*Words* 33–35). The magazine published the story in 1932; it was the first work of fiction by Eando Binder. Although Earl and Otto's collaboration only lasted until 1936, Binder would continue to use the pseudonym for his science fiction work for the rest of his career.[16]

As his reputation grew in the close-knit science fiction fan circles of the 1930s, Binder eventually found work as an agent for writer Otis Adelbert Kline's literary agency, a firm that represented pulp writers who have now become legendary, including Lovecraft and Howard. When Binder met Lovecraft in New York, the creator of the Cthulhu mythos, according to a letter Otto mailed to Earl in the winter of 1936, remarked, "You're half of one of my favorite authors!" In another letter from June of that year, Binder, impressed with Howard's output, describes Conan's creator as "a rough and ready Texan" who "claims he wears no underwear because there's no sense to it!"[17] In response to these letters from Otto, Earl, back in the Portage Park neighborhood on the northwest side of Chicago, was both protective and encouraging: "I have read a lot, Otto, perhaps more than you would give me credit for. I know a writer when I see one. You have it in you. It may be the pulps for some years yet but you will emerge from that, take my word for it."[18] Through the science fiction fan circles, Binder met two other young men, Julius Schwartz and Mort Weisinger, who would become lifelong friends. In the 1950s and 1960s, after the demise of Captain Marvel, Binder wrote scripts for the Weisinger-edited Superman comics at National. A study of Binder's critical role in shaping the Superman mythos in the 1950s and in the 1960s would require its own book.[19]

Binder's most enduring and best known science fiction stories are the Adam Link series, the first of which appeared in the January 1939 issue of *Amazing Stories* (*Words* 59–62). "Binder was always a great, iconic, early tech days science fiction name," remembered Harlan Ellison, who compared him to such obscure figures as Ed Earl Repp and Stanton A. Coblentz.[20] "I, Robot," Adam Link's first appearance, along with Lester del Rey's 1938 story "Helen O'Loy," inspired Isaac Asimov's "Robbie." In 1950, Asimov was about to publish a collection of his popular and celebrated robot stories under the title *Mind and Iron* when his publisher suggested they change the title to *I, Robot* (Asimov, *The Caves of Steel* xi). Asimov, recalling the first Adam Link story, was initially uncomfortable with the switch, but Binder, according to Schelly's biography, asked only that Asimov send him a signed copy (Schelly, *Words* 121). Asimov was always quick to credit Binder's narrative as a precursor to his robot tales and later included Adam Link's first appearance in a collection of significant science fiction from 1939. "My book is now the more famous," Asimov wrote in his introduction, "but Otto's story was there first" (Asimov, *The Great SF Stories* 11).[21]

According to his 1964 *Alter Ego* letter, Binder wrote "some two million words of science fiction pulps published between 1932 and 1945" (Binder,

"Special!" 111). He began writing comics in 1939 for Harry "A" Chesler and wrote his first Captain Marvel story in 1941 (Steranko 12; Schelly, *Words* 67, 78). In Beck's fictional account of their first meeting from "The World's Mightiest Fat Head," artist Wally Baker is a huge fan of Landro, the legendary science fiction writer (Beck, "Fat Head" 1, 42). When Baker asks the veteran writer if he's looking forward to writing for comic books, Landro responds, "Well—it's a job," one that pays pretty well: "Two bucks a page is better than nothing. I figure I can turn out two or three stories a week, eight to ten pages per story . . . it'll keep me from starving" (Beck, "Fat Head" 1, 42). By 1953, Binder, who kept a careful record of his published work, had written 529 stories featuring Captain Marvel, Mary Marvel, or the Marvel Family. "My present-day home in Englewood, New Jersey," he noted, "was dedicated at a Fawcett party as being 'The House That Captain Marvel Built'" (Binder "Special!" 111).

An essay Binder published in 1941, around the same time that he began writing for Fawcett, suggests that, even early in his comics career, he sensed great possibilities for this new form of storytelling. In "A New Medium for Fantasy?", Binder refers to comics as "an intriguing new medium of writing," one that might eventually attract older, more sophisticated readers (Binder qtd. in Schelly, *Words* 78). "Admittedly, the comics appeal to a very juvenile audience, but gradually they are growing up, I believe. The possibility is that eventually the picture-medium may be used to tell far better stories—even good science fiction!" (78). In the early 1950s, Binder began writing scripts for EC Comics based on his earlier fiction. In a 1952 letter to fan and editor Sam Moskowitz, he echoes the sentiments of this 1941 essay as he praises EC's science fiction titles. Binder urges Moskowitz to "pick up a copy of *Weird Fantasy* or *Weird Science* comics sometime and read them" because "the comics are not too far behind the pulps in well-plotted stories, believe it or not!"[22]

While Binder is best remembered for the work he did at Fawcett and later at National, he produced scripts for a variety of other publishers over the course of his long career. "If you like indigestible facts," Binder noted, reflecting on his work from 1941 until the late 1950s, "my *total* comics output—all publishers and all characters—up to the end of 1957 was 2,227 stories for 18,100 pages, or approximately 100,000 panels" (Binder, "Special!" 112). Binder wrote prolifically for National until 1960, when he focused his attention on editing *Space World* (Binder, "Special" 112). By the mid-1960s, he was writing comics again, including the post-apocalyptic *Mighty Samson* for Gold Key, as well as the short-lived *Fatman* and *Super Green Beret* for Milson (Schelly, *Words* 195). In the 1960s and early 1970s, he also wrote nonfiction books that owed a debt to his earlier science fiction work, most notably *What We Really Know About Flying Saucers*, which he dedicated to his late daughter Mary, who died in 1967 at the age of fourteen after being struck by a car outside her school (*Words* 198–99; Uslan, *Batman* 88–89). He and his wife, Ione, had a second child, Robert, who was born in 1955 with Down syndrome (*Words* 140).

According to Schelly, the trauma of Mary's death was one of the factors that brought Binder's comics career to an end. Roy Thomas remembers speaking with Binder not long after the accident. Binder had lost "the enthusiasm" and "hinted that with his daughter's death, it was a little too painful, and he would just as soon forget about comics" (Thomas qtd. in Schelly, *Words* 205). In Steranko's *History of Comics*, Binder confesses that, by the 1960s, writing for comics "was tough sledding," in part because of endless rewrites and revisions, especially for Weisinger (Steranko 21). At the end of Steranko's chapter on Captain Marvel, Binder also makes a poignant reference to Mary's death, a tragedy that prompted him and Ione to relocate from Englewood to Chestertown, New York (see also Schelly, *Words* 206).

In the epilogue to *Words of Wonder*, Bill Schelly describes Binder's tremendous impact on comics fandom in the 1960s and early 1970s (234). As I mention in the introduction, Richard Lupoff and Don Thompson dedicated the 1970 collection *All in Color for a Dime* to Binder. Sam Moskowitz had already dedicated *The Coming of the Robots*, a 1963 anthology that also features Lester del Rey and Isaac Asimov, to him, calling Binder the "[p]opularizer of the 'modern' robot" (Moskowitz, *Robots* 5). Even after the tragic loss of his daughter, Binder continued to share his memories with comic book fans, including, in the early 1970s, an aspiring artist named Frank Miller (*Words* 218). Binder's generosity to fans, even those that criticized his work, no doubt was rooted in his experience with science fiction fandom in the 1930s.

While working in comics, Binder sometimes longed for the closer relationship between writers and readers fostered by the science fiction fan community where he had begun his career. In "Memoirs of a Nobody" and in letters to Moskowitz from the early 1950s, Binder nostalgically recalls those years. By the early 1950s, Binder found himself writing for a different audience than the one that had read his work in the 1930s. As a result, editor Horace Gold from *Galaxy Science Fiction* and Oscar J. Friend, Binder's agent, offered him advice on how to transition back to writing prose for a new generation of science fiction fans. Binder's responses to these letters, and his correspondence with Moskowitz, suggest that the scenes of a frustrated Mr. Tawny laboring fruitlessly at his desk were glimpses of Binder's struggle to adapt to a marketplace that had changed enormously in the years since he'd made the jump to comics in the 1940s.

"YOU'VE GOT A LOT OF SPLASH PANELS AND CAPTIONS TO GET OUT OF YOUR SYSTEM"

Tawny might have struggled with writer's block, but at least he didn't know the agony of rejection slips. In 1953, H. L. Gold responded to Binder's new fiction with advice on how to transition back to prose after a decade primarily devoted to comics. "It's good hearing from you again," Gold wrote, "but it's also disturbing to see what writing comics has done to your style, characterization, and dialogue." Gold concedes that the story's concept "is all right" (Gold does not name the Binder story in question in the letter). The writing and "execution," however, are "hysterical, overdrawn, grotesquely characterized, and blatantly melodramatic." In closing, Gold reassures Binder and offers encouragement: "You've got a lot of splash panels and captions to get out of your system—a painful [process]."[23] In a letter of response dated less than a week later, on February 21, 1953, Binder writes, "Ouch! Too bad you haven't got a comics book [*sic*] you could have used that last ms in. Didn't think my slip showed that much."

Binder faced a couple of obstacles. First, he was accustomed to working in a hybrid medium in which "captions" work in tandem with visuals provided by an artist or a team of artists. Binder enjoyed working collaboratively. In a 1952 letter, he even invites Moskowitz to send him ideas or pitches. "Now I have no prima-donna qualms about accepting ideas from an editor[,]" he explains. Doing so, he noted, would not "violate" his "lone-wolf sensibilities."[24] To prove his point, he offers an example from his experience in comic books, where the "editor and writer often whip up ideas between them." A sudden return to "lone-wolf" status must have been jarring for Binder, especially after so many successful years writing for Fawcett.

Binder faced another more serious challenge, one also reflected in the Tawny stories. Styles and tastes had changed. A new generation of writers was now producing a more stylish, and, in some cases, more experimental and self-consciously literary form of science fiction.[25] Like Gold, Binder's agent, Oscar J. Friend, suspected that the "juvenile" quality of one of Binder's new stories could be attributed to all those years of writing comic book scripts: "Hold it, pal!" Friend wrote in a letter to Binder dated July 6, 1953. "No criticism of comics is meant; just the frank statement that such work naturally affects your serious and adult science fiction output."[26]

Always persistent, Binder responded with two other stories in August. While Friend sensed some "improvement," Binder still had a lot of work to do. In reference to "Where Is Thy Sting?" and "Memory World," Friend wrote, "The ideas are clever enough, but your quality of actual writing needs toning or tooling up." Just as Earl had encouraged his younger brother almost twenty years earlier, Friend had faith that Binder could make the necessary changes to meet the market's demands, but the writer would have to do his homework. "Study a few Bradbury, Sturgeon, Kuttner, and Leinster shorts for sheer quality of writing style and you will see what I mean," Friend suggested. "Their stuff is no better than yours, but their writing is more polished and adult."[27]

Gold, Friend, and J. Francis McComas from *The Magazine of Fantasy and Science Fiction* all agreed that Binder's ideas were strong and worth developing. By the end of 1953, he reported a few sales to Oswald Train, who had published Binder's pulp serial *Lords of Creation* as a book in 1949 (Schelly, *Words* 119–20).[28] "Comics still occupy most of my time," Binder wrote to Train, noting that "good old Captain Marvel was finally sued out of existence by the Superman people," which enabled him to write for Mort Weisinger's Superman titles. Despite the setbacks and rejections in the summer of 1953, he managed to place stories in *The Magazine of Fantasy and Science Fiction* and *Universe Science Fiction*.[29] "I intend to keep writing and selling (I hope) at a modest pace," Binder confided to Train. "Fun to be back at it."[30]

Based on letters from 1952, however, it is not entirely clear that Binder ever intended to write what Friend called "serious and adult science fiction," the kind being produced by Henry Kuttner, C. L. Moore, or Alfred Bester. In an exchange with Moskowitz, Binder wondered if the readers who enjoyed Captain Marvel might also develop an interest in science fiction. Why not publish a science fiction magazine for those young fans? Binder had a specific age range in mind, too, one based on Fawcett's "statistical tabulation" of its readership. After conducting research on those fans, Fawcett, according to Binder, had discovered that their comics attracted readers "from 6 to 18," with most of those boys and girls falling into the "9 to 14" range, what Binder then describes to Moskowitz as "a big pit into which you can pour endless comics and never fill it up."[31] Why spend so much time worrying about older fans when most editors ignored this large demographic of younger readers? The following passage from this letter offers an insight into how Binder understood that audience. He had no intention to simplify his writing. Rather, he sought ways to engage the interest and attention of readers who were young but hardly ignorant or unsophisticated:

> I may be wrong, but don't most stf [science fiction] mags and editors always strive to reach an "older" reading group? Thus hoping to jack up circulation. Maybe a better answer is to reach "down"—toward those avid kids of 9 to 14.

Anyway, Binder argued, "what's wrong with *entertaining kids*? (And also thereby 'training' them to buy 'adult-type' stf as they grow older?)" As Binder stressed several times in this letter, he was not suggesting that a magazine for this age group should be "'written down' or corned up," but instead offered some of Robert Heinlein's fiction as a model. Read in the context of these letters, the Tawny stories provide an example of the kind of fiction that Binder hoped to produce: stories that would appeal, like some of Heinlein's writing, "to many an adult as well as [a] kid."

Binder's emphasis on characterization, especially in Tawny's adventures, might be traced back to a suggestion the writer received early in his career. In 1938, John W. Campbell, editor of *Astounding Science-Fiction*, offered Binder advice on how to write a story that would sell. In response to one of Binder's submissions, Campbell wrote, "Every time your people have life and reality, you'll have a check from Street & Smith [*Astounding*'s publisher, perhaps best known in the pulp market for *The Shadow* and *Doc Savage*]. But I'm going to ask for more character in characters in the future—more than heretofore—in every story."[32] Anticipating some of the comments from Gold and Friend in the early 1950s, Campbell admits that he's concerned that Binder's work "may be getting a little wooden," as tastes began to change even in the late 1930s. As a freelance writer, Binder could not afford to disappoint his editors or his readers.

Binder's introduction to "The Teacher from Mars," a story first published in *Thrilling Wonder Stories* in 1944 and included, along with fiction from Murray Leinster and Henry Kuttner, in the 1949 anthology *My Best Science Fiction Story*, suggests that he took Campbell's advice seriously. "Too many science fiction stories overplay cold science and underplay human characters," writes Binder ("Teacher" 19). When he created Mun Zeerohs, the Martian teacher bullied by his human students, he "wanted to break away from this restriction and produce a living, breathing character. One whose emotions and innermost thoughts you could follow and sympathize with" (19). In order to do this, he established an affinity with this creature of his imagination: "At least, while writing the story, I was a Martian," Binder writes, "and I was beginning to hate the whole human race for mistreating 'my people!'" ("Teacher" 19).[33] In the Tawny stories, Binder performs this same experiment, as the tiger expresses those frustrations that Binder was unable to voice in his other writing. With Tawny as his voice, Binder experienced the freedom not available to him in his fiction or in his other comic book scripts.

Beck believed that "anonymity" was one of the strengths of those working in comics in the 1940s because, like a ventriloquist, "you can say a lot of things under a dummy's name that you could never say yourself" (Beck qtd. in Groth 61). The Tawny stories are among the highlights of Binder and Beck's work because they represent a fusion of their artistic sensibilities. As he noted in the essay that accompanies "The Teacher from Mars," Binder valued "'human interest'" in his fiction (19). By using himself as model for Tawny,

Binder humanized what otherwise could have been a faceless, mechanical, or "anonymous" work of popular fiction. Binder's is the still, quiet voice calling out from beneath Tawny's mask. Once Tawny passed through Beck's "fabric of illusion," the character began to take on a life of his own, one grounded in the quotidian details of Binder's otherwise unremarkable routine but suddenly transformed into something strange, other, and mysterious. In a 1953 interview with Gerry De La Ree for the *Bergen Evening Record*, Binder explained the challenge of coming up with so many "unusual plots or situations," a "gimmick or twist" that readers would not expect (De La Ree 3). The "gimmick" in "Mr. Tawny's Quest for Youth" is a simple one: even though his best friend is a superhero, and despite the fact that he has a good (if boring) job and a nice home, Tawny discovers that he cannot, like Dr. Sivana, travel through time. No matter the intensity of his desire to relive the past, his body will not allow him to forget that he, unlike Billy, has grown old. The "gimmick"? The kids in the story, like the reader, learn that, one day, they'll grow old, too. And it will hurt.

"A REGULAR FELLOW"

It's a figure of pure joy: Tawny, arms outstretched, eyes closed, paws firmly planted on a carpet of green grass. The figures behind him stand in silhouette against a clear, bright, yellow sky. Tawny, a canteen hanging on his (prominent) waist, a pack on his shoulders, wears a white Captain Marvel Club turtleneck. The tiger, no longer trapped in his study, lifts his face to the sun. "Already I feel ten years younger!" he exclaims (fig. 2.4).

This panel from "Captain Marvel and Mr. Tawny's Quest for Youth" (from *Captain Marvel Adventures* no. 131, dated April 1952)[34] appears not long after a thought balloon in which the tiger recalls the circumstances that led to his membership in the club.[35] His goal? To feel young again, to "recapture youth!" In the second panel on the second page of the story, Tawny conjures an image of himself from only "a few days ago," as the tiger, dressed in his green sports coat, walks with his back bent, weighted down by his briefcase. He narrates that image for Billy and for readers: "I was gloomy and tired, not getting any fun out of life!" Worst of all, he explains, he "felt old!" (fig. 2.5).

In this story, feelings of nostalgia result in a series of setbacks and comic failures. "Oh, to be young again!" reads the caption that introduces the story. "Such is the cry of many an older person, dreaming fondly of his childhood days!" In the splash page that opens the story, Captain Marvel is critical of Mr. Tawny's fixation on youth. Tied to a tree, a toy arrow jutting from his forehead, Billy's alter ego asks a question that the reader would no doubt like

2.4 In an early panel from "Captain Marvel and Mr. Tawny's Quest for Youth," the talking tiger joins the other members of the Captain Marvel Club on a hike. From *Captain Marvel Adventures* no. 131 (April 1952). Captain Marvel and related characters © 2016 DC Comics.

answered, too: "What's this, Mr. Tawny? Your second childhood?" (figure 2.6). In the panel, the tiger is dressed as a "big Indian chief" with a headdress and a bow and arrow. He is partaking of one of the rituals of a 1950s suburban childhood, dressed as a nightmarish pulp-fiction parody of a Native American. His costume makes the panel doubly strange, a talking animal disguised as a Tonto-like fantasy, or a cartoon image crossed with a page from *The Boy Scout Handbook*. "The animal has been emptied of experience and secrets," John Berger writes in a discussion of Buffon and eighteenth-century zoology, "and this new invented 'innocence' begins to provoke in man a kind of nostalgia" (Berger 10). The headdress and the bow and arrows might be read as part of the same "*receding* past" that Berger describes, a perceived oneness with nature associated with stereotypical images of Native Americans. An allusion to Tarzan later in the story reinforces these notions of an ideal, exuberant, and youthful past.

How would Captain Marvel's readers, those kids between the ages of nine and fourteen that Binder described to Moskowitz, have responded to Mr. Tawny's lament over his lost youth? Binder is inviting those readers to imagine what middle age might be like and how they might respond to it. "Can Mr. Tawny, the Talking Tiger, recapture the joy of the days when he was a carefree

2.5 Mr. Tawny dreams of a life beyond the museum in a panel from "Captain Marvel and Mr. Tawny's Quest for Youth." *Captain Marvel Adventures* no. 131 (April 1952). Captain Marvel and related characters © 2016 DC Comics.

cub?" The caption implies that the tiger, as his behavior indicates, has lost "his sanity." Captain Marvel's mission is to bring Mr. Tawny back to his senses.

The backgrounds of the panels in "Quest for Youth" reinforce questions about youthful idealism, middle age, and pending mortality. For every lush evergreen, there is a barren and skeletal tree filling the horizon. On his first outing with the club, its members vote Tawny as their leader. Like the school children in "The Teacher from Mars," two of them set out to ridicule and sabotage him. They fill his knapsack with rocks and tie his striped tail to a tent that almost carries him away in a strong wind. Captain Marvel knows the kids are up to something and spends most of the narrative saving Mr. Tawny's life and trying to figure out which of the boys is making trouble.

The story is filled with images of both youth and decay. On page four, Captain Marvel warns Tawny against racing the kids. "Oh, pish posh, Captain Marvel!" says the tiger. "Youthful energy surges within me!" Mr. Tawny is the first in a line of silhouettes. Like the fifth panel on page two, it's a joyous, almost manic image (fig. 2.7). Only two panels later, he's flat on his back and unable to move. "He's just winded!" Captain Marvel assures the boys. Later,

2.6 Captain Marvel appears skeptical of his friend's nostalgia on the first page of "Captain Marvel and Mr. Tawny's Quest for Youth" from *Captain Marvel Adventures* no. 131 (April 1952). Captain Marvel and related characters © 2016 DC Comics.

things get worse when Tawny goes swimming and lands in a pool of mud. At least Captain Marvel takes care of the hornets.

Tawny slowly realizes that he's better off living in the present. His home study might be dull, but at least it's free of bugs, storms, and mean little kids. "Oh, me!" he sighs. "I've had all the joys of youth I can stand!" It turns out that two kids named Red and Freckles did all the "hazing": "We can't let two other guys take the blame!" says Freckles. When it comes time for Mr. Tawny to pass judgment on the troublemakers, he instead predicts their future. No path, no matter how sunny and green, will lead back to the wonders of childhood, he warns. The boys will learn that soon enough. "Someday you'll grow up and try to recapture your youth!" declares Tawny. "*That'll be punishment enough!*"

2.7 Despite his enthusiasm, Mr. Tawny tires quickly in these panels from "Captain Marvel and Mr. Tawny's Quest for Youth" in *Captain Marvel Adventures* no. 131 (April 1952). Captain Marvel and related characters © 2016 DC Comics.

2.8 Mr. Tawny is satisfied to be "a regular fellow" in the conclusion of "Captain Marvel and Mr. Tawny's Quest for Youth" from *Captain Marvel Adventures* no. 131 (April 1952). Captain Marvel and related characters © 2016 DC Comics.

No matter how dangerous the predicament he finds himself in, Tawny always ends up safe and sound. Maybe that's the curse of the life he leads, another part of his routine. In the final two panels of the story, home at last, he walks with a cane and rubs his back (fig. 2.8). A photo of two real boys, not much older than those in the story, appears on the opposite page in an advertisement for a *Handbook for Model Builders*. Like the children in the story, the two boys in the photograph sit outside in the sun. The story has already given readers a warning: this summer day—the leaves, the grass, the sunlight—won't last either.

At least there's some good news. The boys, guilty, have a gift for the tiger, a plaque that declares him "A Game Guy and a *Regular* Fellow." Tawny smiles, and calls this award "one of the real joys of all life—to be called a regular fellow!" There's no glory for Mr. Tawny, no magic powers or eternal youth. For the tiger, there's only the promise of home, the quiet of his room, and the comfort of his dressing gown. To be "a regular fellow" is to contend with time, which inevitably leads to loss and often to loneliness. The resolution of Tawny's "quest" is not especially comforting. Even the image in the final panel is flat and unremarkable. Billy, holding the plaque, stands with Mr. Tawny in a circle of light. Is this really all these kids can hope for? If the boys in the story, and Mr. Tawny's readers, are lucky, maybe one day they'll grow up and become "regular fellows," too.

"IMPORTANT AND WORTHWHILE THINGS"

The Tawny stories are a living archive of Binder's fears and doubts. They also provide a record of his humor, his optimism, and his pride. Binder, in a note included with his papers at Texas A&M University, makes clear the seriousness with which he and Beck took their work on *Captain Marvel Adventures*. A memo labeled "*Questions—on what to do about CMA from now on. . . .*" includes a list of ideas for his editors and for Beck.[36] Someone, presumably Binder, has drawn a large X in pencil on the page. It is unclear whether or not the writer ever shared these notes, but the memo remains an important record of his approach to writing these comics, especially during Captain Marvel's final years in the early 1950s. While Binder advises that the team include "Korean war and horror stories" in order to remain competitive, he also makes clear his and Beck's affection for the series. In a "Note to editors," he writes, "It may be redundant to say it, but writers and artists, if they have any pride, *want* to give their *best* work. I believe Beck and I have always had pride in CMA." One of Binder's strategies for countering the title's decline in popularity and sales is an emphasis on more realistic stories: "I think on this point we can all agree—the stories should have *more of Billy Batson* and his doings and problems. I'm trying to get more BB in." Binder's desire to feature Billy more prominently in *Captain Marvel Adventures* is another example of his philosophy of generating "human interest," of writing what he once called "a 'tear jerker'" ("Teacher" 19) in order to move an audience.

As these notes indicate, Binder had a sense of the lasting significance of the work he and Beck had produced. Those images of a frustrated Tawny working in his study also hold the promise of eventual praise and recognition. "Mr. Tawny's Fight for Fame" ends not with the gloom of the tiger's "Quest for Youth" but with a fantasy as compelling as Billy's first visit with Shazam—at least for a writer. At the end of the story, Tawny learns that readers have begun to take notice. His dissertation on hibernating animals, it turns out, is filled

2.9 Mr. Tawny's dreams come true in the final panel of "Mr. Tawny's Fight for Fame" from *Captain Marvel Adventures* no. 126 (November 1951). Reprinted in *Shazam!* no. 14 (September–October 1974): 58. Captain Marvel and related characters © 2016 DC Comics.

with "patient, plodding genius!" A group of scientists promise to publish it. Once it appears in print, "Mr. Tawny's fame will never tarnish for a thousand years!" His research, and the hard work that went into it, are "important and worthwhile": "This book was my claim to fame all the time and I didn't know it!" he tells Billy. In the final panel of the story, Tawny looks very pleased as he holds the manuscript in his paws (fig. 2.9).

In the late 1940s and early 1950s, Binder expressed his hope that science fiction readers would enjoy and respond to his work. One of the things he missed most about the pulps were the fans, those dedicated readers who wrote in response to his fiction. Although the name Eando Binder appeared as a byline for the Jon Jarl backup stories in *Captain Marvel Adventures*, Binder, unlike Beck, was not credited on Billy's adventures. As a pulp writer, Binder had thrived on his interaction with readers, the give and take that let him know he was not alone: "But as I say," he writes in "Memoirs of a Nobody," "letters like that kept me in a warm glow. They hadn't forgotten me, those loyal fans! They hadn't ignored me and left me shivering out in the cold." Binder repeated this sentiment in one of his letters to Moskowitz in the fall of 1952, where he again mentions the "rosy glow" that accompanies a response, good or bad, from a reader. "Ah, those letters. . . . favorable or otherwise. . . . how I miss them . . ."[37] Just as Binder depended on those letters for inspiration, Tawny, in the character's final Fawcett appearance in 1953, eventually learned that a solitary life, especially for a "regular fellow," will never be rewarding or complete.

In "Mr. Tawny . . . Hermit," published in the second-to-last issue of *Captain Marvel Adventures* (no. 149, October 1953),[38] Tawny, at last, acts as the narrator. "Hello folks!" he says on the first page as he stares back at the reader. "This

2.10 Mr. Tawny offers one final lesson for his and Billy's readers in "Captain Marvel in Mr. Tawny . . . Hermit." *Captain Marvel Adventures* no. 149 (October 1953). Scan from an UberScans CD-ROM of the complete *Captain Marvel Adventures*. Captain Marvel and related characters © 2016 DC Comics.

is my story, told in my own words!"[39] Tired of his notoriety, the tiger makes his way to the forest where, no longer able to live in the wild, he accidentally causes a wildfire to burn out of control. Captain Marvel once again comes to his rescue. On the last page, after Tawny is nearly trampled by a bull, he makes up his mind to return once again to his home. This is the tiger, after all, who made a name for himself by writing a book about hibernation.

In the final two panels, Tawny is back in his "working clothes"—his robe— as he stands and talks with Captain Marvel. The setting is familiar: a mirror on the wall behind him, yellow curtains on the window. Mr. Tawny's forgotten just one thing, his birthday, but his friends have a cake for him. Although it is not clear whether or not Binder knew that this would be Tawny's final appearance in *Captain Marvel Adventures* (like the other Marvel Family characters, the tiger would return in *Shazam!* in the early 1970s),[40] the tiger's closing thoughts bring his journey to an end. His final lesson for Captain Marvel's young readers? It might be an obvious one, maybe even a little "corned up," to borrow Binder's phrase, but it's worth considering: "People are more fun than anybody!" he exclaims. "Why try to avoid them? Might as well have a good time and live a little!" (fig. 2.10).

The Tawny stories are a remarkable record of Binder's life as a writer. Not strict autobiographies, they are instead a series of sense impressions that provide indirect access to the man who wrote them. Just as Walt Kelly used his hometown of Bridgeport, Connecticut, as a model for Pogo's Okefenokee Swamp,[41] Binder documented the ups and downs of his life and his career as a writer in many of Tawny's adventures. As a result, he explored the potential of comics as a medium for meditations on the self. By the 1960s and 1970s,

Binder, through his contact with comics fandom, had a sense that his writing might outlive him, but Mr. Tawny's creator would never be entirely free of doubt and a certain longing for what he'd left behind.[42]

In a letter published in DC's *Shazam!* no. 4 (dated July 1973), a little over a year before he died at age sixty-three, Binder thanked editor Julie Schwartz for getting him a copy of the first issue, the one that includes the writer's brief encounter with Billy Batson. Just as he had a decade earlier in the pages of *Alter Ego*, Binder wistfully writes about his career: "The comics seem like some long-ago dream and I have no slightest hankering to go back to them, in case you're wondering." The next line of the letter suggests that Binder, like Beck, looked back on those days with sadness, wonder, and resignation: "I see that C. C. Beck has the same old 'magic' touch he used to have with the *Big Red Cheese*," Binder writes. After decades of work in the pulps and in comics, Binder's legacy was secure. Like Tawny, however, he must have known that youth, like the bag of rocks on Tawny's back, is too heavy a burden to carry into adulthood. A record of the multiple intersections between the popular and the personal, the Tawny stories are examples of those "important and worthwhile things" that persist, and inspire, long after the dream has ended.

Chapter 3

"BROTHER, THAT AIN'T IMAGINARY!"

Billy Batson and World War II

In November of 1945, the members of the Captain Marvel Club received a letter of thanks and celebration from Captain Marvel himself. At last, the war, now over, was set to become another page in a history book, a memory, and there was plenty of good news for Captain Marvel fans. With the end of wartime paper shortages, Fawcett could return its entire comics line to a monthly publication schedule. "Dear Pal," begins the letter, which includes a list of Captain Marvel merchandise,

> Now that the great struggle of World War II is over, all of the Fawcett comic book characters want to join me in a salute to you and all the rest of [your] fellow-club members in appreciation of the fine job you did to help win this epic victory. Maybe you think that buying War Stamps and War Bonds, saving scrap metal and waste paper were of minor importance, but all those little things put together by a lot of people like you working in cooperation add up to a tremendous contribution.[1]

The letter assures Captain Marvel's loyal readers that their efforts were essential and decisive for the Allied cause. As soldiers returned home, a new era of abundance was just around the corner; it would be a kind of paradise, with an endless supply of new comics, not to mention Captain Marvel-approved clothes, toys, and hats. Taking a cue from his alter ego, Billy Batson, the skilled radio reporter, Captain Marvel pauses for a commercial break, reminding club members about "Captain Marvel's dandy new suspenders," available at department stores like J. C. Penney's and Grant's. If you already have a belt or a favorite hat, the Captain adds, you might consider the "lovely dresses, bags, sweaters, [and] skating cap and scarf combinations" designed by Billy's sister,

73

Mary (also known as Mary Marvel). Any of these items would "make ideal Christmas gifts for your sisters or girl friends!"[2]

Beck hated these toys so much that, in his first essay for the Critical Circle, he suggested a link between Captain Marvel's role in the war effort, the marketing of these products, and the hero's eventual decline. As Fawcett "insisted that he be made more convincingly real," Beck wrote, the less appealing he became (Beck, "What Really"). This push for greater realism began when Billy's alter ego started "visiting the front lines and leading bayonet charges," but things only got worse when Captain Marvel appeared on mobiles, shirts, hats, pins, and pennants. "The merchandising of Captain Marvel was awful," Beck wrote, in part because of "ads drawn by artists who distorted him all out of shape" (Beck, "What Really"). From Beck's perspective, Fawcett's legal battle was only one of the many factors that brought Captain Marvel's career to an end. His discomfort with these "realistic" depictions of the hero—in World War II adventures, for example, or as a pitchman for various toys, games, and clothing—provides a test case on Beck's theories of comic art. If, as Beck explained to the Critical Circle, "comic strip characters can't appear in real life and be convincing" ("What Really"), why did readers by the millions flock to newsstands in the 1940s to read Billy's stories, imaginary or otherwise?

Don Maris, for example, includes "Captain Marvel in the World of If," one of Billy's many encounters with Adolf Hitler, in the same 1970s "best of" collection that includes the fan club letter advertising various Captain Marvel toys. "Millions of kids like myself felt that we knew and lived with the Big Red Cheese," Maris recalled of his experience reading these stories in the early 1940s.[3] For Beck, however, only a veiled realism, like the kind on display in Binder's autobiographical Mr. Tawny stories, had a place in comic book art.

The three stories I discuss in this chapter, Beck would no doubt agree, lack the innovative quality of those postwar narratives. Nonetheless, as scholars including Bradford Wright and Christopher Murray have argued, the superheroes that appeared in comic books in the early 1940s no doubt filled a psychological need for some readers, especially children terrified by the war and its impact on their families and communities.[4] These works of the imagination, even deeply flawed ones like "Capt. Marvel and the Mark of the Black Swastika"—in which Billy takes on both Hitler *and* Satan—are easy to dismiss because of their crudeness, predictability, and sentimentality, but they provide points of access for historians studying the social and psychological impact of the war on soldiers and on civilians. Beck later remembered comics like these with skepticism and even disdain. "Real life problems have no simple solutions and cannot be solved as neatly as comic book situations can be solved," Beck argued in "Good Taste in Comic Art," the second of the Critical Circle essays. What Beck failed to understand is that, for many readers, even the *idea* of another world in which good guys like Captain Marvel always win is satisfying and often reassuring, especially in the midst of upheaval and chaos. As Maris pointed out, he and the other "kids" who read these stories looked forward with great "anticipation" to "seeing [Captain Marvel] each month."[5]

In the stories I discuss in this chapter, Captain Marvel is often more child-like—prone to mistakes, silly, and immature—than Billy Batson is. I would argue that Billy does not transform into "an adult superhero" (Murray 28); rather, Shazam's magic enables him to revert to a more innocent state of being. As Bradford Wright puts it, the hero often behaves "like a bumbling overgrown child" (19), one still trying to come to terms with his powers. Then again, if the adult world is filled with villains like Hitler, Goebbels, and Göring, all of whom Billy encountered during World War II, what good is a magic word that forces him to grow up? Captain Marvel, that descendant of King Arthur, behaves more like J. M. Barrie's Peter Pan, the little boy free from the vanity, petty hatreds, and the evil of adults. Captain Marvel's popularity, I suspect, was a function of a form of "innocence" historian Michael C. C. Adams describes in his book *The Best War Ever*. American soldiers during World War II, he writes, especially those "who had not been in combat," often "seemed immature because they had not grown up amid war and because their parents had worked to prolong in them the sheltered innocence that Americans feel is a part of their national dream" (Adams 91). Although Beck attributed Captain Marvel's "success" to Billy's skills as a storyteller ("Real Facts"), this "sheltered innocence" no doubt played a role in the character's popularity. Put more simply, Billy and the Captain offered a measure of hope. The war would end and, once concluded, the United States would return to that earlier state of being. That's Billy's story. He's in no rush to become an adult; he just wants to go home. Of all the powers that Shazam grants Billy, the greatest is the ability to rebuild the comfortable life that his greedy uncle had destroyed.

The story of Captain Marvel, and the nostalgia for the character expressed so poignantly in the fanzines of the 1960s and 1970s, might be understood in the context of how American soldiers were trained during World War II. Captain Marvel, whose innocence all but guaranteed his success over numerous Axis villains, would later become the perfect spokesman for those Captain Marvel Club toys, games, and clothes. After all, he'd had plenty of practice during the war. "The infantilized soldier was utterly independent of his family," writes historian Susan J. Matt, and, now "utterly dependent on the army," would therefore be "willing to subordinate his own needs to 'institutional ends'" (Matt 202). Matt describes the essential role that consumer goods played in this process of infantilization, as "nearly 8 million soldiers who flocked to the PX" bought everything "from soft drinks and candy bars to *Time* magazine," and, of course, large numbers of comic books and other "potent reminders of home" (Matt 208; see also Murray 112).[6] The military hoped that these "commercial comforts" would appeal to soldiers and "assuage their homesickness" (Matt 208). By the time fans like Richard Lupoff and Don Maris began writing about their memories of the hero in the 1960s and 1970s, Captain Marvel already had plenty of experience as a focal point for nostalgia. The soldiers who'd read these comic books in the early 1940s had gotten there first.

While comics, as reminders of home or as entry points to a world of fantasy and power, often brought relief to these soldiers, comic book heroes and their exploits could also be painful reminders of what had been left behind or destroyed.[7] In his 1989 book *Wartime*, Paul Fussell highlights a passage from Barry Broadfoot's *Six War Years, 1939–1945: Memories of Canadians at Home and Abroad*. Here, a Canadian soldier who saw combat in Normandy and in Holland recalls his return following the end of the war. Volunteers for "the Red Cross or the Sally Ann, some girls," he remembers, met him as he disembarked from his ship (qtd. in Broadfoot 392). To mark the occasion, the young women offered each soldier "a little bag" filled with "a couple of chocolate bars in it and a comic book." Rather than taking comfort from these items, the solider found them strange and unnerving: "Here, we had gone overseas not much more than children but we were coming back, sure, let's face it, as killers. And they were still treating us as children. Candy and comic books" (Broadfoot 392; qtd. in Fussell 288). In this passage, "candy and comic books" are markers of a disconnect between the returning soldiers and the Red Cross volunteers. It's a sad, almost meaningless gesture that is nonetheless poignant, one that appears to ignore the trauma and the horror these veterans experienced overseas. But what choice do the volunteers have? This scene encapsulates the compelling power of nostalgia and of memory. The bag filled with candy and comic books, the young women hope, will serve as a welcome for these soldiers. It is an act of faith, an assurance that *things will return to normal*; it is a promise of renewal and stability, reminders of a time before the war. The returning soldier, puzzled and rendered speechless, glimpses, for a second, the boy he was *before* he entered the service. Unlike Billy, he has no magic word that will restore to him everything that he, and the Red Cross workers, have lost.[8]

Captain Marvel reached the height of his popularity at a time when, as Michael C. C. Adams points out, the American public consumed a wide variety of media, from radio shows and movies to magazines and comic books— forms that anticipated the explosion of mass popular culture in the mid-to-late twentieth century: "The public's concentration span and ability to tolerate any but optimistic messages were being eroded," Adams writes of the war, especially in its final stages. And it was this "media age," Adams continues, that "also spawned comic books, whose superheroes further simplified the issues and made them black or white" (Adams 10–11). Like Beck, I'm not certain that placing a fantasy character such as Captain Marvel in the middle of a combat zone makes for good comics. Nonetheless, the terrible contrast between Billy's fantasy life and the terror of the war itself—the fear of sabotage, the bloody reality of combat, the horror of the concentration camps—challenges us to remember and to articulate the complexities of an era that, despite its continued presence in popular culture, remains as vexing as those "candy and comic books."

In the closing pages of *Wartime*, Fussell expresses his dissatisfaction even with his own account of World War II and with his writing about his experiences as a veteran. He argues that "the enormousness of the war and the unmanageable copiousness of its verbal and visual residue" leave "the revisitor of this imagery" with no choice other than "to indicate a few components of the scene" (296). In Captain Marvel's battles with Hitler, readers will discover fragments or, to borrow Binder's phrase once again, "tiny flashes" ("Special" 112) of the war itself,[9] one imagined by artists like Beck and Marc Swayze and their other colleagues at Fawcett. In Billy's fantasy world, home is never very far away. All it takes for him is a magic word and he's back with his sister, or with the wizard Shazam, or even with his friend Steamboat. That is Billy's greatest talent: to imagine himself as a being more innocent and childlike than he, or his readers, can ever hope to be.

"BY GOSH! I'LL GO WITH YOU! I'M PATRIOTIC, TOO!"

Billy Batson and Captain Marvel volunteered for the US Army in June 1942. Just six months after Pearl Harbor, the United States military, already at war in the Pacific, had not yet finalized its plans for Europe. One of the government's goals was to prepare American citizens for the demands of wartime. In the summer of 1942, as Billy volunteered for service, the army introduced the Army War Show, an exhibition designed to boost support for the war effort (Banas 31). The War Show, which performed at stadiums across the East Coast, Midwest, and South, including cities such as Philadelphia, Chicago, New Orleans, and Atlanta, offered audiences a means of imagining what the war might look like and what America's soldiers would face when they ventured overseas. The show featured new recruits, many of whose battalions eventually saw combat in North Africa and in Europe in 1943.

In the summer and fall of 1942, however, these newly recruited and trained soldiers toured the country, performing mock battles and showing off the new

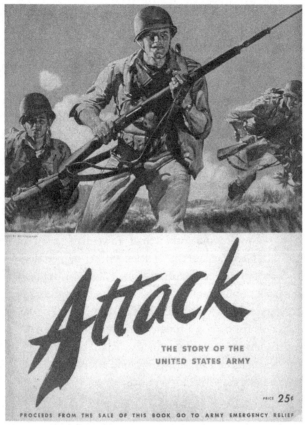

3.1 The cover of *Attack: The Story of the United States Army*, a souvenir booklet that documents the 1942 Army War Show performances. From the author's archive.

technology of war in the form of machine guns, flamethrowers, jeeps, and tanks. Major General A. D. Surles, in a memo on the War Show dated April 22, 1942, explained the purpose of these public spectacles: "The expositions will not only raise large sums for Army Emergency Relief, but they will enable our people to see their Army at first hand and thereby be inspired to greater effort in supporting it with full confidence in its leadership and purposes."[10] The War Show made its debut at Municipal Stadium in Baltimore on June 12–15, 1942 (fig. 3.1), around the same time that *Captain Marvel Adventures* no. 12, dated June 26, first hit the newsstands.[11]

Like "Captain Marvel Joins the Army," the first story in *Captain Marvel Adventures* no. 12, a souvenir booklet from the War Show seeks to inspire and to comfort readers uncertain about what the war might bring. The booklet, *Attack: The Story of the United States Army*, appeals, like the War Show performance itself, to the imagination of the reader. What is the military? Its

3.2 A War Show ticket from the Soldier Field performances held in Chicago in September 1942.
From the author's archive.

history? What will soldiers experience once they've completed their training? In a section of the program titled "Here's YOUR Army!" we learn that these young soldiers

have been gathered together from the North, the South, the East, and the West to present to you not a circus—not a light-hearted display of touring troupers—but a glimpse here, and a picture there, of the battle-bound millions of American youth. These particular men of the Task Force of the Army War Show have been chosen to represent a cross-section of the Army, and they present this action tonight with a deep sense of serious responsibility to their country and to you.[12]

While the War Show, according to newspaper accounts of the era, was indeed a circus-like spectacle, despite what the anonymous writer of the program might claim, it did not entirely shy away from depicting the inevitable consequences of combat. Every night, as an article in the *Chicago Daily Tribune* from September 2, 1942, describes, Private Teddy Tedesco from Brooklyn was killed in a mock battle ("City Gets Taste").[13] In a ticket issued for the War Show performance at Soldier Field in Chicago in early September 1942, we see a soldier wearing combat fatigues and carrying a rifle. Grim but determined, he is a man of action. In the other corner of the red, rectangular ticket (fig. 3.2), we see an image of home as a dark-haired young woman cradles a baby in her arms.

Next to her, in blue letters, the ticket tells us to "Take the load off his HEART!" Buying this ticket to attend a performance of the Army War Show will assist the soldier as he fights for freedom and defends the US and the rest

3.3 Captain Marvel takes action in Marc Swayze's cover for *Captain Marvel Adventures* no. 12 (June 26, 1942). Captain Marvel and related characters © 2016 DC Comics.

of the world against the evil of the Axis powers. The show is a spectacle but, like Marc Swayze's drawing of Captain Marvel leading a line of soldiers into battle on the cover of *Captain Marvel Adventures* no. 12, it's a necessary fiction, one that transforms the energy, enthusiasm, wonder, and concern of the audience into a shared sense of urgency and action.

Swayze's iconic drawing served the same purpose as these War Show performances—and the tickets, booklets, and other souvenirs that accompanied them. This is what the war *might* look like: the sky behind Captain Marvel is the color of a bruise, but, in the lower left-hand corner, there is daylight. While the cover might at first appear absurd, it embodies the hopes and fears of its readers and of its creators. There's only one problem. As Swayze himself later pointed out, Captain Marvel and the soldiers look like they're still fighting World War I (fig. 3.3).

In an article written for the *Fawcett Collectors of America* in 1997,[14] Swayze recalls the atmosphere in the Fawcett offices in early 1942. "Fawcett, like most publishers, jumped onto the war stories without delay," Swayze explains. "After all, the comic book super-heroes were out there scrambling to be the first to be involved in the US effort" (75). The heroic cover of *Captain Marvel Adventures* no. 12, Swayze points out, is filled with anachronisms. "I was assigned a wartime cover so early on that the US infantrymen Captain Marvel was leading over a battlefield wore World War I helmets!" (75). The soldiers-in-training in this issue's title story wear the same uniforms.[15] If a being like Captain Marvel joined the army, he would of course become an officer because of his superior strength and intellect, not to mention his boyish exuberance. The other soldiers would look up to him as their leader, and the enemy wouldn't have much of a chance. But, as Beck argued in his first Critical Circle essay from 1988 ("What Really"), once Captain Marvel is placed within a realistic setting, writers and artists face the challenge of blending cartoon fantasy with an uncertain, terrifying, and bloody reality.

The cover of the War Show booklet, the drawing on the ticket from the Soldier Field performance, and Swayze's image for *Captain Marvel Adventures* no. 12 provide us with a constellation of iconic figures: the soldiers in battle, the brightly costumed hero in action, the mother caring for her child. These examples, taken one at a time, are meaningless without context, but, when viewed together, allow access to a community that shared and celebrated these images in the first place. In this case, to borrow a phrase from Guy Debord, the "spectacle" here is the idea of the war, and all the fear and anxiety that accompany it. Each one of these drawings, from the painted cover of the souvenir booklet to the sketch on the back of the ticket to Swayze's dramatic (if speculative) image, as Debord might have argued, are not in themselves interesting or compelling: "The spectacle is not a collection of images, but a social relation among people, mediated by images" (Debord n.p.).[16] Each drawing asks, *What will this war look like?* and, more important, *Who will fight it?* By mixing reality and fantasy, each artist, from the illustrators who worked on the War Show materials to Swayze and his colleagues at Fawcett, reveals the limits of popular culture in responding to rapid historical change.

Following the dramatic, two-page spread that opens "Captain Marvel Joins the Army," the first story in *Captain Marvel Adventures* no. 12, the reader sees Billy Batson at his desk, a line of skyscrapers visible through the window behind him (fig. 3.4).

Billy's friend Whitey Murphy is planning "to enlist in the Army and smash the Axis!" Inspired, Billy replies, "By gosh! I'll go with you! I'm patriotic, too!"

3.4 Billy sits at his desk before following his friend Whitey Murphy to the US Army recruiting office. From page 4 of *Captain Marvel Adventures* no. 12 (June 26, 1942). *Captain Marvel* and related characters © 2016 DC Comics.

Billy, the sergeant explains, is too young to join: "We'll take you, buddy," he explains to Whitey, "but the other kid better go home and grow up a little!" (4).[17] On the window behind Whitey and Billy is a sign that reads, "Men Wanted for U.S. Army." It appears again in two of the next three panels. Billy, however, can only grow up by speaking his magic word and even then, as I've argued, he remains a kid, albeit one with impossible strength and invulnerability. He calls on his magic powers, as he explains it, to "show that overgrown sergeant!" (5). I read the image at the top of the page as another of Billy's fantasies, one in which the exact details of the war are not yet known. In this daydream, Captain Marvel leads a line of soldiers across an expanse of barbed wire, a scene from no man's land. The sky is filled with explosions and dark clouds of smoke and fire. One of the Nazi planes has been hit and plummets to the ground. As we can see from the first narrative panel on the story's opening page, Billy is an upstanding member of society, successful and respected. We know this because of the items on his desk and the file cabinets that line the walls of his office. But to prove himself as a man, he must do more than sit behind a desk. He must spring into action and use his gifts to fight an enemy that threatens the life he has created since that first meeting with Shazam.

On the next page, Captain Marvel enters the recruiting office and, under the name M. R. Vell, volunteers for duty along with Whitey (6). He soon

3.5 Billy inspires a group of new recruits in a scene from page 9 of "Captain Marvel Joins the Army" (June 26, 1942). Captain Marvel and related characters © 2016 DC Comics.

discovers that his drill sergeant is in fact a German spy sent to undermine the confidence of these newly recruited soldiers. In a meeting with other "enemy aliens," a mug of beer in his hand, the evil sergeant explains his intentions: "I am busy convincing the men they cannot become good soldiers! For instance, today I made fools of two privates—Vell and Murphy!" (8). These saboteurs kidnap Billy after he speaks to an assembly of newly recruited soldiers. The spies attempt to coerce the star reporter into broadcasting propaganda for them, but he eventually manages to speak his magic word. In a single-page fight scene, Captain Marvel easily clobbers the villains (15).

Early on, Billy reminds readers that he's a magical storyteller. His narratives, he hopes, will counteract the negative propaganda of America's enemies. As the duplicitous sergeant attempts to undermine these new recruits, Billy's words offer comfort and inspiration. In the final panel on page nine, a caption informs us that "Billy, always a forceful speaker, pleases his audience immensely!" (fig. 3.5).

At the start of his speech, he admits that it is not his place to dictate how the war will be fought or won: "I'm not going to tell you how to do it . . . Americans learned to fight and win wars long ago!" After references to "big bad Nazis" and "little yellow Japs," Batson urges the soldiers to "teach them a lesson they won't forget for centuries!" In this horizontal panel that closes page nine, he speaks to a room filled with young, white, uniformed soldiers, all of them grinning and ecstatic. "You said it, Billy!" "That's the talk!"

A few pages later, after Captain Marvel has defeated the saboteurs, and soldiers have arrived to take them into custody, Captain Marvel learns that even his mentor, the wizard Shazam, has joined the fight. Billy is shocked to see the old man wearing a general's uniform. "I, too," Shazam explains, "am in the

3.6 Shazam explains his wartime "plans for Captain Marvel" on page 19 of "Captain Marvel Joins the Army." Captain Marvel and related characters © 2016 DC Comics.

service of the greatest country in the world! I've arranged for Private Vell's transfer to special service—out of uniform!" (19). Puzzled and disappointed, Billy says, "Captain Marvel wanted to fight the Axis!" In the next panel, Shazam, his long white beard covering his uniform, explains his intentions in more detail: "I have plans for Captain Marvel that extend even beyond the armed forces of the United States! He'll see more action than any soldier possibly could!" (19). This explanation seems reasonable enough to Billy, who replies, "I see what you mean now!" (fig. 3.6).

Although Billy might understand what Shazam intends to do, the inability of the hero's editors, writers, and artists to predict what the future will hold is made clear in this clumsy, inconclusive ending. Captain Marvel, of course, cannot leap from the panel and join the US Army. By introducing this note of uncertainty, Beck's "fabric of illusion" begins to unravel. Captain Marvel is a creature of the imagination, a being of possibility. The war in Europe and the Pacific is a sign of the limits of human imagination, a perversion of this faculty for destructive ends. The problem here is not so much, as Beck might have argued, that a cartoon character like Captain Marvel is about to confront a real-life menace like Hitler (he'll do that in the next story I discuss, as Billy takes on the Devil with the help of a few spirited French children). Rather, in these last few panels, Shazam speaks for Fawcett's writers, artists, and editors;

this is not an easy story to tell, they seem to say, since the war itself, as it takes shape, remains a mystery.

Shazam's explanation fills a word balloon that dominates the second-to-last panel of the page. In fact, there's a lot more talk than action as the story comes to a close. The balloon fills a space that Fawcett's artists would otherwise have left blank. Since the wizard does not reveal all of his "plans" for Captain Marvel, he leaves it up to Billy, and to the reader, to imagine what kinds of "action" the hero will see. The advertisement at the bottom of the page is an example of Billy's only viable mission, as a mouthpiece for war bonds and stamps, the role of salesman that he will take up again after the war. The soldiers in that advertisement, like the ones lined up behind Captain Marvel on the issue's cover, look like extras left over from World War I.

Billy's magic word allows him to exist in a permanent, idyllic, carefree state of wonder and innocence. The orphan newsboy, now a respected and successful broadcaster and a minor celebrity, is more worldly and sophisticated than his godlike counterpart. The alluring dream at the heart of Captain Marvel's origin is very American: Billy, despite his age, is a hero driven by his rich fantasy life. In that sense, he is a harbinger of an obsession with youth and vitality that will continue to define American culture for the rest of the twentieth century. Meanwhile, "Capt. Marvel and the Mark of the Black Swastika," dated January 22, 1943, might be read as a variation on Stephen Vincent Benét's "The Devil and Daniel Webster" (1937), another popular short story that, like James Thurber's "The Secret Life of Walter Mitty," explored notions of heroism at the close of the 1930s.

"WHAT MANNER OF MAN IS HE?"

The first page of *Captain Marvel Adventures* no. 20 includes a text box that names the "Editorial Advisory Board of Captain Marvel Adventures."[18] The board includes Eleanor B. Roosevelt, "Past President, Girl Scouts Council of Greater New York"; Richard E. Byrd, "Noted Explorer, Aviator, and Author"; Dr. Allan Roy Dafoe, "The famous Quintuplet doctor"; and the Reverend John W. Tynan, a member of the "Fordham University Faculty." Fawcett's president, W. H. Fawcett, Jr., assures readers that these advisors have helped the publisher "maintain high standards of wholesome entertainment" (4).[19] The list draws on the social and moral authority of the medical profession, academia, and the clergy.

This authorization reflects the standards of conduct that governed Fawcett publications. Chip Kidd and Geoff Spear include a copy of the company's "Code of Ethics" in their recent book *Shazam! The Golden Age of the World's*

Mightiest Mortal. These 1942 guidelines include injunctions against "scenes of actual sadistic torture"; "[v]ulgar language"; "a humorous or glamorous treatment" of divorce; or "dialects and devices" used "to indicate ridicule or intolerance of racial groups" (although, as Kidd and Spear point out, this last stipulation did not prevent Billy's friend Steamboat from appearing in the comics until finally being removed in 1945). The first in these guidelines is a rule against any depiction of a challenge to the existing power structure:

> Policemen, judges, officials, and respected institutions must not be portrayed as stupid or ineffective in such a way as to weaken respect for established authority. Crimes against the law shall never be presented in such a way as to throw sympathy with the crime as against law and justice or to inspire others with the desire for imitation.[20]

Captain Marvel is a force for good. That goodness, in fact, blinds him to the being who, in the first story of *Captain Marvel Adventures* no. 20,[21] grants Hitler evil powers for the first time. In this narrative, Captain Marvel's childlike nature makes him immune to the Devil's evil ways. Here is a version of the infantilization described by Susan Matt: Captain Marvel's victory, like that of the United States, is assured because of this innocence, an unwillingness to engage with an adult world filled with cruelty, brutality, and corruption. Unlike the villains in the story, as we shall see, Billy and Captain Marvel have a sense of humor. As readers, we laugh with Billy and the Captain, but we spend most of the story laughing *at* Hitler and his henchmen. By the end, even the Devil seems to find the Nazis and their vanity a little silly and tiresome.

"Capt. Marvel and the Mark of the Black Swastika" begins with images of the Blitz. Nazi airpower attacks London as Captain Marvel arrives to aid the British forces (4–5). The opening pages of the story feature a dramatic image of Captain Marvel flying over a burning city: in the distance, spotlights, antiaircraft fire, and explosions frame an image of Big Ben (fig. 3.7). On the devastated street below, small figures struggle to douse the flames as a crew of ambulance workers point to the familiar red-costumed figure: "Wot's that flyin' up there, a man?" one shouts. Another, pointing to the incoming Nazi bomb, replies, "Duck, 'arry! That bomb's gonna hit 'im!" The last figure, standing over a wounded civilian lying on a stretcher, reminds his fellows that they have no need to fear, as the "flyin'" man has arrived to rescue them: "Don't worry. That's Captain Marvel!" (4).

Captain Marvel's presence in the foreground of the image highlights the hellish landscape looming before him. The artists and letterers have arranged the title of the story in such a way that the reader must scan the accumulated horror of the flames, the demolished buildings, and the falling bombs.

3.7 Captain Marvel arrives to help British soldiers and medical personnel on pages 4 and 5 of "Capt. Marvel and the Mark of the Black Swastika" from *Captain Marvel Adventures* no. 20 (January 22, 1943). Captain Marvel and related characters © 2016 DC Comics.

First, on the left-hand side of the spread, "Capt. Marvel" appears in bold letters; then, in the lower right-hand corner of the next page, the words "and the Mark of the Black Swastika" complete the title. Above this yellow caption there appears a solitary, cloaked figure on the roof of the only building still standing. Although he remains in shadow, his clawed hands and horned head suggest that supernatural forces are at work.

As readers open *Captain Marvel Adventures* no. 20, they are no longer in a world of imagination. This opening shot of London in flames is not a memory of World War I or an illustration of how the war *might* look. This is a hellish vision of the city, complete with falling bombs, burned buildings, and clouds of toxic orange smoke. The presence of Captain Marvel and the Devil adds a touch of fantasy to an otherwise grisly and largely realistic landscape. These panels provide a test case not only for Beck's resistance to realism in comic art, then, but also for Scott McCloud's discussion in *Understanding Comics* of the relationship between comic book characters and the spaces they inhabit.

McCloud argues that characters drawn in an "iconic" style sometimes inhabit "unusually realistic backgrounds" and, as a result, promise a unique sensory experience (42). This "combination" provides readers with an opportunity to "*mask* themselves in a character and safely enter a sensually stimulating world" (McCloud 43; emphasis in the original). In this case, Captain Marvel guides his readers through this terrifying depiction of London in flames. Captain Marvel's colorful presence offers security and assurance in two different forms.

First, Fawcett's writers and artists have transformed the horrors of the war into cartoon images, promising a kind of mastery over this violence and destruction that, as Beck argued, is not possible in real life. Drawing the Nazi leaders as caricatures serves the same purpose, as readers laugh at their absurd and self-serving behavior. Secondly, Captain Marvel's presence is a dreamlike inversion of these terrors and anxieties. The "mask" the story offers the reader is one of ease and control. The panels at the bottom of these two pages, complete with the origin stories of Hitler and Goebbels, suggest that these men were *never* innocent, even as children. As boys they dreamed of violence and world domination. To return to McCloud's argument, a "cartoony" figure with a "realistic" background results in a complex reading experience: "One set of lines to *see*. Another set of lines to *be*" (43). As the reader observes these evil figures, and witnesses the aftermath of the Blitz, the fantasy of Captain Marvel suggests another way of *being*: one in which lies, physical violence, and the pursuit of material wealth are desires and fantasies best left to adults. The Nazis, after all, are only thinking of themselves, whereas Captain Marvel—the boy whose magic word guarantees that he'll never grow up—acts selflessly, offering support to these British soldiers and to the medical personnel.

On the lower portion of these split pages, Captain Marvel's alter ego, Billy Batson, introduces the flashback sequence featuring the two Nazi leaders. Standing before the microphone at WHIZ, Billy explains, "Folks, this is a strange story whose real beginning was way back 30 or 40 years ago, and whose real ending is not yet in sight" (4). The subsequent panels illustrate parallel incidents in Germany and in Austria. Two young boys named Joseph and Adolph make deals with a red-cloaked, pointy-eared figure who promises them power and prestige. The first one, Joseph, who later in the story is revealed as Goebbels, expresses his ambition to become "der biggest liar in der vorld!" (4). Off-panel, the Devil, his words framed in a floating, disembodied word balloon, replies: "Excellent, my boy! A commendable ambition!"

In the next panel, the demon places a mark on Joseph's chest, promising, "There! I have put my mark on you! You will go a long way, now, my young friend! Someday you will be the greatest liar in the world!" (5). The devil then pursues the young Adolph Hitler, who has just beaten up another boy half his size. After being shamed by his fellow villagers, Adolph wanders off and, beneath a dead tree and its bare, skeletal branches, he swears, "Bah! Phooey! Someday I kill dem all! Someday I vill be boss uf der whole world, den I show them!" On the next page, as he places another mark on the boy's chest, the

3.8 Captain Marvel struggles to figure out the identity of his adversary from page 9 of *Captain Marvel Adventures* no. 20. Captain Marvel and related characters © 2016 DC Comics.

Devil predicts the future: "You will go a long way now, young Adolph! A 1-o-o-on-n-gg way!" (5). These panels indirectly refer to Billy's origin story from 1940. In contrast to these young men, Billy, with every right to be bitter and angry after being swindled and disowned by his uncle, is a practical, hard-working, and honest kid, whose only ambition, until he meets Shazam, is to make a living and survive as best he can.[22] In "Capt. Marvel and the Mark of the Black Swastika," Billy's first encounter with the Devil also illustrates his essential goodness.

In his zeal to rescue the citizens of London, and because of his innocent nature, Captain Marvel fails to recognize the Devil, who plays coy with the befuddled hero: "Well, let's just say that I'm . . . er . . . director of the underground heating system!" (8). After being struck by a bomb, Captain Marvel turns to the reader and appears to ask for help (he might also be talking to himself): "He—he really can change the course of a bomb! What manner of man is he?" (9) (fig. 3.8).

A few pages later, the Nazis once again capture Billy, but soon find themselves fighting Captain Marvel (apparently the saboteurs from *Captain Marvel Adventures* no. 12 were unable to send word back to their colleagues in Europe about Billy's talent as an escape artist). Just as he is about to destroy the Nazis' radio equipment in the same dramatic fashion that he destroyed Sivana's radio-silencer just a few years earlier, Captain Marvel flies to France at the Devil's request (15). There, the hero finds Hitler squabbling with his subordinates. The bomb he drops on them seems to have had no effect because,

3.9 Captain Marvel and his French allies have some fun with Satan on page 18 of *Captain Marvel Adventures* no. 20. Captain Marvel and related characters © 2016 DC Comics.

as the Devil explains, "[t]hey belong to me, and cannot be killed until I order it!" (17). In the last two pages of the story, three French children notice that Old Scratch is on fire and try to put out the flames (fig. 3.9). Screaming, "Don't be good to me—I can't stand it!" (18), the Devil, like Margaret Hamilton in *The Wizard of Oz*, slowly melts, then disappears. Why? Captain Marvel, a child himself, explains, "You children killed him with kindness!" (18).

As this summary of the story suggests, all of the characters are ridiculous. The hero cannot identify the villain. Captain Marvel's confusion, however, serves an important function: his ignorance allows readers to identify the source of this evil and destruction for themselves. So, *the Devil himself* is behind this! Captain Marvel, like the French children at the end of the story, cannot fathom or even recognize pure evil. He has no name for it, no language with which to express it. When he finally confronts the Devil, he asks, "Who are you? And what are you doing here?"[23] Although the villain's true identity remains something of a mystery, the French children have no trouble identifying the story's hero: "You know who zat was? Eet was ze American *Capitaine Marvel!*" (19).

The defeat of the Axis, the narrative implies, is inevitable. Those in charge would rather fight amongst themselves and serve their evil master than pursue a path to victory. As they argue, Hitler shouts, "Am I not der boss—der Fuehrer? Does not efferyt'ing belong to me? Haff I not told you so a million times?" Joseph replies, "Yah-h! Ve know, Adolph! Ve let you think so, because you are der biggest stuffed shirt of us all!" (15). Not only are the Nazis narcissistic fools, but they are also, Goebbels must admit, a little *stuffy*. They lack the humor and good will of Captain Marvel and his three French allies, a girl and two boys so kind and naïve that they'll offer a helping hand to Satan himself.

Captain Marvel embodies an innocence that has lost its resonance and appeal for contemporary readers. While in the last decade Hollywood has produced a series of financial and sometimes critically successful superhero films, including Christopher Nolan's Batman trilogy and Joss Whedon's big-screen reinvention of The Avengers, it has yet to produce a Captain Marvel movie, although, as of this writing, one starring Dwayne Johnson as Captain Marvel's nemesis Black Adam appears to be on the horizon.[24] Most recent Hollywood adaptations of popular superhero characters attempt to reinvent these heroes for a more adult audience—that is, for filmgoers already familiar with and nostalgic for these existing properties.[25] The essence of the Captain Marvel myth, the boy who turns into a man who is more boyish and innocent than the child himself, is perhaps a remnant of that era of "candy and comic books."

Attributing Captain Marvel's popularity during the war years solely to this dream of innocence would be too easy, and perhaps misleading. But the hero's adventures, despite their frequent absurdity, might reveal the workings of that dream. After the death of his parents, Batman seeks revenge. When Superman's planet explodes and his rocket ship finds its way to Earth, the child eventually seeks opportunity and fame in his new home. Unlike these heroes, when Billy Batson discovers the underground subway tunnel, he finds the strength to rebuild what's been taken from him, to return to the world of comfort on display in the Historama.[26] His reward for discovering that lost, secret self lies in the infinite possibility offered by childhood play.

"AND AS LONG AS THERE IS CAPTAIN MARVEL AROUND, THINGS JUST *CAN'T* GO WRONG!"

In January 1945, the unthinkable happened: Captain Marvel turned traitor and joined forces with Adolph Hitler. Old Scratch had nothing to do with this lapse in the hero's judgment. Rather, Captain Marvel's simplicity and good humor, which had served him so well in his battle with the Devil, almost thwarted the Allies and their cause. The story appeared in *Captain Marvel Adventures* no. 42 (January 1945),[27] a holiday issue with a message of "Season's Greetings" from the hero on its cover. The first page of the comic, which names Beck as the magazine's "Chief Artist,"[28] includes another advertisement for war bonds and stamps. It also urges Captain Marvel's young fans to "Order in Advance!" as paper shortages will result in Fawcett printing fewer copies of each issue. "Every now and then a magazine *will* be late, even though we'll do our best to avoid it. We're cooperating! Will you?"[29] Even the full-color advertisement for Wheaties that appears on the inside front cover reminds readers of what is at stake: four soldiers, three of them with helmets, are grappling

with a coconut tree because, as one remarks, "Milton likes milk on his Wheaties," that "Breakfast of Champions." As the war rages on, commerce and pa-
triotism intersect. The reader might show his or her loyalty to the cause by
purchasing bonds *or* by requesting copies of *Captain Marvel Adventures*.

In the opening panels of "Captain Marvel in the World of If," a scientist
named I. Q. Putter discusses his most recent invention, a nickelodeon-like
machine that produces short movies of alternate histories. What the professor
doesn't suspect is that his assistant, Carl, is another Nazi saboteur. Professor
Putter, it appears, is not a regular Fawcett reader. Otherwise, he would know
that most assistants with German names in World War II-era Captain Marvel stories turn out to be spies, with the remarkable exception in this story
of a few brave resistance fighters. Putter explains that his fantastic machine
"shows, mathematically, *two* or more ways for any event to happen, each of
which might produce a *different* kind of future! There is the normal world—
and then there is the *world of if*—the world that *might be!*" Carl wants to learn
what might happen if "the famous Captain Marvel *joined the Nazis!*" Once he
learns of how those events unfold in that alternate timeline, the spy will bring
that terrible reality here to our reality, the one in which Captain Marvel and
the Allies will eventually defeat the Axis.

Several pages later, Carl, posing as a fan seeking Captain Marvel's auto-
graph, tricks the hero into signing a pledge that reads, "I, Captain Marvel, here
by [*sic*] agree to denounce America and help Hitler!" Feeling bound by the
document, Marvel flies to Berlin, where he meets with Hitler, Goebbels, and
Göring, the cartoon villains from "Capt. Marvel and the Mark of the Black
Swastika." Goebbels and Göring are just as petty and narcissistic in this story
as they were in *Captain Marvel Adventures* no. 20. The Devil, perhaps still under the watchful eyes of those plucky French children, is nowhere to be seen.
This time, robbing Göring of his medals, Hitler offers Captain Marvel a pro-
motion. As second-in-command of the German forces, the hero will now be
known as Field Marshal Marvel. "Thank you, mein generous Fuehrer," replies
the former Captain, still honoring his pledge.

Despite the hero's behavior, Billy Batson, the narrator assures us, "has *not*
turned Nazi, along with his counterpart!" Instead, once he discovers what
Captain Marvel has agreed to, he throws himself on the bed in his quarters
and begins sobbing: "Oh, this is terrible! Just because he signed that paper, he
thinks he has to go through with it! And I can't do a thing myself!" In the next
panel, Billy plots his escape: "Suddenly the brave boy sits up in determination!" reads the caption in the second-to-last panel of the story's eighth page.
"I know what I'll do! I'll get that paper and tear it up! Then Captain Marvel
will come to his senses!" (fig. 3.10). On the next page, Hitler, confident in Field

3.10 Billy is determined to break Captain Marvel's pact with Hitler in a scene from "Captain Marvel in the World of If" from *Captain Marvel Adventures* no. 42 (January 1945). Captain Marvel and related characters © 2016 DC Comics.

Marshal Marvel's loyalty, tears up the document before Billy has a chance to do so. Released from his obligations, Captain Marvel socks Hitler on the jaw and takes the tyrant into custody.

We soon learn that these panels are merely images generated by Professor Putter's machine. With the action of the story now safely back in our reality, the hero rescues Putter from Carl, just before the machine, short-circuited by "the strain of showing Captain Marvel as a Nazi," explodes with a "Poof!" While the professor does not explain why, even in an alternate universe, Captain Marvel would ever agree to join forces with the Nazis—unless, of course, we are meant to understand that he is *always* as good as his word, even when he's been duped—he does offer words of advice and assurance to Captain Marvel's readers.

The machine's sudden inability to project anything other than an Allied victory suggests, just as Billy promised at the start of the war, that the eventual defeat of the Axis is inevitable. Even a work of science fiction—a fantasy of other possible realities—folds in on itself when faced with Captain Marvel's role in the Allied cause. Just before his machine explodes, Putter insists that the device has already "made the greatest and most wonderful prediction in the world! It shows that no matter *which* way the world goes—into no matter what kind of *world of if*—there can be no *if* world that goes bad! *Not while*

there is a Captain Marvel!" In the final panel of the story, just before an ad for
the Captain Marvel Club, Billy, with the same storytelling skills that inspired
those young recruits in 1942, reiterates Putter's optimistic message:

> Yes, folks! There are many possible branches of *if* worlds! But in *all* of them,
> no matter which one fate chooses to follow, there is always Captain Marvel!
> And as long as there is Captain Marvel around, things just *can't* go wrong!

Billy's closing thoughts echo the rhetoric of victory popular in the United
States and in England in the first months of 1945. As Paul Fussell points out,
Harold Arlen and Johnny Mercer's "Ac-Cent-Tchu-Ate the Positive" was a hit
for Bing Crosby and the Andrews Sisters "in the early spring of 1945," a time
"when everyone's 'morale' needed a special boost, the war having gone on
months (or even years) longer than expected" (Fussell 143).

Perhaps Beck's claim that a character like Captain Marvel, a being that exists in the realm of fantasy, has no role to play in fighting real-life forces like
those of the Nazis is too sweeping a generalization. Rather, a character like
Captain Marvel might be understood as an essential figure in the "ideology"
Fussell describes, one that grew even more pervasive after the war.[30] This desire, as Johnny Mercer's lyrics put it, to "latch on to the affirmative" lost none
of its appeal after the Allied victory. In fact, the ascendancy of American consumer culture in the late 1940s and early 1950s might be traced in part, according to Fussell, back to the Allied propaganda machine (164).[31] As Fussell
notes, even by the late 1980s, the United States had "not yet understood what
the Second World War was like and" as a result was "unable to use such understanding to re-interpret and re-define the national reality to arrive at something like public maturity" (Fussell 268). American popular culture's continued fascination with superheroes from the 1940s might be read as a symptom
of this inability to confront the nature of a war that, seventy years after its
conclusion, continues to shape our national discourse. Its true violence and
trauma, Samuel R. Delany writes, "circulated as an unstated and inarticulate
horror whose lessons were supposed to be brought back to the States while
their specificity was, in any collective narrativity, unspeakable, left in the foreign outside, safely beyond the pale" (Delany 186). Those who returned from
combat, like those who mourned the dead, had to invent a new language to
record and to express what had been lost.[32]

As far as Beck was concerned, of course, Captain Marvel had no business
taking part in combat, and he dismissed Billy's participation in the war effort
in the same way that he criticized those "tie clips, whistles," and other products ("What Really"). When meeting "various mayors, magazine distributors,"
as well as other "local celebrities," Captain Marvel, Beck believed, was not

3.11 In an alternate reality, Field Marshal Marvel captures a couple of German resistance fighters in a panel from "Captain Marvel in the World of If." Captain Marvel and related characters © 2016 DC Comics.

"convincing": "The contrast between a normal human and a cartoon character is too great; one or the other will always look phony" ("What Really"). One of these unsettling "phony" moments takes place in the middle of "Captain Marvel in the World of If," in which Field Marshal Marvel, wearing his medals, captures two "free Germans of the underground movement" who are trying to assassinate Hitler. When the fighters question Captain Marvel's loyalty, and accuse him of being a traitor to the American cause, this alternate-universe version of the hero shouts, "Shut up, dogs! America is no longer my country! I hate America!" On the next page, holding the two men by the backs of their necks, he offers them to Hitler, who commands, "*To der concentration camp mit dem!*" This panel echoes the collision of fantasy and realism in that two-page opening sequence from "Capt. Marvel and the Mark of the Black Swastika"; in both examples, the writers and artists introduce a comic book hero to mitigate the true horror that inspired each image—the bombing of London or, in this case, the reality of the camps (fig. 3.11). The look on one of the conspirator's faces—stiff and wide-eyed, drops of sweat spilling from his forehead—creates a rupture or a crack in Billy's world. This scene undermines the story's neat, predictable conclusion. Meant to illustrate just how far Field Marshal Marvel has fallen, the reference to the concentration camp alludes to the unspoken and to the unknown, to a violence that reduces everything in its path to silence and anonymity.[33]

Why, then, should we read these stories today, decades after the historical moment that produced them has passed? Their Chief Artist, after all, found narratives like these unsatisfying and even distasteful, as they tended to violate his rules of effective and appealing comic book art and storytelling. As records of the war, they also come up short, remnants of that "realm of myth" (Murray 101) also inhabited by Captain America, Superman, and the other comic book heroes who fought against Germany, Italy, and Japan.[34] Accounts of the war fill bookstores, libraries, and digital archives. Why spend any time on these comics and what Beck described as these "phony" scenarios, absurd and impossible meetings between Captain Marvel, a being who never existed, and cartoon versions of historical figures? These comic books, like a box of photographs, or a stack of postcards, or a dress uniform tucked away in the back of a closet, serve as reminders of what still remains unsaid, not only by those who lived through these years in the first place, but for those of us who have inherited a legacy not only of victory and abundance but also of shame and uncertainty.

"AN IMAGINARY RIVER"

I am looking at three relics from the past arrayed before me on my desk: first, a photograph of my grandfather standing with another soldier, Private K. L. Brodeur, on a street outside the YMCA in Pittsburgh in June 1942. Members of the Coast Artillery Battery, they've just spent a few days with the War Show at Franklin Field in Philadelphia. They'll celebrate July 4th with a performance at the University of Pittsburgh. I've opened my grandfather's Army War Show yearbook to a list of dates and locations of the eighteen stops on the tour, from Baltimore in early June to Atlanta just before the Christmas holidays. Next to the photograph and the yearbook lies a brittle, coverless copy of *Captain Marvel Adventures* no. 20, which I found on eBay a few years ago as I started working on this book. By February 1943, not long after Billy first met Old Scratch and those French children, my grandfather and the rest of his battalion were in North Africa, where he would be stationed until the spring of 1944, according to his service records. Having survived the war, he died in January 1960, thirteen years before I was born. I know him only through photographs, newspaper articles, war records, and family stories. As I look at the photo, the yearbook, and the comic book, I am searching for the links between family narrative, United States military history, and popular culture.

Unable to feel nostalgia for any of these items, I wonder how I might arrange them to recognize a pattern or to communicate, somehow, with the dead. It's impossible, of course, and foolish. Then again, that's also part of Billy's story—his ability to reclaim and to understand the past. Here, again, Captain Marvel serves as a "companion" (Lupoff, "Big Red" 68), a guide to these forgotten spaces. Like Shazam's room of wonders, they've been here all along, waiting to be discovered. Still, I have to wonder what my grandfather would have made of this conversation between the two of us, his small but essential role in this book, as I tell a story that once belonged only to him.

On Wednesday, September 2, 1942, he was one of the soldiers performing in the rain at Soldier Field in Chicago. In a program booklet for the show, I notice that they've misspelled his last name, adding an *e* where the *o* should be at the end of *Stango*. Even now, as I write this, I am trying to correct a small piece of history that no one outside my family would notice. In an article published in the *Chicago Herald-American*, David Camelon describes a few of the highlights of that September 2 performance. The engineers, he writes, were a hit: "The announcer said they would erect a pontoon bridge across an imaginary river," a display of their readiness for combat and of the Army's so-phisticated new weapons and equipment (Camelon 6). Before they could do so, however, "a voice cried: 'Brother, that ain't imaginary!'" Like a superhero, of course, Private Tedesco would return for the next night's performance. Eventually, all of the soldiers, Camelon writes, would pack up and "put their show on in other cities. And then, some day, they'll put it on in earnest on some battlefield" (6).

Swayze's cover for *Captain Marvel Adventures* no. 12, the records of the War Show, these comic books, Beck's essays, even this chapter—each one, I think, is an attempt to build that "bridge across an imaginary river" of time and history.[35] Or maybe, like that care package of candy bars and comic books, each one is nothing more than another gesture, an offering to those men and women whose absence—like their hopes, fears, and desires—still shapes our present.

Chapter 4

STEAMBOAT'S AMERICA

Tied to a burning candle, Captain Marvel is standing on a birthday cake, his yellow boots covered in white frosting. Sivana, holding another pale blue candle, threatens him, and Billy's alter ego, the brave soul who faced Hitler and Goebbels and Satan himself, looks terrified. Sivana grins. *This time*, the mad scientist must be thinking, *I've got him*. But can any of this be real? The title gives it away. "Captain Marvel and the World's Mightiest Dream!"—published in *Captain Marvel Adventures* no. 48 (Aug.–Sept. 1945)[1]—gives the reader a look at Captain Marvel's nightmares. Although he's the World's Mightiest Mortal, even he has bad dreams sometimes. It's not his birthday either. In the inset panel to the right, Billy and other WHIZ employees sing to Sterling Morris, their boss. To Billy's left is a character who first appeared in a Captain Marvel adventure in 1942, just two years after Billy's debut in *Whiz Comics* (fig. 4.1).

This strange but otherwise unremarkable story is notable because it marks the final appearance of Steamboat, a regular cast member until 1945. As Billy and the other two men sing to Mr. Morris, Steamboat joins in, but he is the only character in the panel staring directly at the reader. Billy's friend and servant, he is what Frantz Fanon might have called "an object among other objects" (Fanon 89; see also Gilroy 8), the embodiment of an illusion, a cruel fantasy—in other words, a kind of dream, but one far more destructive than the nightmare which startles Captain Marvel from his sleep. Like the images of blackness in advertising that Fanon responded to in his work, Steamboat, to borrow a phrase from theorist Paul Gilroy, represents an "abbreviated (Fanon's term for this would be 'amputated') conception of human subjectivity," like the other stereotypical figures that populated a "twentieth-century dreamworld" in which blackness "began to acquire commercial value" (Gilroy 8–9; Fanon 89). That inset panel on the first page of "Captain Marvel and the World's Mightiest Dream!" tells the story of that "dreamworld," an ideal,

4.1 The first two panels of "Captain Marvel and the World's Mightiest Dream!" from *Captain Marvel Adventures* no. 48 (Aug.–Sept. 1945). Captain Marvel and related characters © 2016 DC Comics.

comfortable existence filled with the markers of material success and prestige: the table, the birthday cake, the men in suits, the painting, and, in the center, Billy's "valet" (Lupoff, "Big Red" 70).

Steamboat only appears in the first five panels of the story. After Morris's party, he and Billy head home to their apartment. Having eaten too much cake, Billy worries that he might have a "nightmare," but Steamboat has more pressing concerns: "Ah's got a nightmare right now!" he says. "Ah's got de feelin' dat somebody is shadowin' us!"[2] Looking wary and frightened, he turns his head to see if anyone is following them, but Billy replies, "Nonsense, Steamboat! It's your imagination!" In the next panel, the reader learns that Billy's friend has been right all along. As they enter the door to the apartment building, Sivana—the madman himself, not the dream figure holding the glowing candle—emerges from an alley and, in a thought bubble, reveals his grisly plan. As soon as Billy falls "asleep," Sivana will go to work with his "little hatchet!" Steamboat can do nothing to stop him (fig. 4.2).

4.2 Captain Marvel finally wakes up from his nightmare at the end of "Captain Marvel and the World's Mightiest Dream!" *Captain Marvel Adventures* no. 48 (Aug.–Sept. 1945). Captain Marvel and related characters © 2016 DC Comics.

After the first panel on the story's second page, Steamboat disappears, but not before turning out the light. "G'night, Mistah Billy! How does yo-all feel now?" The room is bright and comfortable, with red, patterned curtains, matching lamps, nightstands, and a bed with a headboard. More dream images fill the next several pages—a talking birthday cake, for example, a giant bird's nest, and trees with eyes and mouths. At the end of the nightmare, Sivana, seated on the cake, like a demon from a fairy tale, appears again with his hatchet, eager to murder Billy. "I'm going to chop off your head!" the scientist says with a laugh. The nightmare, it appears, was a premonition, as the real Sivana lurks in the darkness. But Billy's magic word works just as well at night as it does during the day: "Once more, both in the dream and in real life," reads a caption, "the magic lightning comes!" Captain Marvel's head is so thick and invulnerable that the blow fails to wake him up at first. Then, in the final three panels of the story—printed almost entirely in blue to suggest the darkness that fills Billy's room—Captain Marvel springs out of bed. "Gosh, what a horrible nightmare Billy and I had!" he remarks, until he finds Sivana's hatchet, and a broken lamp, on the floor.

That Steamboat's final appearance should introduce a story about paranoia, hallucinations, and nightmares is fitting, given that he is a creature of illusion, one shaped by discourses of white supremacy that permeated the popular culture of the United States in the 1940s. The character, a version of the "coon" figure that Donald Bogle describes in his history of African American stereotypes in Hollywood cinema (Bogle 7–8), suggests a significant flaw in the dream logic of Beck's theories. If Billy exists in a land of pure fantasy, one in which he can will himself into an ideal state of being, why is he unable to imagine his friend Steamboat as anything other than a "coon," a servant, a sidekick? Novelist and cartoonist Charles Johnson refers to the "Ur-images of blacks" that appeared in animated films, comic strips, and comic books in the early twentieth century as "a testament to the failure of the imagination (and often of empathy, too)," figures that "tell us nothing about black people but *every*thing about what white audiences approved and felt comfortable with in pop culture until the 1950s," when the Civil Rights Movement began to usher in significant political and cultural advances (Johnson 13). While Steamboat's presence represents that "failure of the imagination" on the part of Fawcett's writers and artists, the character's removal provides an example of how action on the part of readers can bring about small but significant social change. The real heroes of Steamboat's story aren't Billy, Captain Marvel, and Shazam, but a group of New York City junior high school students who, as part of a program called Youthbuilders, visited Executive Editor Will Lieberson in 1945 and argued for Steamboat's removal.

This chapter, then, tells Steamboat's story, and the significant role he played in Billy's early adventures. As an "object" in Billy's world, Steamboat provided evidence that the newsboy, after that first meeting with Shazam, had mastered the strange, sometimes ominous world in which he lived. After receiving his magic word and securing a position at WHIZ, the character, as Richard Lupoff points out in "The Big Red Cheese," "lived in a comfortable apartment, alone save for his Negro valet," a character who "was the exemplification of the racial stereotype of the era," one found in "pulp magazine stories, radio dramas," and "motion pictures," as well as "other popular media" (70). Steamboat, along with Billy's job and that "comfortable apartment," served as markers of the boy's remarkable transformation from homeless orphan to popular celebrity. Billy was never wealthy, but he possessed a measure of power and social capital, on display in his relationship with Steamboat, who, Lupoff writes, is "obviously a grown man in the employ of a half-grown boy," an adult who "always addressed his employer as 'Mist' Billy'" ("Big Red" 70). While, as Lupoff points out, the comic books, comic strips, and pulp magazines of the era are filled with characters like Steamboat, there are what Erika Frensley calls "notable exceptions" (Frensley 6-7), including The Shadow's Jericho Druke and The Avenger's Josh and Rosabel Newton, African American characters who use these stereotypes to their advantage as they assist in solving various crimes.[3] These three pulp heroes are unusual in the popular media of the late 1930s and early 1940s, but their presence, like Oscar Micheaux's films and detective novels or the Youthbuilders' response to Steamboat, serve as reminders of the progressive voices that critiqued these images at the height of World War II.[4]

While it is not possible to tell Billy's story without Steamboat and his role in the hero's transformation, there is also a danger in reading Billy's valet as a relic of racism in the United States in the 1940s, an era we might dismiss as less enlightened than the one in which we live. In doing so, we run the risk of ignoring these images, or ones descended from them, in the popular culture that surrounds us. A note in the Table of Contents for volume 4 of *The Shazam! Archives*, published by DC Comics in 2003, for example, cautions readers that the stories included in the collection "were produced in a time when racism was more overt in society and popular culture both consciously and unconsciously" (4). The note also assures readers that these comics, including Steamboat's debut in *America's Greatest Comics* no. 2 from 1942, "are reprinted without alteration for historical reference" (4). In writing about Steamboat, I take as my example the Youthbuilders and their resistance to the discourses of racism and white supremacy. Not merely a figure of "historical" interest, Steamboat represents a pernicious ideology that persists in the cultural and political landscape of the United States. The students who visited the Fawcett offices in 1945 imagined a world very different than the one on display in the pages of these comics. If Billy's story is about the unlimited potential of the imagination, why should readers settle for a character so ugly and limited as Steamboat? The students took these comic books seriously, and asked that their creators do the same.

In her 1943 book *Children Object*, social worker and Youthbuilders founder Sabra Holbrook explains that the program encouraged students to engage with various social and cultural issues in a three-step process, one that begins with "*free discussion*," continues with "*exciting investigation*," and ideally ends with "*concerted action*" (Holbrook 167; italics in the original). Forty years later, in the early issues of *Miracleman*, Alan Moore would also address the historical, cultural, and psychological impact of the ideology of white supremacy in comic books. While Moore's Evelyn Cream, a black spy who guides and defends Mike Moran, Miracleman's alter ego (and a variation on both Parker and Beck's Captain Marvel and Mick Anglo's Marvelman), is not a direct response to Steamboat, the writer introduced the character as a critique of the images of blackness that had filled superhero comics for decades. If Steamboat had dreams, they might look something like those that haunt Evelyn Cream, who reflects on the stereotypes and discourses that have shaped him and his relationship with the book's hero. In the first half of this chapter, I discuss Steamboat's role in two of Billy's adventures from the 1940s before turning my attention to Holbrook, the Youthbuilders, and Moore, each of whom offers a glimpse of an alternate future, one in which there is no place for Steamboat and all he represents.

The stories featuring Steamboat reflect the petty hatreds, unexamined hostility, and dangerous ignorance that, as Charles Johnson has suggested, represent a "failure of the imagination" (13), one that mirrors the flaws in the wartime stories I discussed in the last chapter. But Steamboat's America is much closer to us than we might care to admit. Only by engaging with it, and by critically assessing these images, can we identify the contradiction that, as Ralph Ellison once noted, lies at the heart of these racial stereotypes. In a 1953 essay, Ellison argues that

> whatever else the Negro stereotype might be as a social instrumentality, it is also a key figure in a magic rite by which the white American seeks to resolve the dilemma arising between his democratic beliefs and certain antidemocratic practices, between his acceptance of the sacred democratic belief that all men are created equal and his treatment of every tenth man as though he were not. (Ellison 45–46)

In examining these stereotypes and their place in the history of American racism, I also hope to introduce a set of reading strategies that might be applied to other works of comic art. As Ellison implies, that "dilemma" at the heart of American democracy cannot be resolved, based as it is on falsehood and denial. By examining this "magic rite" more closely, however, especially as manifested in these comic books, we might begin to dismantle a power structure that thrives on illusion.

To build the kind of society Holbrook and her teachers and students once imagined, we must contend with these existing structures, especially those we have inherited. Comics scholarship has the potential to provide insight into how we might continue to challenge and resist the "antidemocratic practices" embodied by cartoon figures like Steamboat. In a recent essay, scholar Qiana Whitted, for example, addresses Will Eisner's discussion of "stereotypical images" in *Graphic Storytelling and Visual Narrative* (Eisner 17–20):

> Conventional wisdom states that comics are made up of stereotypes of human behavior, due in no small part to the material demands for economy and efficiency on the page. Too often, however, this line of thinking is extended to include *cultural* stereotypes in which the comics industry is said to be as irrevocably bound to the status quo as it is to the spatial dimensions of a panel grid. (Whitted 97)

If the form is as flexible and promising as both Eisner and Beck argue in their critical work, then it offers the means and the opportunity to subvert these "*cultural* stereotypes," which, when present, serve as reminders of that "real world" that Beck so often dismissed. In other words, if Billy's stories should enable us, for a few moments, to leave those "dull and stupid things" behind us (Beck, "Real Facts"), Steamboat's presence prevents us from doing so. In an interview with Tom Heintjes, Beck, like Eisner, admitted that he used these visual shortcuts as a way to simplify these narratives: "To keep readers from having their attention drawn away from stories," he explained, "I deliberately used characters, settings and props that would be instantly recognized by everyone everywhere . . . in other words, stereotypes" (Beck qtd. in Heintjes). This strategy, at least for the students who spoke with Lieberson in 1945, did not work, as Steamboat's role in these stories proved to be a distraction, a reminder of the ignorance and intolerance of the adult world.

In order to, as Whitted writes, "repurpose hegemonic racial discourse," to imagine the medium as a site of "cultural intervention" (97), we must first identify the nature and origin of these stereotypes. My analysis of the Steamboat stories I discuss in this chapter is, like Whitted's work, based in part on Toni Morrison's discussion of an "Africanist presence" in American literature (Morrison 6–7; Whitted 80). In *Playing in the Dark*, Morrison introduces the phrase "American Africanism," which she defines "as a term for the denotative and connotative blackness that African people have come to signify, as well as the entire range of views, assumptions, readings, and misreadings that accompany Eurocentric learning about these people" (6–7). Later in the book, after providing examples of this presence in the works of authors ranging from Edgar Allan Poe and Herman Melville to Ernest Hemingway and William Faulkner, Morrison offers a list of "common linguistic strategies employed in fiction to engage the serious consequences of blacks" (67). The first of these, what she calls the "[e]conomy of stereotype," is especially relevant when writing about characters like Steamboat, as its use "allows the writer a quick and easy image without the responsibility of specificity, accuracy, or even narratively useful description" (67). This "quick and easy image," as Charles Johnson has also suggested, has nothing to do with African American culture or history. Rather, as Morrison points out, it is a projection, a fantasy, one whose only purpose is to enhance the heroic characteristics of a story's white protagonist.

Consider again the final panel in which Steamboat appears: the doors, the nightstands, the shades, the curtains, the windowsill, the bed. Each of these "objects" (to borrow Fanon's word again) tells part of Billy's story (fig. 4.3).[5] Steamboat has no agency, no subjectivity. Once Billy lies down and falls asleep, Steamboat is gone. Imagine, however, a different ending to "Captain Marvel and the World's Mightiest Dream!" As Captain Marvel picks up Sivana's hatchet, the door to Billy's room opens. Steamboat turns on the light, but his grotesque features have disappeared. Such a transformation might have been possible. After all, just a few years later, Captain Marvel, as John G. Pierce has pointed out, would confront a group of villains dressed like members of the Ku Klux Klan in one of Mr. Tawny's early appearances (Pierce, "Levity" 77).[6] But what if Steamboat, and not Tawny, had rented that house in the suburbs and, with Captain Marvel at his side, then faced the hatred and violence of those hooded figures? This question might appear to be nothing more than

4.3 Steamboat gets ready to shut off the light and close the door in his final appearance in a Captain Marvel story. From "Captain Marvel and the World's Mightiest Dream!" *Captain Marvel Adventures* no. 48 (Aug.–Sept. 1945). Captain Marvel and related characters © 2016 DC Comics.

idle speculation, or theory without the "*doing*" that Holbrook called for in her work with teachers and with students (161). That last page of "Captain Marvel and the World's Mightiest Dream!" remains troubling, not because of its predictable twist ending—*was it all just a dream?*—but because of its inability to answer any of the questions that it raises. What happened to Steamboat? The answer to that question, of course, is simple: Lieberson agreed with the students, and called for his immediate removal (Lieberson 94). With all of Captain Marvel's Fawcett adventures easily accessible online, however, the character, like Billy's persistent nightmare, remains with us, a reminder not just of the 1940s but a warning about the consequences of what Ellison calls that "antidemocratic" impulse.

"MUCH LIKE A THOUGHT BUBBLE"

Steamboat, from his first appearance in 1942 to his sudden disappearance in 1945, embodies many of the qualities of what Donald Bogle describes as an "uncle remus," a variation on the "coon" figure that made its debut in blackface minstrel performances of the nineteenth century (Hamm 124).[7] The *uncle remus*, whose name Bogle borrows from the storyteller in Joel Chandler Harris's popular series of local color tales, "distinguishes himself by his quaint, naïve, and comic philosophizing" (Bogle 8). These stereotypes, Bogle notes, were in "full flower" in "the 1930s and 1940s with films such as *The Green Pastures* (1936) and *Song of the South* (1946)" (8). Like the "coon" figure that preceded it, the "uncle remus," Bogle writes, "has always been used to indicate the black man's satisfaction with the system and his place in it" (8). Steamboat bears the hallmarks of this "crazy, lazy, subhuman" figure (8). Like Billy, his origin story from 1942 involves his search for a new job. In *Whiz Comics* no. 2, however, Billy, despite the challenges he faces, appears eager and ready for a change. Steamboat, on the other hand, with his horse and wagon, appears ill at ease in the urban spaces that Billy has mastered.

In an interview with Matt Lage, Otto Binder recalled Steamboat's introduction to Billy's supporting cast: "We were always creating new side characters, most of which became just one-shots if they turned out to have no appeal" (60). According to Binder, "Steamboat was the creation of Ed Herron," in his opinion "the greatest early Captain Marvel editor" (Binder qtd. in Lage, "We Were" 60). In later interviews, Binder and Beck discussed Steamboat and the decision to remove him from the pages of Fawcett's comics. In his conversation with Lage, Binder places that decision in a larger context.

The character, he explains, "was dropped during a wave of criticism of any anti-minority leanings that came up in that period," not only in comic books but also in "newspapers, movies, and all the media" (60). Although he supported these changes, Binder admits that he had some reservations. From his perspective, Steamboat was comparable to other "dialect" characters in the series. Here, Binder alludes to Steamboat's speech patterns but not to the character's physical appearance. In reference to the decision to eliminate Steamboat from the comics, Binder explains, "I was all in favor, actually, of anti-discrimination so it didn't bother me, except that we did sigh once in awhile because it was fun to depict such dialect groups. We never meant to degrade them, merely play them for humor" (60). Beck echoes Binder in his interview with Tom Heintjes for *Hogan's Alley*.

The cartoonist explains that "Steamboat was created to capture the affection of [N]egro readers" (Beck qtd. in Heintjes). After a reference to the Youthbuilders and their meeting with Lieberson, he insists that Steamboat "was always a cartoon character, not intended to be realistic at all," although "he was taken seriously by some, sadly enough" (Beck qtd. in Heintjes).[8] In his meeting with the students who participated in the Youthbuilders program, Lieberson, according to an article written by the Associated Negro Press and published in several newspapers in the spring of 1945, at first argued that "white characters too were depicted in all sorts of ways for the sake of humor [. . .]" ("Negro Villain"). The students, however, "retorted that white characters were both heroes and villains while 'Steamboat,' a buffoon, was the only Negro in the strip." The final paragraph of that news report not only anticipates Morrison's discussion of the "economy of stereotype," but also serves as a response to Binder and Beck's reflections on the character. According to the article, a young man, while speaking with Lieberson, "produced an enlarged portrait of 'Steamboat' and said, 'This is not the Negro race, but your one-and-a half million readers will think it so'" ("Negro Villain"). Even a comic book character like Billy, to use Morrison's phrase, possessed a "specificity" that Steamboat lacked. Billy is capable of great heroism, but he and his alter ego often make silly mistakes. While he is still a "cartoon" character, he has a more complex personality than Steamboat, who does not possess the "human interest" that Binder, in his introduction to "The Teacher from Mars," identified as the secret to good writing (Binder, "Teacher" 18–19). What Binder and Beck failed to understand is that Steamboat embodied a form of realism.[9] As the embodiment of what Whitted would describe as a deadly set of "*cultural* stereotypes," Steamboat proved to be a distraction from that "fabric of illusion" which Beck sought to create in his work. If Billy's potential is so unlimited, why should one of his closest friends be so limited in his range of emotion and behavior?

Steamboat first appears in *America's Greatest Comics* no. 2, dated February 11–May 13, 1942. Volume 4 of DC's *Shazam Archives* does not identify the story's writer but attributes the art to Beck, Dave Berg (best known for his later work on *Mad*), and "The Fawcett Captain Marvel Art Staff" (4).[10] The urban landscape of Captain Marvel's first appearance in *Whiz Comics* no. 2 and "The Park Robberies" are remarkably similar, but the opening page of Steamboat's first appearance is much more atmospheric.[11] As the large figure of Captain Marvel stands guard over the city, "an elderly man," the caption at the bottom of the page tells us, moves "warily" beneath "the shadow of a bridge" (3).[12] The page does not begin with the simple, rectangular panel that opens Billy's first adventure. Rather, the artists have created a complex portrait of an urban landscape, one with Captain Marvel at the top of the page and the old man, and that mysterious tunnel, at the bottom (fig. 4.4).

While the streets in *Whiz* no. 2 are curiously empty, except for the men who pass Billy in the rain, the park in *America's Greatest Comics* is a fully realized setting, complete with narration that might have appeared in one of Walter B. Gibson's Shadow novels of the 1930s: "Here, in the very midst of civilization, young savages lurk in the darkness to pounce upon unsuspecting prey—and an occasional scream is the only evidence of their murderous deeds" (3).[13] In the next panel, a figure shouts, "Git his dough!" as a group of young men beat the old man with clubs. The narrator has given us some assurance—we can expect that our hero will soon appear "on another of his mercy errands!" (3)—but even Captain Marvel can't save the man from the terrors of this "jungle," one inhabited by these "savages" who "lurk in the darkness" and threaten innocent bystanders (3).

In order to put a stop to the youth violence plaguing the park, Captain Marvel disguises himself as a police officer. Billy's alter ego even adopts an

4.4 The splash page of *America's Greatest Comics* no. 2 (Feb. 11–May 13, 1942). Reprinted in *The Shazam! Archives* volume 4 (175). Captain Marvel and related characters © 2016 DC Comics.

Irish accent so that no one suspects his true identity: "Top o' the marnin' to ye, gents," he says to two men sitting on a park bench in what the narrator tells us is "the most dangerous part of the park!" (13). Captain Marvel goes on patrol in the hope of capturing some of the young men he calls "kid gangsters" (13), the hooligans who have been beating, mugging, and otherwise terrorizing honest, law-abiding citizens.

One of these citizens, we learn on the next page of the story, is Steamboat Bill. He first appears in the second panel of page fourteen (fig. 4.5). Napoleon, his horse, draws a carriage covered in advertisements for "Hamburgers" and "Pop." Although the horse and carriage dominate the frame, we can see the

4.5 Steamboat enters the park with his horse on page 14 of *America's Greatest Comics* no. 2 (Feb. 11–May 13, 1942). Reprinted in *The Shazam! Archives* vol. 4 (186). Captain Marvel and related characters © 2016 DC Comics.

white circle of Steamboat's lips. Gray silhouettes of buildings line the horizon. Aside from his features, Steamboat's accent marks him as different from the other characters that surround him. Just as Captain Marvel spoke in an Irish accent, Steamboat speaks in the dialect of the minstrel stage: "F'hevvins sakes!" he exclaims (14). One young man screams, "Yaaah! Ice cream! An' hamboigers!" while another shouts, "Grab 'em, gang!" In the next two panels, the boys try to hold Steamboat's horse, but they fail, and the animal breaks loose from his harness and dramatically gallops away, even jumping over a baby carriage. Steamboat pursues him, but only Captain Marvel has the strength to stop the old and frightened animal: "Getting winded eh, old fellow? You should know better than to dash around like that at *your* age!" (15). Steamboat returns again a few pages later, as he and Napoleon save one of the police officers from certain death at the hands of an adult gangster. Just as a man in a trench coat is about to murder the officer by "pumpin'" him "fulla lead!" (21), Steamboat and Napoleon knock the villain into a small pond. Steamboat, barely in control of the horse and carriage, shouts, "Heah's me ag'in, folks! Gangway!" As he falls, the gangster expresses his anger and frustration: "The blankety blank!" he exclaims (21).

At the end of the story, the former gang members, once the victims of those adult gangsters, join the Captain Marvel Club, an organization that will enable them, as Billy puts it, to assist in the hero's "fight against crime!" (22).[14] In the story's final panel, Steamboat asks Billy for help. Their conversation

4.6 Billy plans for his future at the end of his origin in *Whiz Comics* no. 2
(February 1940). Script by Bill Parker and art by C. C. Beck. Reprinted in *The
Shazam! Archives* vol. 1 (32). Captain Marvel and related characters © 2016
DC Comics.

echoes Billy's first meeting with Sterling Morris. Having assisted in the ar-
rest of the gangsters who'd caused all the trouble in the park, Steamboat now
faces troubles of his own: "Mistuh Billy," he says, "I done cracked up my wagon
com-plete when I busted up dem gangstuhs!" Billy offers to help, and invites
Steamboat to "come down to the broadcasting studios in the morning" for "a
new job!" That "new job," however, will look a lot like his old one (22).

On the final page of Captain Marvel's first appearance from 1940, Billy
shakes his fists with joy (fig. 4.6). No longer a victim of his uncle's greed,
he now has friends and a promising career. "Billy Batson, radio reporter!"
he shouts. "Boy, oh, boy! Here's where we go to town!" In the last panel of
"The Park Robberies," however, Steamboat doesn't learn what his next job
will be, but his chef's hat—worn throughout the story—suggests that, while
he might have an opportunity to leave his old horse and his wagon behind
him, he will remain what he already is (fig. 4.7). Whereas Billy undergoes a
transformation that changes his personality and his perspective on the world,
Steamboat, when he appears in "Captain Marvel and the Warrior of Wai" in
Captain Marvel Adventures no. 10 (May 1, 1942), is still wearing that cap (see
p. 45 of the comic).[15] He remains a cook, Billy's assistant. Although Billy lives

4.7 Steamboat finds a new job at the end of "The Park Robberies" from *America's Greatest Comics* no. 2 (Feb. 11–May 13, 1942): 22. Reprinted in *The Shazam! Archives* vol. 4 (194). Captain Marvel and related characters © 2016 DC Comics.

in a charmed, dynamic, and often exciting universe, Steamboat remains fixed and unchanging. That static quality is one of the key features of any stereotype, especially visual ones: they imply an inability to change, to adapt to one's circumstances.[16] As Ellison and Bogle have argued, these stereotypes are projections, ones that assure the viewer that Steamboat, and the community he allegedly represents, is content "with the system" as it stands (Bogle 8). While Billy spends his origin story learning how to survive in his new environment—observing each tunnel, street, and skyscraper carefully, claiming each one as his own as he prepares to "go to town!"—Steamboat, in his first appearance, spends his time defending himself from the gang of kids or chasing after his horse. His act of heroism, as he and Napoleon prevent the gangsters from murdering the old police officer, is also a moment of slapstick comedy. While Billy has many roles to play in these stories, Steamboat has only one, that of the comic sidekick whose presence assures white readers that Billy's valet is grateful for the life that he now leads.

In his essay "Looking at Whiteness: Finding Myself Much like a Mugger at a Boardwalk's End," philosopher George Yancy argues that white supremacy cannot exist without this *fantasy* of blackness. In a passage on his experience of white drivers locking their car doors when he approaches on a city street, Yancy writes, "I am the 'proof' that they concocted to confirm their superiority" (33). In the last chapter, I noted that when Billy says his magic word, he, like a superheroic Peter Pan, is often more innocent and childlike than he is as a newsboy or radio reporter. His dream is to stay a child forever. In racial discourse in the United States, Yancy argues, "whiteness is a form of make-believe, a game played by children who refuse to grow up, though the existential stakes are high for black people" (Yancy 33). Later in his essay, Yancy employs an image borrowed from a comic strip or comic book to describe his encounters with the white drivers who are terrified of what they *think* he represents. As he walks past them, and as they lock their doors, he experiences a form of dissociation, a version of the "double-consciousness" that W. E. B. Du Bois defined in *The Souls of Black Folk* in 1903 (Du Bois 3). Suddenly, Yancy writes, he feels as though he is "floating like a phantasm in their imaginary—much like a thought bubble" (35). A phantasm is also a ghost, a dead thing, a being whose nature is already fixed and defined. While a phantasm cannot be called back from the dead, however, a thought bubble can be edited, revised, erased. A physical thing, both word and image printed on a sheet of paper, it can also be rejected, or brought into juxtaposition with other images, ones that comment upon it or redefine it. The work of the writer, artist, critic, and scholar is to question these found images, to deny their claims, to reveal the ideologies that made them possible in the first place.

STEAMBOAT AND THE "BACKWARD SOUTH"

In his nostalgic summary of Captain Marvel's various friends and adversaries, published in a fanzine called *The Rocket's Blast Special* no. 8 in the early 1970s, Gene Arnold describes Steamboat as "basically lazy" and "cowardly," a character "with an accent you could cut with a knife" (Arnold n.p.).[17] That accent, especially in stories like "Capt. Marvel and the Voodoo Showboat," published in *Captain Marvel Adventures* no. 22 (dated March 26, 1943),[18] implies Steamboat's Southern origins.[19] His first appearance in "The Park Robberies" marks him as an inhabitant, with his ancient horse and wagon, of another time and space, an agrarian lifestyle associated with the US South. In the story, Steamboat's "long-lost grandma" (21) doubles as both Voodoo Annie, Sivana's accomplice, and as Showboat Mammy, her "real self" (28). His grandmother, we learn, would love to be famous as a jazz singer. First, however, she must escape Sivana's clutches.

The South as figured in *CMA* no. 22 is just as strange and impossible as Steamboat himself. Filled with references to voodoo, zombies, showboats,

4.8 Billy listens to Axis radio chatter as Steamboat reads a book on voodoo from the first page of "Capt. Marvel and the Voodoo Showboat" in *Captain Marvel Adventures* no. 22 (March 26, 1943): 21. Reprinted in Don Maris's *The Best of* (1975). Captain Marvel and related characters © 2016 DC Comics.

"slaves" (30), and plantations, the narrative introduces a territory still haunted by the ghosts of the Civil War, a world apart from Billy's city, that cross between Chicago and New York. In the introduction to her 2006 book *The Nation's Region*, Leigh Anne Duck refers to Edward Said's *Orientalism* as she provides an overview of discourses about the South and its role in US history. After referencing Said's discussion of "imaginative geography" (Said 55), Duck argues that "when national discourse has acknowledged the conflict between southern conservatism and national democracy, it has typically done so in ways that localize this conflict," pitting "a 'backward South'" against "a modern or 'enlightened nation,'" an ideological conflict with race at its center (Duck 2–3). Duck points out that "this pattern" is especially "apparent and destructive" when it appears "in political and legal representations of southern racial segregation," which often "disavowed both the contemporaneity of the South with the larger nation and the presence of apartheid in other areas of the country" (Duck 3). This notion of the South as "backward" (3) is evident on the first page of "Capt. Marvel and the Voodoo Showboat," in which Billy sits listening to Axis broadcasts on his shortwave radio. It's a babel of voices, from "Achtung!" and "Capish!" to "blabber" and "blah" (20). Steamboat, reading a book, sits to Billy's right. "Just the usual Axis malarkey from all over!" Billy remarks, before the reader turns the page and Steamboat offers a lesson on the living dead (figure 4.8).

That "hair-raising book" is filled with information about zombies and "voodoo," which Steamboat warns is "turrible stuff!" (21). His hair standing on end, Steamboat, eyes wide, sweats as he reads this account of what the caption on the previous page refers to as "bad magic." "You don't *believe* in it, do you??"

4.9 Examples of the "southern aristocracy" from page 27 of "Capt. Marvel and the Voodoo Showboat" from *Captain Marvel Adventures* no. 22 (March 26, 1943). Reprinted in Don Maris's *The Best of* (1975). Captain Marvel and related characters © 2016 DC Comics.

Billy asks. The image in the second panel answers that question before Steamboat has a chance to respond. His posture communicates his distress. Pointing at the cover of the book, he leans forward (fig. 4.8). Although he derives his abilities from "good magic" (as he explains in the story's introduction on page twenty), Billy is also at ease with modern technology. As Steamboat tells the tale of Showboat Mammy, Billy, sitting at the radio, wears a set of headphones and continues to listen to the Axis chatter (21). For now, at least, he doesn't have time to spare on his valet's fears and superstitions.

By the next page, Voodoo Annie's broadcasts have transformed Billy (and therefore Captain Marvel) into a zombie. Meanwhile, Sivana reveals that, in his never-ending quest "to become the rightful ruler of the universe," he plans to throw a "showboat party" (26), one that will give him the opportunity to hypnotize white Southern land owners. "*All* will become my slaves!" he exclaims. "I'll own *all their land*! My new empire will be *launched!*" (28). The first of two horizontal panels on page twenty-seven includes a drawing of a "Kunnel" on horseback. In the distance is Sivana's newly refurbished showboat, which, a caption explains, "blazes forth as in its day of glory!" (27). A white-haired man wearing a straw hat and suspenders asks the mounted "Kunnel" if he will be "goin' to th' showboat pahty too?" to which the old soldier responds, "Yeh man! Ah ain't had no fun a-tall since it closed down, fohty yeahs ago!" (27). These characters, like the showboat Sivana has brought into the present, are markers of the past and of that long-lost (and fanciful) "day of glory." In the next panel, we see "the lavish showboat party" as it "goes into full swing, attended by the plantation-owners and Southern aristocracy of the region!" (fig. 4.9).

4.10 Showboat Mammy reveals her "real self" on page 28 of "Capt. Marvel and the Voodoo Showboat" from *Captain Marvel Adventures* no. 22 (March 26, 1943). Reprinted in Don Maris's *The Best of* (1975). Captain Marvel and related characters © 2016 DC Comics.

After Sivana reveals his plan, Steamboat learns that Voodoo Annie, Sivana's accomplice, is none other than his grandmother, Showboat Mammy (29). As her name suggests, she is another stereotype common in the popular culture of the era, the "mammy," a figure "closely related to the comic coons" but notable for "her fierce independence" and "cantankerous" behavior (Bogle 9). As the story progresses, we understand that she is performing a masquerade, one in which "Voodoo Annie," as she explains, is "a sideline" or "a hypnotist act!" (28). She reveals her other self by removing the knotted green handkerchief that has covered her head since her first appearance on page twenty-one. This doubling echoes Billy's own transformation, but unlike our hero, Showboat Mammy/Voodoo Annie closely resemble each other (fig. 4.10). Although she now wears make-up, pearls, and bracelets, as her name suggests, she remains a "mammy" figure like the ones described by Bogle.

4.11 A jazz record sets the "southern aristocracy" free on page 30 of "Capt. Marvel and the
Voodoo Showboat" from *Captain Marvel Adventures* no. 22 (March 26, 1943). Reprinted
in Don Maris's *The Best of* (1975). Captain Marvel and related characters © 2016 DC Comics.

Steamboat plays a role in defeating the evil scientist, but in his capacity as
the story's coon figure, he is not an active agent in the villain's defeat. After
his reunion with his grandmother, she leads him to Sivana's quarters, where,
she says, "He got all dis radio junk heah—!" (24). The fourth panel on page
twenty-four echoes the earlier scene in which Steamboat explains the nature
of "bad magic" or "voodoo" to a skeptical Billy. Worried about his friend, he
is unable to understand the purpose of the machines arrayed before him,
with one important exception. "Waal, anyways," he says, "let's have some
music out of dis radio-phonograph! Music allus soothes me!" The record,
a Cab Calloway-like scat number, does the job, not just for him but also for
the aristocrats under Sivana's control. On the next page, as Sivana cracks a
whip and commands his "slaves" to "bow down" before him, the music has
the same effect on the Southern aristocrats as it did on Steamboat. Suddenly,
they are free of Voodoo Annie's spell (30). No longer zombies, they "joyously
go into a jam session!" Musical notes over their heads, they dance in silhouette (fig. 4.11), oblivious to Captain Marvel's nemesis and his commands. Just
as Sivana is about to whip Steamboat and Showboat Mammy for ruining his
plans, Captain Marvel, also set free by the music, returns and, predictably,
punches the villain in the jaw (31). As in many of the other stories in which

4.12 Billy and Steamboat prepare to return home in the final panel of "Capt. Marvel and the Voodoo Showboat" from *Captain Marvel Adventures* no. 22 (March 26, 1943): 31. Reprinted in Don Maris's *The Best of* (1975). Captain Marvel and related characters © 2016 DC Comics.

he appears, Steamboat plays an important role in the story's resolution, but he does so only by happenstance. Driven by narcissistic urges—in this case, his desire to calm his nerves after losing track of his friend and unexpectedly rediscovering his grandmother—he lacks Billy's wits as well as Captain Marvel's brute strength and authority.

The final caption of the narrative assures readers that Steamboat and Billy, having once again thwarted Dr. Sivana's plot to rule the universe, will now return home: "Back to the city and his job once more goes Billy Batson. Where—who knows?—perhaps an even greater adventure may be waiting for him!" (31) That final panel neatly summarizes Steamboat's role in this and in other Captain Marvel stories. Caught between that "imaginative geography" of the South and Billy's "city," Steamboat, the image suggests, exists in both worlds but belongs in neither. As he walks across the plank leading to shore, his grandmother sits in a rocking chair (fig. 4.12). Although the record managed to rescue the planters and Captain Marvel, that music, and her ambitions, cannot save her. According to the logic of the story, she must remain where she is, unable to follow her grandson to the city and, by implication, into the future. When Steamboat asks if she'd like to accompany him, she replies, "No, ah's gwine lib an' die here on dis yere old showboat!" (31). No longer in her hat and pearls, she once again wears a yellow, polka-dot blouse, an ankle-length black dress, and the knotted handkerchief that covers her white hair. She remains in the chair while Steamboat waves goodbye. As she explained to her grandson a few pages earlier, she has been on the boat all these years because she "couldn't bear leavin' it!" (29).

These closing images, and Showboat Mammy's masquerade, all suggest the relationship between images of stereotype and a sense of place. Just as characters such as Superman, Batman, and Captain Marvel are defined by their relationship to the city, Steamboat and his grandmother remain tethered to fantastic images of the South and its history. Billy Batson and his alter ego represent a modernity characterized by urban spaces, a territory of steel and glass filled with automobiles, skyscrapers, record players, radio broadcasts, and magical subway trains. Billy is a master of that domain because, as the opening panels of this story suggest, he is comfortable with technology and with various forms of discourse, no matter how nonsensical, like the Axis voices he listens to on his shortwave radio. Unlike Steamboat Mammy, he is also in control of his "real self." While she is unable to inhabit that second, somewhat secret identity, her voodoo, though powerful enough to ensnare even Captain Marvel, is, like the voices on that radio, chaotic and ill-suited to the modern world. Easily manipulated, she must give up her Voodoo Annie persona so that the story reaches a neat, orderly conclusion. After she promises no longer to work her magic, Billy—standing on shore and ready to head home—remarks, "Good for you, Mammy! No harm done—but it *might* have hurt a lot of people!" (31).

The various forms of masquerade in this story are also worth noting, as even Sivana disguises himself as a member of that nearly vanished "Southern aristocracy." As Marc Singer has argued, over the last seventy years, "the generic ideology of the superhero" demands that "exotic outsiders" often "work to preserve America's status quo" (Singer 110). As a result, he continues, an "examination of race in superhero comics must consider these innate tensions," ones that reveal "the genre's most radical impulses and its most conservative ones" (110). In this story, only Billy's double identity allows for real freedom because of its links to modernity and to whiteness. His ability to move with ease from one shape to the next—from an innocent boy to a hero and back again—would not have been possible without his access to the subway tunnel and to Shazam. Voodoo Annie is just as powerful—perhaps even more capable than he is—but, unable to harness those forces effectively, and unwilling to leave that wreck of a ship (and the region it represents), she will remain where she is, locked in place, the subject of what Singer, in a reference to Fanon's writing about black stereotypes, describes as "a psychological, existential sentence rather than a social one" (Singer 108; see also Fanon 18).

In placing limits on these characters, Fawcett's editors, writers, and artists also also underestimated their readers. "The artist is no freer than the society in which he lives," concludes Ralph Ellison in "Twentieth-Century Fiction and the Black Mask of Humanity," "and in the United States the writers who stereotype or ignore the Negro and other minorities in the final analysis stereotype and distort their own humanity" (60). By dismissing Steamboat, or by ignoring the ugliness and "distortion" in these stories, we also run the risk of forgetting those who responded to these narratives in the first place. These images did not exist in a vacuum; to suggest otherwise would be to deny the imaginative power of that group of students who visited the Fawcett offices in 1945. By saying "no" to Steamboat and what he represented, they offered a model for the future, a way of being in the world, and an example of the compassion and curiosity lacking in these comic book narratives.

"THE WORLD WE WANT TO LIVE IN": SABRA HOLBROOK AND THE YOUTHBUILDERS

In the spring of 1945, just a few months before Steamboat's final appearance in *Captain Marvel Adventures*, Youthbuilders founder Sabra Holbrook visited the PTA at Newton Bateman Elementary School on the north side of Chicago. According to an article in the *Chicago Tribune* for March 18, she was there to deliver a lecture titled "The World We Want to Live In," a presentation that would be followed by a "film on the same subject" courtesy of "the Chicago Round Table of Christians and Jews."[20] At the end of the evening, the school's band, conducted by Helen Gedelman, was also set to perform. A couple of years earlier, Viking had published Holbrook's *Children Object*, a book that offered advice and suggestions to other teachers and school districts interested in the Youthbuilders program. The title of Holbrook's lecture at Bateman provides a concise summary of her philosophy of education, one that set out to imagine and then build a more functional world than the one she and her students faced in the early 1940s.

An article in the *Nassau Daily News*, published just a few days after her visit to Chicago in March 1945, explains that while Holbrook did not train to be a teacher, "her major interest in life lies in the field of American education, specifically the education of young people for responsible citizenship in a democracy."[21] Holbrook was a native of Massachusetts, where her father, Robert W. Rollins, was the president and general manager of the Worcester Electric Light Company (Kerr 13).[22] After undergraduate work at Vassar, she served as a social worker for the Judge Baker Foundation in Boston where, according to an article published in the *Spokane Daily Chronicle* in 1947, she worked "with delinquent children" (Kerr 13). Working closely with Byrnes MacDonald, Holbrook developed the idea for Youthbuilders after a meeting with William Jansen, New York's assistant superintendent of schools, who "sent her into a junior high school to visit with the youngsters and find out what interested them" (Kerr 13; see also "Youthbuilders, Inc."). In contemporary terms, Youthbuilders appears to have functioned like a club or an after-school program, an extracurricular activity designed to engage students and build a sense of community.

In the second chapter of *Children Object*, Holbrook describes the students who took part in these forums, which reflected the racial and ethnic make-up of New York City in the late 1930s and 1940s. One group of children, students at "a co-educational junior high school in which thirteen different nationalities were represented," addressed the issue of prejudice in one of their discussions. As they debated and researched the problem, Holbrook writes, they realized "that their prejudices were handed down to them at home by their parents" (27-28). Their solution? The students called for the school's PTA "to put on a forum, for the parents' entertainment, on the subject 'Are All Men Brothers?'" (Holbrook 29). Holbrook admits that, despite the best efforts of the students and their families, they were unable to solve the problem completely, but they did succeed in opening a dialogue that eased some of the tension at the school. "I can't say the situation in that community today is Utopian," Holbrook writes, "but I can say it is a lot healthier than it was before the children went to work on themselves *and* their parents!" (30). Idealistic but pragmatic, Holbrook's discussion of her educational philosophy is remarkably contemporary, especially in her emphasis on student engagement, inquiry, and debate. In an ideal learning environment, Holbrook argues, students must take ownership of their education and of their community, both at school and back home. Best of all, in the "Utopian" space she describes, group discussions would take the place of pedantic speeches: "That's one of our rules and perhaps it would be a good rule to use with adults, too—'no lectures'" (Holbrook 159).

One of the challenges instructors faced was finding topics that would interest students. Some of the children participating in forums across the city lived in neighborhoods plagued by gang violence. In her description of a Youthbuilders meeting at a school in the Bronx, Mary Jean Kempner, in a profile published in *Vogue* in 1946, writes, "I had been told that this was a neighborhood where extortion gangs of fifteen-year-olds preyed on other children and fought gang battles" and "twenty-two children had been killed by other children in about two years" (Kempner 181). At the meeting, Kempner discovered "thirty-odd tough boys and girls" who "were talking about a settlement house. How to raise money to build one. How much money had already been banked" (181). Teachers in the New York City schools had to contend with the violence and poverty students experienced at home. That lack of structure and stability, and the fear it produced, often made its way into the classroom. Teachers also had to deal with other distractions, notably ones from the popular culture of the period. In a 1948 article published in the *New York Post*, Fern Marja points out that instructors aimed "to transfer the excitement and stimulation youngsters usually find in the unreality of comic strips and radio serials to the reality of the world they live in" (Marja, "Youthbuilders Units"). While students, as Marja notes, developed a number of initiatives in the New York schools, ranging from "a rat extermination drive" to "the establishment of veterans' recreation centers" ("Youthbuilders Units"), one of the most common issues the program and its various forums addressed was that of racial prejudice.

In the appendix of *Children Object*, Holbrook advises that "in handling discussions of intercultural relationships it is necessary to be exceedingly cautious in the way in which you deal with 'differences'" (186). She argues in favor of a form of assimilation in which students of various ethnic and racial backgrounds define themselves first as "American," but also recognize "that the American heritage" includes "many different strains and ideas" (186). In a piece of advice that anticipates the Youthbuilders' conversation with Lieberson in 1945, Holbrook cautions against objectifying students of color. A teacher, for example, asked Holbrook to "send some Negro members of Youthbuilders out to discuss 'Negro Culture' with her students." Holbrook "refused," she explains, because,

> "[t]hat would be putting glass cases over their heads, setting them off as specimens and labeling them as 'different,'" I said. "It would be exceptionally bad for the Negro children, and almost as bad for the white." (Holbrook 186–87)

The students at Junior High School 120 would have been trained by their teacher to be cautious and skeptical of false "specimens" of "difference" like Steamboat. In a conversation with Marja for the *New York Post*, Holbrook called Youthbuilders an example of "aggressive education instead of progressive education," one designed "for the complete translation of learning into living" (Holbrook qtd. in Marja, "Youthbuilders Teach"). The Associated Negro Press article from the spring of 1945 picks up on Holbrook's insistence that adults have a lot to learn from children. For the Youthbuilders, youthful enthusiasm and childhood play were potential starting points for activism.

The first line of the Associated Negro Press story from the spring of 1945 suggests that "[o]ldsters" could learn something "in their fight against racial prejudice" from the students who visited Will Lieberson. They liked Captain Marvel comics just "fine," but were certain that Steamboat would "go far to break down all that anti-bias groups are trying to establish" ("Negro Villain"). The article makes clear that those students wanted to do far more than eliminate the character from Billy's supporting cast. They wanted Lieberson to understand the impact Steamboat might have on black *and* white readers. Like Holbrook, those students, with the guidance of their teacher, imagined a "world they wanted to live in," one with comic books free of racial caricatures.

The students proved themselves to be more forward-thinking and imaginative than some of the adults at Fawcett. For his part, Lieberson, in his interview with Matt Lage, also expressed his distaste for Steamboat: "I always found the character objectionable and when I took over Rod Reed's position I exercised my prerogative as executive editor and ordered him out of all future scripts" (Lieberson 94). While Steamboat's removal proved to be an important victory for Youthbuilders—a 1948 article edited by Elsie S. Parker in the *National Municipal Review*, for example, lists it as one of their achievements (Parker 391)—its significance has yet to be fully understood or appreciated. In entering into a dialogue with Lieberson, the Youthbuilders provided an example of how discussion, informed by research and debate, might bring about positive change. In Kempner's *Vogue* article, her sense of enthusiasm for the program and its potential still resonates. At its best, she writes, Youthbuilders offered "tangible proof that almost any group confronted with objective facts and the time to consider them will, as a group, hand down an unprejudiced and just decision" (Kempner n.p.). In the conclusion of her book, Holbrook seeks to inspire her readers, but she reminds teachers that change is only possible as a result of hard work and compromise (188). In other words, there's no magic to it, no inevitable neat and happy ending as there would be, say, in a comic book (Beck, "Good Taste").

Imagine, then, yet another possible ending to "Captain Marvel and the World's Mightiest Dream!" and it might look something like this: when Steamboat switches off the light, and leaves Billy's room, he finds himself in Lieberson's office, surrounded by a group of boys and girls, comic book fans. The young man still holds that "enlarged portrait" of the character ("Negro Villain"). Like the Devil who encounters the French kids at the end of "Capt. Marvel and the Mark of the Black Swastika," Steamboat is no match for them. Standing before a mirror-like image that reflects all of the cruelty and ignorance that he represents, he slowly fades from view, leaving behind copies of the now old and brittle comics in which he appeared. In asking their questions, in challenging Fawcett, the students followed Holbrook's example, but they were also walking, at least indirectly, in Billy's footsteps. He gains his power, after all, not by right of birth or through violent struggle, but because of his curiosity, his willingness to ask questions, like the one he asks Shazam when they first meet in the subway tunnel: "H-how do you know my name?" If he'd been a real kid and not an imaginary one, Billy would have made a great student leader in the Youthbuilders program. Maybe he didn't need that magic word in the first place. As Holbrook argued, children bring a point of view, and a desire for change, that is too often dismissed by adults. Her advice? "So keep your mind open and approach the children with as much of a desire to learn as a desire to teach" (188). Shazam himself, who had faith in Billy, Mary, and their friend Freddy, couldn't have said it any better.

STEAMBOAT AND EVELYN CREAM

What if Steamboat, upon leaving Billy's room, found himself traveling through time, forty years into the future, suddenly inhabiting the body of a comic book character who'd become friends with another Captain Marvel-like superhero? In the early installments of Alan Moore's *Miracleman*, first serialized under its original title *Marvelman* in Dez Skinn's *Warrior* magazine in England and then published in color by California-based company Eclipse Comics beginning in 1985, Evelyn Cream befriends Mike Moran, a character based on Parker and Beck's Billy Batson.[23] Created by Mick Anglo for a British audience in the 1950s, after Fawcett canceled all of its Marvel Family titles, Moran and Marvelman, his alter ego, filled the vacuum left by Captain Marvel's sudden disappearance. In his proposal for *Warrior*, Moore explained that, by reviving this character from his childhood, he wanted to create "something quite innovative and breathtaking" (Moore, "Proposal" 24). His goal was to write "the definitive Marvelman" and "the definitive super-hero strip as well" (24). In order to do so, he noted, he would have no choice but to engage with "nostalgia" for the character (his own and that of his readers) by retaining "the naïve and simplistic Marvelman concept of the Fifties" but moving it forward in time to "a cruel and cynical Eighties. The resultant tension will hopefully provide a real charge and poignance" (24). His inspiration, he explained in a later interview with George Khoury, was Harvey Kurtzman and Wally Wood's "Superduperman," a parody of Superman and Captain Marvel first published in *Mad* in 1953. As a young man, years before he began his career in comics, Moore imagined what might happen were Moran to forget his magic word— *Kimota!* which is *atomic* reversed and spelled with a *k* (see Khoury 11 and Moore, "M*****man" 31). In the first issue of *Miracleman*, Moran, struggling to recall his past, cannot escape the dreams and nightmares of a childhood that still haunts him.[24] Following Kurtzman's example, Moore's ambition was to "apply sort of real world logic to a kind of inherently absurd super-hero situation," to create a narrative both "startling" and "dramatic" (Moore qtd. in Khoury 11–12).

Early in the series, after Moran accidentally rediscovers his powers, the British government contacts Evelyn Cream, an agent for the "Spookshow," to neutralize the hero before he becomes a threat to national security (the government also wants to keep Miracleman's true origin as a botched military experiment a secret).[25] Cream, who soon joins forces with Miracleman, at times serves as a stand-in for the reader, especially in his first encounter with the hero in issue no. 3 (November 1985). On page six of that story, drawn by Alan Davis, Cream describes the hero: "Out of the dark, the dark of legend, into the harsh lamplight of modern reality . . ." He trails off, until another caption completes this thought: "and he is still unbelievable."[26] Soon after this meeting, Cream begins having nightmares that he attempts to understand. In order to do so, he confronts the bloody images that begin to haunt those dreams. As the story progresses, Cream, especially in his role as narrator, explores his relationship to the caricatures and stereotypes that have shaped his existence.

Until his death in issue no. 6 (February 1986), Cream acts as both an assistant to Miracleman and as a mentor for the often hapless Mike Moran. For American readers, this relationship would have been a familiar one. Donald Bogle lists the many "buddy" movies that proved popular at the box office in the late 1970s and early 1980s, including *Rocky II* with Sylvester Stallone and Carl Weathers (1979), *Stir Crazy* with Richard Pryor and Gene Wilder (1980), and *48 Hrs.* with Eddie Murphy and Nick Nolte (1982) (Bogle 272, 277, 281–82). Bogle argues that, from "Will Rogers and Stepin Fetchit" to "Frank Sinatra and Sammy Davis, Jr.," "buddy" films "have been wish fulfillment fantasies for a nation that has repeatedly hoped to simplify its racial tensions" (Bogle 271–72). As a writer working with a fantasy narrative based on American popular sources, Moore had to address these patterns in order to create "the definitive super-hero" story. Like the history of American film in the twentieth century, superhero comic books are also filled with these "buddy" narratives, from Billy and Steamboat to the more progressive but no less complex relationships between heroes such as Captain America and the Falcon.[27]

Although he "wasn't even aware of the 'Steamboat' character," Moore developed Cream as a direct response to other racial stereotypes that remained commonplace in superhero comics in the early 1980s. Moore explains, "I wanted to create a complex black character who was also a villain, to avoid the covert racism behind the smattering of condescendingly noble and heroic black characters featured in conventional comics at the time."[28] Until his death in issue no. 6, Cream functions more like Dr. Watson in a Sherlock Holmes mystery. Without his narrative presence, Miracleman would be too

4.13 Evelyn Cream reflects on the "mysticism" that haunts him on the first page of *Miracleman* no. 5 (Eclipse Comics, January 1986). Script by Alan Moore and art by Alan Davis. Miracleman and related characters © 2016 Marvel Characters, Inc.

alien, too powerful. Meanwhile, Cream's internal monologues call attention to the stereotypes embedded but too often ignored in the superhero genre.

In issue no. 5 (January 1986), "The Approaching Light," Moore and Davis begin with a five-panel sequence (fig. 4.13).[29] The first establishes the title of the story. Over the next four panels—each one long and rectangular—Cream, in a series of captions, describes his dreams, which, in the next issue, are revealed as premonitions of his violent death while assisting Miracleman in

4.14 Cream's restless sleep from *Miracleman* no. 5 (Eclipse Comics, January 1986). Script by Alan Moore and art by Alan Davis. Miracleman and related characters © 2016 Marvel Characters, Inc.

rescuing Liz, Moran's wife, from the clutches of Dr. Gargunza, the strip's version of Dr. Sivana. Cream, cleaning a gun, sits in a pool of light at the bottom of the first of these four panels. "I dreamed of death and jungle," he explains. Then: "It is laughable. *I* am laughable. Can we *never* rise above our stereotypes?" he wonders. There is another break before the next caption. A pause. "Perhaps tonight I shall dream of cotton balls and water melon and awaken to find myself singing 'Mammy.'" These captions lead the reader to a small image of Cream, muscular and stone-faced. "This *mysticism*," he concludes. "This weak and hysterical mysticism. It will destroy me." In the next panel, in which Davis includes a close-up of the right side of Cream's face, the character realizes that his death, when it comes, will have nothing to do with "mysticism": "*He* will destroy me," he thinks. Right now, Gargunza is the least of his worries. More terrifying is Miracleman and what he represents.

"The Approaching Light"—like "Captain Marvel and the World's Mightiest Dream!"—includes a scene, just four pages after this opening sequence, in which Cream and Miracleman, bathed in blue and purple light, try to sleep (fig. 4.14). Miracleman has no problem, but the spy, anticipating the encounter with Gargunza, is restless. He stands over the hero's bed before lying down. Slowly, he dreams again, this time in a four-panel sequence that echoes the first page. As he tries to sleep, Cream remarks again on "the superstition, the *mysticism*." In the next caption, he remembers another image from the minstrel stage, or from the advertisements Fanon describes, or from Hollywood: "Why not sit and roll your eyes in the dark, Mr. Cream? Why not shiver and

say, 'Lawsy! I'se spooked!'" In the final two triangular panels at the bottom of
the page, Davis includes images that artist Chuck Beckum will repeat in issue
no. 6, just before Cream's death: lynched black men hanging from tree trunks,
then a skeleton in a white top hat and tails—a ghastly, Zip Coon-like figure.
Cream understands the role he must play in this narrative, but he is unable to
extricate himself from it. In other words, he can identify the frame, trace its
edges, but, unlike Captain Marvel or Miracleman, he cannot break it.

Whose dream is it anyway? In issue no. 6 (February 1986), just before his
death, Cream offers readers a confession. Staring at the nightmare image of
the lynchings and of the top-hatted ghoul, he explains, "I wanted the *white
miracle*" (5).[30] A few captions later, he concludes that this "whiteness" is not
that "of hot steel" and "sanctity" but of "death." With growing terror, Cream
finds himself trapped not in his dream but in someone else's. It could be that
of the editor, the writer, the artist, or the reader (fig. 4.15). What does the white
reader want from this black figure? If Cream is part of that "magic rite" Ellison
described (45–46), his fate is certain. The hero, and therefore the story, will
continue without him, just as Billy and Captain Marvel continued for almost
a decade after Steamboat's departure.

Moore, like the Youthbuilders, sets out to reveal all that whiteness has
eclipsed, both in the present and in the past. In Mary Jean Kempner's *Vogue*
article, she concludes with a description of her visit to a school on New York's
Lower East Side where students debated "the Negro question." Kempner
writes that a thirteen-year-old named John, "blond and matter of fact," summarized the "violence" that filled the conversation. During the forum, John
said, "Wait till my brother gets home from war, he'll put them in their place."
John's teacher then asked the class if any of them could offer any "personal
experience" that provided evidence "that all Negroes were bad," to which they
replied, "No, but we know all right" (Kempner n.p.).[31] But what did these children "know"? What had made them so certain of their role and of their place
in society? And why did any form of difference provoke feelings of aggression
and anger? *"No, but we know all right"*: In that moment, whiteness reveals itself not only as a form of play, like the one that Yancy described, but as a void,
one whose lack of shape and form makes it both unpredictable and deadly.

◊ ◊ ◊

Look again: the scene has changed. The curtains, now blue, are covered in
circular patterns. The green windowshade obscures the glass of the window,
the frame. One lamp lies shattered on the dresser, but the other one remains
intact. The carpet, like the headboard, is a shade of purple. Our hero, leaning
forward, touches the hatchet that lies on the carpet (fig. 4.16).

4.15 Cream faces the nightmare of "the *white miracle*" in *Miracleman* no. 6 (Eclipse Comics, February 1986). Script by Alan Moore, art by Chuck Beckum, letters by Wayne Truman, colors by Ron Courtney. Miracleman and related characters © 2016 Marvel Characters, Inc.

4.16 Captain Marvel stands in the darkness of his room in the final panel of "Captain Marvel and the World's Mightiest Dream!" from *Captain Marvel Adventures* no. 48 (Aug.–Sept. 1945). Captain Marvel and related characters © 2016 DC Comics.

He is alone. Where's Steamboat? After *Captain Marvel Adventures* no. 48, Gene Arnold writes, Fawcett provided "no explanation of what happened to him. He was just conveniently written out of future scripts and there was no reference made to him again. It was as if he had never existed" (Arnold n.p.). In this chapter, I've attempted to make Steamboat visible again, to imagine, for a few moments, what might have happened after he switched off the light in Billy's room and closed the door. When the Youthbuilders visited the Fawcett offices, they took control of Steamboat's story, revealed him for what he'd been all along, a being more cruel, and therefore more powerful, than Billy or Shazam and all the rest. Leave Billy's room. Close the book. Then, consider again the young men and women holding that "enlarged portrait of 'Steamboat.'" Seven decades later, they ask the same question they first posed in Fawcett's New York offices in the spring of 1945: What do you see?

Chapter 5

WERTHAM'S LITTLE GOBLINS

Captain Marvel, Fanzines, and the Art of Nostalgia

In one of his final essays for the Critical Circle, mailed in the summer of 1989 just two months before his stroke, C. C. Beck remembered the 1920s, that "remarkable decade," as his "golden age" (Beck, "Golden Ages"). Like the simple drawings in a Captain Marvel adventure, he vividly described everything from "pocket flasks filled with bathtub gin" to "raccoon coats" and "ukuleles." Beck recalled the dances, too, "the Black Bottom and the Charleston" (Beck, "Golden Ages"). In an expanded version of the essay published in *The Comics Journal* in the spring of 1990, just a few months after Beck's death, he argued that "a golden age is purely a matter of opinion" (Beck, "Are We" 117). And what about the Golden Age of comics in the United States, the years when Superman and Captain Marvel and Batman and Wonder Woman thrilled and delighted readers? Best to leave it a "memory," a thing of the past, where his and Parker's hero, as far as Beck was concerned, "should have remained" ("Are We" 118). Billy's fans did not agree.[1]

In the 1960s, Captain Marvel returned in the pages of fanzines, amateur publications devoted to the history of comic books and to the editors, writers, and artists who created these heroes. As they wrote about Captain Marvel, those fans, some of whom would go on to work for Marvel and DC Comics, also wrote about themselves and key moments in their lives in which these characters played a role. After their disappearance from the newsstands in 1953, however, Billy and Captain Marvel did not officially return to comics until the early 1970s, when DC licensed the characters from Fawcett. In the meantime, other Captain Marvels had appeared to take their place, including Carl Burgos's campy hero and Stan Lee and Gene Colan's alien warrior.[2]

This final chapter, concerned with theories of nostalgia and with Captain Marvel's afterlife in the fanzines, is not so much about comic books—what they are and how they work—as it is about how and why we *remember* certain images and objects from childhood. Although Bart Beaty, in his assessment of the "second wave" of comics fandom in the US, argues that "fandom and nostalgia are not inherently linked" (154), a closer examination of the relationship between the two, and of fandom's influence on comics scholarship, is worth exploring. A significant figure in the history of comics in the United States, Captain Marvel appears in Jules Feiffer's *The Great Comic Book Heroes* and in the collection *All in Color for a Dime*, two foundational texts for comics studies in the United States. As Thierry Groensteen has argued, perhaps the field needs to be honest with itself by acknowledging nostalgia as a source of strength and vitality (Groensteen, "Why Are" 11). In writing about the relationship between comics, memory, and childhood, we're in good company. As C. C. Beck implies, what we might now call *nostalgia* has fascinated poets, philosophers, scientists, artists, and scholars for centuries. In the final published version of "Golden Ages," Beck writes, "As far back as we have written records writers were complaining about how awful everything is," all of them repeating the same thing, "that the world has gone to the dogs since the days of their ancestors" (Beck, "Are We" 117).

These feelings of nostalgia are often associated with a specific location. In his "Shop Talk" interview with Beck, Will Eisner recognized the link between this sense of place and a work of comic art. Early in that interview, Eisner asks a number of questions about Beck's training in Chicago in the late 1920s, the era Beck later identified as his "golden age." Why was Eisner so interested in the details of Beck's life before Fawcett and the success of Captain Marvel? "The reason I'm questioning you about that is that I believe geographic origin impinges on style of art considerably," Eisner explained (Eisner, "Shop Talk" 55). Read the essays about Captain Marvel published in the fanzines in the 1960s or interviews with his creators and a pattern begins to emerge. A memory of Captain Marvel, and of the comics in which he appeared, is often an autobiographical starting point. As a writer remembers that first encounter with the hero, a map of the past, as detailed as Beck's recollections of the 1920s, becomes visible. What Eisner calls "geographic origin," then, not only "impinges on style of art," but also on memory itself, on those narratives we tell about ourselves in an effort to define who we are and what role we play in our communities.

Given the complex and elusive nature of memory and its relationship to how we read and study comics, I have divided this chapter into three sections. First, I provide an overview of nostalgia studies with highlights from the fields of medicine, psychology, and literature. After a brief history of the word *nostalgia*, and its origin in Hofer's 1688 dissertation, I examine more recent studies of what was, in Hofer's time, considered a terrible disease. In addition to the historical and cultural work of Svetlana Boym and Susan J. Matt, I also touch on recent psychological studies of nostalgia and its possible impact on human evolution and civilization.

In a 1987 essay, Edward Casey, in reference to Hofer's work, argues that "the past at issue in nostalgia is the past of a world that was never itself given in *any* discrete present moment" (366). In other words, Casey suggests, the imagination goes to work and transforms those lived realities into something else—an uncanny blend of fact and fiction. As Marianne Hirsch, whose work has had a tremendous impact on memory studies and on comics scholarship, has argued in an essay about Art Spiegelman's *Maus* and W. G. Sebald's *Austerlitz*, these "surviving images from the past" always "require a particular kind of visual literacy, one that can decode the foreign language that they speak" (Hirsch, *Generation* 52). That is, we must learn to read the past as a text, one filled with tensions, contradictions, and discrepancies. In any act of translation, of course, something will be lost. This sense of loss permeates the field of memory and nostalgia studies as scholars, writers, and artists ask a simple question: Why do we remember what we remember? And how has technology—from cameras to iPhones—shaped our ability to recall what we once were, both individually and as a culture?

I devote the second part of this chapter to a discussion of Captain Marvel's presence in the fanzines of the 1960s. Even in today's era of social media, zines continue to play a small but significant and sometimes visionary role for those in a variety of communities, from do-it-yourself cartoonists and musicians to political activists. The popularity of conventions such as the Chicago Zine Fest, for example, highlights a renewed interest in zines as "a special form of communication," to borrow a phrase from the title of Dr. Fredric Wertham's 1973 study of the medium.

While Wertham is notorious in comic book circles for his 1954 book *Seduction of the Innocent*, his work on fanzines remains an overlooked contribution to the history of comics scholarship.[3] Although Wertham was not convinced that fanzines could serve "as a counterforce," "an answer to the problems of society," or as "a remedy for its frailties," he was fascinated by these obsessive, idiosyncratic publications, which he believed contained "genuine human voices outside of all mass manipulation" (35). The title of this chapter alludes to Wertham's description of fanzines and their "impact" on popular culture (36). Early in the book, Wertham tells the story of "a little goblin" that swaps "all the solemn church bells" in Rotterdam "with tinkling sleigh bells" (36). Here, Wertham suggests that the revolutionary potential of these amateur magazines lies in their sense of fun and mischief:

The citizens were awakened in the morning by the jingling sound instead of the stern clamor of the usual bells. They took it as a special message of cheer and optimism. Having had to read so many solemn professional and professorial publications in my life, the unconventional fanzines reminded me of the cheery sleigh bells of Rotterdam. (Wertham 36)

The goblin is the mischievous outsider, the one who effects a small but joyful change in consciousness. If fanzines—many of them filled with stories of favorite childhood characters and comic books—are these "cheery sleigh bells," then the editors and writers who produce them are the "little goblins" sending this vital and often exuberant "message." The goblin, that practical joker, is also an artist, one with a utopian vision of a community in which the past is *always* present.

In the final part of this chapter, I consider Captain Marvel's impact on comics scholarship itself. Billy's role in those early, foundational texts, in which fans combined first-person narrative with detailed studies of their favorite comic books, suggests that nostalgia, as Groensteen has argued, is an essential component of the discipline, a fact to be honored rather than feared or dismissed (Groensteen, "Why Are" 11).

Any act of scholarship is always an act of recovery. It is a statement of faith in the meaning and persistence of the past. Captain Marvel's disappearance in 1953 left many fans feeling unsettled, but his sudden end should not have come as a surprise. A descendant of King Arthur, Billy's story would not have been complete without the loss of his kingdom. Perhaps Billy was only fulfilling the destiny Parker and Beck had outlined for him. Shazam might be ancient, but he is not immortal. One day, according to the logic of the story, Billy will be old and weary, too, and pass along those powers to another worthy young person. That sense of the inevitable passage of time is another quality that distinguishes Captain Marvel from the other heroes of the 1940s; although Billy might live in a world of fantasy and illusion, he, like his mentor, is a human being. In a summary of Billy's "powers" included in the fanzine *The Rocket's Blast Special* no. 8, Beck notes that the hero is "[a]ll mortal, as CM was the World's Mightiest Mortal, nothing more."[4]

In Billy's origin story, history has weight and substance in the form of the "massive granite block" that "hangs" over Shazam's head on "a slender, frayed thread" (fig. 5.1). When Billy says the wizard's name for a second time, the block falls. Shazam, of course, later comes back as a ghost (or, in "Captain Marvel Joins the Army," as a general in the US Army), but, with Billy now playing the role of the hero, the wizard is a disembodied presence. When Billy needs help, he returns to the subway tunnel or to the Rock of Eternity, Shazam's otherworldly home, for advice and assurance. Old comic books,

5.1 As the "massive granite block" hangs over him, Shazam explains his plans for Billy in *Whiz Comics* no. 2 (February 1940). Script by Bill Parker and art by C. C. Beck. Reprinted in *The Shazam! Archives* vol. 1 (24). Captain Marvel and related characters © 2016 DC Comics.

fondly remembered, also provide a measure of comfort. For some writers and fans, they offer a set of coordinates in space and in time. For others, they establish a link to that lost world, what editor Kim Thompson described as that "golden thread strung through the decades," connecting a present self with one that existed during childhood (Thompson n.p.). But nostalgia, like the "granite block" that hangs over Shazam's head, can also be a burden, so looming and massive that it shadows what we have become. In writing about their relationship to these comic book stories, fanzine writers came to understand what Shazam already knew: the past has its limits. No matter how many times we might revisit and imagine it, history is not infinite in meaning or possibility. But it remains all that we have, our only possible guide, no matter how flawed, to a better and more lasting present.

COMIC BOOKS AND NOSTALGIA

Nostalgia, like Billy Batson, has an origin story, one almost as magical as his encounter with the stranger and his journey to meet Shazam. It begins with Johannes Hofer's dissertation, which is available in an English translation by Carolyn Kiser Anspach published in the *Bulletin of the Institute of the History of Medicine* in 1934.[5] In his study, Hofer describes a mysterious illness that "lacks a particular name in medicine," an ailment that usually affects those who find themselves far from home and unable to return (Hofer and Anspach 380). By giving the illness a name, Hofer also hoped to find a cure. Susan J. Matt attributes Hofer's investigations partly to the spirit of the Enlightenment.

As religious or supernatural explanations for emotions began to fall out of favor, doctors like Hofer looked for a more scientific understanding of these states of being (Matt 25–26). Hofer admits that while "deliberating on a name," he settled on "the word *Nostalgias*, Greek in origin and indeed composed of two sounds, the one of which is *Nosos*, return to the native land; the other, *Algos*," which "signifies suffering" as well as "grief" as a result of a "desire for the return to one's native land" (380–81). Just as Captain Marvel was at one time called *Captain Thunder* and *Captain Marvelous*, however, Hofer offers two other possible names for the ailment, *nosomanias* and *philopatridomania*, for those readers who might find one or the other "more pleasing" (381).

A later section of Hofer's dissertation reads like a diagnostic manual. A person suffering from this disease will exhibit "continued sadness," "disturbed sleep," a "decrease of strength, hunger," and "thirst," as well as "palpitations of the heart" along with "frequent sighs," all tied "to nothing hardly, other than an idea of the Fatherland" in the mind of the patient (Hofer 386). Edward Casey remarks that Hofer, like other early figures in the study of this illness, does not "identify it as a mode of memory or a form of preoccupation with the personal past" (366). Nostalgia, then, as Hofer first defined it, can be understood as a process, an attempt to return to a specific point from one's past, but also as a kind of surrender. Those afflicted find it impossible to think about, to remember, to imagine anything other than a distant time and place. Casey zeroes in on Hofer's assertion that the illness "is 'symptomatic of an afflicted imagination,' *not* of a disturbed memory" (Casey 366–67). Only the imagination, Casey writes, makes it possible to "make present what is absent" by enabling us to witness moments from the past (367). Notice again the key phrase in Anspach's translation: the patient experiences a "stupidity of the mind" that is the result of "*an idea*" of home (Hofer and Anspach 386; emphasis mine). Nostalgia, then, according to Casey's reading of Hofer, is a state in which imagination and memory work in tandem to create meaning. As Casey puts it, "we have recourse to imagination just where perceiving and remembering fail us—and they always do fail us to some significant degree" (367). The failure of memory, like the block that hangs over Shazam's head, is an inevitable reality.

Today, cultural theorists like the late Svetlana Boym and many psychologists view nostalgia as a powerful tool of the imagination, one with life-saving potential. By the twentieth century, historian Andreea Deciu Ritivoi points out, nostalgia had for the most part lost its "medical sense" and its "negative connotation" (Ritivoi 27). There are some notable exceptions, of course, especially in the United States. In Arthur Miller's *Death of a Salesman*, for example, Willy Loman's obsession with the past dooms him and his family, just as it destroyed Jay Gatsby's dreams. In another example, a soldier struggling with what we would now call post-traumatic stress disorder in John Huston's

1946 documentary *Let There Be Light* uses the term to describe his troubled emotional state.[6] His doctor, looking at his file, notes that the young man has suffered from "headaches" and "crying spells." Somewhat sheepishly, the soldier replies, "Yes, sir. I believe in your profession it's called *nostalgia*." The doctor seems to agree: "In other words," he says, "homesickness." The trigger for these emotions, the young man admits, was a photograph he received from his "sweetheart."

After the war, as "'nostalgia' entered American popular discourse in the 1950s," Ritivoi writes, "the term had lost completely its pathological connotations" (Ritivoi 29). Drawing on the work of sociologist Fred Davis, she notes that this change can be attributed in part to social and cultural shifts during the postwar years when "the very idea of 'home' becomes questionable" (Ritivoi 29; see also Davis 6). As I discussed in Chapter 3, Susan Matt, in her history of homesickness in the United States, locates the origin of these shifts in American culture in the changing patterns of consumption that began during the war. Those "mass-produced and commercialized" items popular with soldiers—such as cigarettes, candy, and comic books—provided soldiers a "sense of place and connection" when they were far from home (208). After the war, these products continued to provide a sense of stability in the constantly shifting landscape of consumer culture in the late 1940s and 1950s (Matt 213). By the early 2000s, what Boym calls a "souvenirization of the past" in the US accompanied by "an obsession with roots and identity" had become "ubiquitous" (Boym, *Future* 38).

At the close of the twentieth century, nostalgia was no longer considered a disease, but its presence in popular culture proved worrisome for some critics. In an essay on "nostalgia films" published in the late 1980s, Fredric Jameson wondered if the popularity of movies like *Star Wars*—the George Lucas blockbuster based in part on Alex Raymond's comic strip *Flash Gordon* and the movie serial it inspired—indicated "an alarming and pathological symptom of a society that has become incapable of dealing with time and history" (Jameson 9–10). Perhaps what Boym called a "souvenirization of the past" was inevitable as consumer habits that first took shape during World War II expanded during the Cold War when Americans, as Herbert Marcuse wrote in the early 1960s, began to "find their soul in their automobile, hi-fi set, split-level home, kitchen equipment" (Marcuse 9). What Marcuse describes is the sort of materialism Harvey Kurtzman and his fellow writers and artists at *Mad* were satirizing in the early 1950s in their sendups of movies, television shows, and, of course, other comic books and comic strips.[7] Clark Bent, the protagonist of Kurtzman and Wally Wood's "Superduperman," the story that inspired Alan Moore to imagine what happens when a superhero forgets his magic word, is an early comic book example of Marcuse's "one-dimensional man."[8]

Despite Ritivoi's and Matt's assurances that nostalgia is no longer a disease, the prognosis for a culture obsessed with the past is up for debate. Billy's first appearance in *Whiz Comics* also sends mixed messages about nostalgia's impact on our lives. On the one hand, Captain Marvel's triumph over the automobile on the cover indicates that, through strength and willpower, we might slow the inevitable progress of history, at least during the brief time it takes to read and enjoy a comic book. Then again, Billy's past is filled with pain and loneliness. Based on the evidence provided by the Historama, the young man has no home to return to because of his uncle's cruelty. Like the protagonist of Chris Marker's *La Jetée*—a film about the process of memory and its relationship to childhood nostalgia—Billy looks to the future for a new life *and* for an escape from the terror and isolation of the present. Jameson and other critics, then, are right to be skeptical of nostalgia. After all, the heroes of American literature afflicted with it have rarely survived, and, as Hofer himself admitted, in his time there was no cure for those unable to "return to the native land" and suffering from a condition that often led to "delirium" and to "mania itself" (390).

Nevertheless, several recent studies suggest that there is hope for those afflicted with a bad case of this "delirium." A 2013 *New York Times* piece brings Hofer's Enlightenment-era concept into the twenty-first century. In the article, which provides a summary of current psychological research on the phenomenon, John Tierney reports that this sense of longing might have a positive effect on human thought and behavior. Tierney explains, "Nostalgia has been shown to counteract loneliness, boredom and anxiety. It makes people more generous to strangers and more tolerant of outsiders" (Tierney). First a disease, then an existential condition, nostalgia has emerged, Tierney suggests, as a superheroic folk remedy of the digital age.

In "Finding Meaning in One's Past: Nostalgia as an Existential Resource," a more formal summary of recent psychological studies, researchers Clay Routledge, Constantine Sedikides, Tim Wildschut, and Jacob Juhl reached conclusions that no doubt would have startled Hofer. According to their work, it appears that "nostalgia elevates positive mood, enhances and protects the self, and strengthens social connectedness" (Routledge, et al., "Finding Meaning" 303).[9] A study by Xinyue Zhou even suggests that nostalgic memories can increase body temperature. The brain's ability to use nostalgia "to maintain physiological comfort," Tim Wildschut explains, "could be an amazing and complex adaptation" because the ability to draw on these memories in times of distress "could contribute to survival by making you look for food and shelter that much longer" (Wildschut qtd. in Tierney; see also Zhou, et al.). In their overview of the current research at institutions including the University of Southampton, Routledge, Sedikides, Wildschut, and Juhl point out that "nostalgia narratives" employed in studies of this phenomenon "are typically focused on the self but are also highly social in nature" as "people write about momentous life events and, in particular, social interactions in which the self is featured prominently" (Routledge, et al., "Finding Meaning" 300). Routledge and his team imply that nostalgic feelings invite us to identify and to negotiate the line between the self and the community of which we are a part (Routledge, et al., "Finding Meaning" 312).

The fanzine writers of the 1960s developed this sense of community by sharing their memories of the Marvel Family and their affection for the writers and artists who created these characters. As Boym's essays and Routledge's research makes clear, it appears that nostalgia only becomes "pathological," to borrow Jameson's word, when it exists merely as an end in itself. The active, adventurous nostalgia that Boym honored in her writing and in her visual art is a survival strategy, an attempt to build community, to create spaces in which people can ask each other, *Do you remember this, too?*

Nostalgia is a cold draft, a closed door, a cracked window, a scrap of paper, a photograph cut in half, the dedication in an old book, a box of coverless comics, the locked drawer of a desk, a stack of postcards in a junk shop. Each image, like a magic word, is an invitation. This is Billy's secret: the name *Shazam* doesn't turn him into the World's Mightiest Mortal. Rather, the word enables him to settle up with his past, to satisfy the longings and desires of those no longer able to speak, those who had no real voice in the first place. In searching for C. C. Beck or Otto Binder, these fanzine writers and editors also went looking for themselves. For Harlan Ellison, nostalgia is "a small child sitting in a small wooden chair in a dark place," one who takes comfort by "remembering a page of a Captain Marvel comic," especially one first read decades earlier ("Nay, Never Will I").[10] For Beck, it is the recollection of a "golden age." For Binder, it is one of those "tiny flashes of light" (Binder, "Special!" 112). For most of us, it is a conversation with the dead, often an apology: I can't bring you back. But, like people of Rotterdam who laugh at the goblin's practical joke, I can listen, which is the next best thing. If comic books, like movies, urge us to look, fanzines insist that we *listen* as we share these intimate stories.

WERTHAM'S LITTLE GOBLINS:
FANZINES, COMIC BOOKS, AND MEMORY

In their introduction to "The Secret History of Chicago Zines," a recent lecture on independent and small-press periodicals, Jake Austen and James Porter joked that fanzines have a long history, one that might be traced back, indirectly, to Tom Paine's broadsides, Ben Franklin's newspapers, and even to the tablets on which Moses first read the Ten Commandments (Austen and Porter; Moore, "Be a Zinester"). Writers including Stephen Duncombe and Amy Spencer offer more concise summaries of the history of the fanzine and its gradual evolution into the zines of today. In the 1980s, Duncombe points out, after fifty years of science fiction fanzines and almost a decade of fan publications dedicated to punk rock, "the 'fan' was by and large dropped off 'zine,' and their number increased exponentially," partly because of the influence of *Factsheet Five* in the United States, which included listings of titles and addresses for a wide range of zine-makers (Duncombe 11). Like Captain Marvel, the fanzine can also trace its origin to the Midwest and, more specifically, to *The Comet*, an amateur magazine devoted to science fiction and published by Walter L. Dennis's Science Correspondence Club in Chicago (Austen and Porter; Spencer 80).[11] Writer Louis Russell Chauvenet introduced the term *fanzine* in 1941, but by then these small-press publications had been circulating for almost a decade (Schelly, *Words* 238; Spencer 80–81).[12]

The fanzines, then, had their roots in science fiction fandom, just as Otto Binder did. As Bill Schelly points out, the letters pages in Hugo Gernsback's *Amazing Stories* enabled science fiction fans to write to each other (Schelly, *Words* 38). In her book *DIY: The Rise of Lo-Fi Culture*, Amy Spencer notes that *Amazing Stories* "sponsored" the Science Correspondence Club (80). As these organizations began to appear across the country, Spencer writes, "it was an obvious progression for sci-fi fans to start writing their own versions of the magazines they were reading" (80). In the letter columns of *Amazing Stories* and in early fanzines like *The Comet* and Allen Glasser's *The Time Traveller*— a publication that featured contributions from Binder's friends and future colleagues Julius Schwartz and Mort Weisinger (Schelly, *Words* 38)—readers "insisted on talking back to the stories being written for them in the new commercial magazines" (Duncombe 114). The science fiction fanzines also established a pattern that would emerge again in the amateur comic book magazines of the 1960s. These early publications offered a venue for young writers and artists to develop their talents (Spencer 81). As Jerry Siegel and Joe Shuster set their sights on the pulp magazines of the era, professionals like Binder contributed essays and articles to these fanzines. Thirty years later, Roy Thomas, Richard "Grass" Green, and C. C. Beck's protégé, Don Newton, to name only a handful of writers and artists, would also get their start in *Alter Ego* and in *The Rocket's Blast*.[13] Binder's close relationship with Roy Thomas and Bill Schelly should come as no surprise given the active role that the writer and his mentor, Otis Adelbert Kline, played in science fiction fandom of the 1930s (Schelly, *Words* 39–40). Comic book fandom in the 1960s must have reminded Binder of the science fiction circles of the 1930s, when, for example, he served as an executive director of the Chicago chapter of the Science Fiction League (Schelly, *Words* 39, 41).[14]

By the early 1950s, as Binder learned, the science fiction market had changed considerably as it slowly moved away from the pulp conventions of the 1930s. As the writers who would later be part of the New Wave learned their craft, the fanzines began to reflect these changing tastes. When Pat Lupoff and Richard Lupoff began publishing the fanzine *Xero* in the early 1960s, they made it their mission to avoid the "fannish" style so common in other amateur science fiction publications of the era (Lupoff, *Xero* 14). Lupoff's "The Big Red Cheese" appeared in the first issue in 1960, introducing what would become a series of articles on the Golden Age of comics in the US. With that essay, Lupoff established the template for other writers, including Roy Thomas, Ron Goulart, and Harlan Ellison, who wrote articles for *Xero* about their favorite comics. At the time, too many fanzine contributors, Lupoff writes in his introduction to *The Best of Xero*, were content with entertaining readers in articles that often "would have *absolutely no substantive content*" (Lupoff, *Xero* 14; emphasis in the original). The Lupoffs urged their contributors to "write about *something*," to combine, as Lupoff and Don Thompson note in their introduction to the collected "All in Color for a Dime" articles in 1970, personal history, archival information, and critical reflections (Lupoff and Thompson 14–15). As a young man growing up in southern Illinois, Roger Ebert, a contributor to *Xero*, sensed the radical potential of the form. For Ebert, the fanzines were "dangerous," often "untamed, unofficial, unlicensed" (Ebert 2). Both visionary and conservative, fanzines, as Duncombe, Spencer, and Anne Elizabeth Moore have pointed out, enable those without a voice in popular culture to be heard (Moore, "Be a Zinester"). The fanzines of the 1960s, especially those focused on comic books, sought to revive and conserve works of art that had vanished, a "backward-looking" tendency that Bart Beaty describes in *Comics Versus Art* (154).

No wonder, then, that Ebert sensed an affinity between fandom and another movement in American culture in the late 1950s and early 1960s: "It was the time of Beatniks and *On the Road*, which I also read," he writes (2). Fanzines and the culture that surrounded them had a "subversive" quality (Ebert 2) that, like the work of the Beats, anticipated the counterculture and the social upheavals of the late 1960s. "Because of fandom," Ebert points out, "we got to 1967 ten years before most of the non-fan world" (10). Ebert's reference to Kerouac is fitting, given the poet and novelist's radical experiments with form and his Proustian longing for a childhood haunted by characters from pulp fiction and comic books. This longing is most evident in his novel *Doctor Sax* (1959), which features a protagonist obsessed with the book's title character, a variation on Walter Gibson's The Shadow. The Beats sought to locate themselves in a literary tradition that included William Blake, Walt Whitman, and Thomas Wolfe, writers whose formal innovations are often inextricably linked, especially in Wolfe's case, to a utopian desire for a dreamlike past that makes possible a visionary future. In a 1959 reading on *The Steve Allen Show*, Kerouac described the combination of fact and fiction in his writing: "All the stories I wrote were true, because I believed in what I saw."[15] That unshakable belief in the narrative arc of one's life and experiences is also central to fanzine discourse. By telling these stories with simplicity and directness, the writer identifies the links between the past and the present, nexus points where the future begins to reveal itself.

Even an artist as forward-thinking as Jimi Hendrix, whose debut album with the Experience was released in 1967, not long before The Beatles' *Sgt. Pepper's Lonely Hearts Club Band*, combined the blues of Muddy Waters and Buddy Guy with the gospel-derived R&B of Curtis Mayfield and Pops Staples. Meanwhile, Bob Dylan, The Band, The Byrds, Joni Mitchell, and other musicians rejected psychedelia in favor of a sound, and a look, based in folk, country, and honky-tonk music. When Ebert describes 1960s science fiction and comic book fandom as an early expression of the counterculture, I suspect he has in mind this dialogue between tradition and innovation, the mixture of past and present that would also inspire the punk fanzines of the 1970s.

In the 1990s, zines, especially within the context of the riot grrrl movement, again offered a means of expression for those alienated from popular culture. Anne Elizabeth Moore describes these publications as a repository of "hidden histories" that "tell the kinds of stories deliberately ignored, glossed over, or entirely forgotten by mainstream media" (Moore, "Be a Zinester"). Moore, a zine-maker herself, points out that the medium continues to attract a diverse range of writers and artists, both professional and amateur, from "prisoners" and "homeschoolers" to "survivors of sexual assault" and "members of the military"—in other words, as she puts it, just about "anyone else who has ever felt that the voices speaking for them in the larger culture weren't conveying their stories" (Moore, "Be a Zinester"). Cindy Crabb echoes this sentiment in "i believe," an essay included in *The Encyclopedia of Doris*, a collection of her writing and drawings.

Like Moore, Crabb, a prolific and popular contemporary zine-maker based in Athens, Ohio, writes about radical politics and the possibility for social change. At first glance, her zine *Doris* might appear to bear no relationship to *Xero*, *Alter Ego*, or the countless other comic book fanzines from the 1960s. Nonetheless, there are many parallels just beneath the surface. "I started writing a zine because I believed in the power of telling secrets," she writes in the opening paragraph of "i believe" (Crabb, *Encyclopedia* 18). Every page of *Doris* is a miniature work of art, a photocopied collage of text, drawings, and found images. Svetlana Boym's phrase "paper architecture" suits Crabb's work, as it establishes a space, what Boym would have called "an imaginary topography" (*Architecture* 6), in which the writer and her community look to the past in order to imagine a sustainable future. A believer in "fundamental social change," Crabb explains that she began writing, drawing, and distributing her zines because she "wanted to live in a world where we were humans and not just consumers, where our voices mattered, where we learned together instead of just arguing" (Crabb, *Encyclopedia* 18). Crabb's vision might appear to be at odds with the at times consumerist tendencies of the 1960s fanzines. What she shares in common with writers such as Richard Lupoff or Maggie Thompson, however, is a fascination with memory, with personal stories and "the small beautiful things" they contain (*Encyclopedia* 18).

The cover of Cindy Crabb's *Doris* no. 31, for example, features a collage filled with three distinct images, each one set against a background that appears to be a page from a lined notebook or a sheet of composition paper. First is a drawing of a heron, then a photograph of a young girl next to a bird in a cage, and then another drawing of a fawn. Each component of the image, from the lined paper to the photo of the girl, is a marker of childhood, fragments of a picture book, a photo album, a school report. In "Cape Cod," the long essay at the heart of this issue, Crabb recalls the time that she and her friend Elliot squatted in an abandoned house in Massachusetts. There, she writes, they experienced "a strange burden in that total freedom life" (Crabb, "Cape Cod"). That "total freedom" is the result of "constant self-examination," the kind of reflection that gives her the strength and courage to go about "really living in the world, not shut off, not cynical" ("Cape Cod"). Filled with comics, typewritten essays, and found images, Crabb's *Doris* echoes the layouts of the 1960s fanzines, but it also resembles a textbook or grade school primer. Consequently, she implies that the innocence that we once knew is, in fact, real, not an illusion, but a state to which we can return.

That lack of cynicism appealed strongly to Fredric Wertham. In this passage from *The World of Fanzines*, the psychiatrist, so charmed by the juxtapositions at work in the obscure publications he studied, sounds remarkably like Crabb, despite not sharing her conviction that fanzines might bring about lasting social change: "Communication is the opposite of violence," writes Wertham in his book's conclusion. "And every facet of communication has a legitimate place" (133). Since he often solves problems with his fists, maybe Captain Marvel could use a lesson or two from these fanzines in the art of open and honest conversation, a means of building community through the sharing of stories and experiences. Meanwhile, as Binder notes in his 1964 *Alter Ego* letter, the kids who'd grown up reading all of those comic books had become "serious, often scholarly, researchers, many of them sporting engineering degrees and professional honors," perhaps because critics like Wertham had failed "to block young minds charging eagerly into the future" (Binder, "Special!" 112). Not all of the fanzine essays, however, were entirely "scholarly" in tone or execution. Writers like Lupoff had another goal in mind: like their childhood hero, they would travel into the past, study it, and bring back what they'd found. It was a fun challenge. Without the aid of a Historama, how much could you remember? It all would be so much easier with a magic word.

"MOSTLY, I REMEMBER CAPTAIN MARVEL"

This book has its origin in Binder and Beck's stories of their time at Fawcett, but also, as I mention in the introduction, in Lupoff's autobiographical "The Big Red Cheese." Lupoff begins his essay with a memory of "the sunbaked village of Venice, Florida" and its "pharmacy," both a long way from "distant, metropolitan Sarasota" (Lupoff, "Big Red" 67). Before providing a history of the character, Lupoff invites the reader to imagine "the sights and odors of that bright day near the Gulf of Mexico," including "the palmettoes," "the scrubby grass," and "the rocky, sandy Florida soil," all of which culminate in a long description of the ice cream he and his brother enjoyed (68). The boys also bought a copy of *Whiz Comics* no. 2. "Mostly, I remember Captain Marvel," Lupoff writes, but the paragraphs that open his essay suggest that, in looking for Billy Batson, he is also searching for this moment with his brother, a narrative from their childhood in a small town in the early 1940s. In the introduction to the collected *All in Color for a Dime*, Lupoff and Don Thompson admit that the *Xero* articles about comic books are less about "'pure' factual scholarship" but focus instead on "recreating and assessing 'those thrilling days of yesteryear'" (Lupoff and Thompson 15), especially for other comic book fans. Lupoff and his fellow contributors, working outside the confines of academia, sought to preserve images, sense memories, and fragments. Most of all, they sought to return to a moment of possibility, one in which the future still existed only in the imagination.

Lupoff's essay, like all good works of nostalgia, is also about place. He describes the space between Venice and Sarasota. He also remembers the distance between himself and his older brother, who is "taller" and more "extroverted" (67). One of the great myths of nostalgia is its promise of wholeness—that a visit to the past or a return home will lead to satisfaction and fulfillment. Here, Lupoff suggests the opposite. What we desire when we set out to reclaim the past is a sense of restlessness, that desire for escape. In other words, Lupoff, recalling this pivotal moment in his life, doesn't long for the ice cream or the comic book. He wants to remember what it was like to feel this excitement and eagerness for the first time. What stories do we tell when we remember the past? What objects or images define these moments? A toy. A beloved book. A piece of clothing. Or a sound: a melody, a loved one's voice. D major strummed on a guitar.[16] A door opening. A sunlit room. What did it *look like?* How did it smell, sound, feel? In "The Big Red Cheese," Captain Marvel plays the same role that Shazam did for Billy Batson or that Virgil did for Dante; the hero, like the poet, leads the writer to that which was lost, to his beloved.

In Bill Schelly's 2003 book *The Golden Age of Comic Fandom*, Lupoff admits that, while writing "The Big Red Cheese," he "did no research whatsoever. It was just plumbing the depths of nostalgic recollection" (Lupoff qtd. in Schelly, *Golden Age* 23). Nonetheless, Lupoff's groundbreaking essay provided an early model for comics studies in the US by highlighting the role that memory plays in shaping our response to the medium. In his assessment of the article, Schelly emphasizes Lupoff's "yearning" tone, an expression of an "almost painful desire" for the "return to the lost innocence of youth" (Schelly, *Golden Age* 24). Lupoff and the other writers who contributed to the "All in Color for a Dime" series, then, offer examples of discourse that contemporary comics scholars might wish to explore more fully. What do these intimate stories tell us about the impact of graphic narratives on young readers?

Of course, as I mention in the introduction, childhood recollections of comic strips and comic books are not prerequisites for an engaged study of the medium. This more personal mode of discourse is just one of many possible responses to an art form that, as Binder noted in his 1964 letter, tends to inspire intense reactions from artists, readers, and critics. Perhaps it's what Hillary Chute describes as the "handmade" quality of these normally "mass-produced" narratives that inspires that sense of closeness and immediacy. "Another feature of the composition of comics," Chute writes, involves "its *handwriting*, which carries, whether or not the narrative is autobiographical, what we may think of as a trace of autobiography in the mark of its maker" (Chute, *Graphic Women* 10; emphasis in the original). Inspired by the writers and artists whose work they adored, fanzine writers no doubt sensed these autobiographical traces even in assembly-line comics like those produced by Fawcett. By studying these popular narratives, fanzine-makers found themselves, quite literally, back where they'd started, with the comics that, in some cases, first gave them confidence as readers and even as fledgling writers.

As one adult remembered the boy who experienced the heat of the Gulf Coast in winter, another recalled a park in Painesville, Ohio, a town named for a Revolutionary War hero. In 1943, nine-year-old Harlan Ellison waited for the next installment of the popular and influential Monster Society of Evil serial. For Ellison, the memory of these stories, especially the revelation of Mr. Mind's true identity, are also tied to a specific location from his childhood. After buying a copy of *Captain Marvel Adventures*, he "would sit on the plinth of [General Paine's] statue" to read the latest issue. In a 2014 interview, he remembered buying his comic books, reading them carefully, and then biking "home, back all the way up Main Street [where it] turned into Mentor Avenue and Mentor Avenue ran all the way through to Cleveland where it became Euclid Avenue," another destination promising a more exciting, impossible future ("Nay, Never Will I").[17] Both Lupoff and Ellison see their younger selves in motion—visiting the drugstore, eating the ice cream, purchasing the comic books, dreaming of fantastic, faraway places like Sarasota or Cleveland.

As I write in the introduction, other Captain Marvel fans also vividly remember their first encounters with the character. P. C. Hamerlinck, for example, in his introduction to the *Fawcett Companion*, recalls seeing Captain Marvel's "smiling" face staring back at him from the cover of DC's *Shazam!* no. 1 at a "local Rexall Drug" in the early 1970s (Hamerlinck, "Introduction" 6). Trina Robbins's memory is less location-specific, but, in her essay about C. C. Beck, she notes her fondness for Billy's sister Mary: "Thus Captain Marvel became the only superhero I read as a girl," she writes, "and a pretty major inspiration for my own art style" (Robbins, "C. C. Beck"). For Lupoff, Ellison, Robbins, and Hamerlinck, Captain Marvel is both a point of departure and marker of home.

Four decades after Ellison impatiently waited for each new installment of the Monster Society serial, and about ten years after Hamerlinck read his first Captain Marvel adventure, Alan Moore offered further reflections on comic books and nostalgia. By the late 1960s, Moore remembered in his 1985 essay "M*****man: Full Story and Pics," he'd become a devoted reader of Marvel Comics, but he rekindled his affection for Mick Anglo's hero after he "came across an old and outdated Marvelman hard-cover annual in the racks of a bookstall on the windswept sea-front at Great Yarmouth" (31). Although he found the stories "amateurish" in comparison "to the work of Kirby, Ditko, and Lee," the fifteen-year-old Moore felt "overcome by that warm glow of nostalgia which is probably the single biggest factor keeping us interested in this medium, whatever amount of intellectual satisfaction we manage to glean on the side" (31). A few years earlier, Moore had read "Superduperman" in a collection of stories from *Mad* (Moore qtd. in Khoury 11). What would happen, Moore wondered, if Mike Moran, Marvelman's alter ego, suddenly forgot his past? What if, all these years later, he'd lost his powers? "I was struck by the image of the eternally youthful and exuberant hero as a middle-aged man, trudging the streets and trying fruitlessly to remember his magic word" ("M*****man" 31; see also Khoury 11). Years later, Moore had the opportunity to develop this idea, and its link to nostalgia, more fully when he pitched a revamped Marvelman to Dez Skinn, editor of the British comics magazine *Warrior*.

In his proposal, Moore foregrounds the role that memory plays in his conception of the character. "Nostalgia, if handled wrong," he writes, "can prove to be nothing better than sloppy and mawkish crap" (Moore, "Proposal" 24). On the other hand, Moore recognizes that nostalgia also has tremendous appeal for readers, especially of comic books: "It's finished. We'll never see it again . . . and this is where the incredible poignance of nostalgia really comes from" ("Proposal" 24). By the time Moore completed his run on *Miracleman* for Eclipse Comics in the late 1980s, what began as an idea for a Kurtzman-inspired parody had become a grand meditation on the relationship between superhero comics and memory.[18]

Miracleman no. 16, Moore's final issue, published in late 1989, begins with a text piece that owes as much to J. G. Ballard, Michael Moorcock, and the space-rock band Hawkwind as it does to Mick Anglo, Otto Binder, and C. C. Beck.[19] The hero, now a benevolent dictator of a comic book utopia, describes a world that resembles the panels from the "naïve and simplistic" comics of the 1950s (Moore, "Proposal" 24), especially Batman's adventures with the Boy Wonder: "I dream a world where everyone has sidekicks and caves to keep their eerie souvenirs."[20] Two pages later, illustrated by one of John Totleben's fantastic floating machines, Miracleman recalls his adventures, now "commercially available" to the citizens of his perfect world, as "mystery plays. Men read allegories into these childish tales, read revelations into every line" (3). Here, Moore no doubt has in mind the comic book fans, critics, and historians who had been searching for these "allegories" since the 1960s.

In this final installment, Moore also asks two vital questions: Is nostalgia worth the trouble? And is the utopia promised by nostalgia worth it, either? Neil Gaiman explored this question more fully when he took over the title after Moore's departure. The answer, however, already lies in Moore's first *Miracleman* story. In its opening pages, illustrated by Garry Leach, Mike Moran wants nothing more than to escape the nightmares of the past that render him sleepless. If only he could remember. What's more simple than that? Like a dream, but not like this one: a nightmare of flying in deep space, UFOs, stars, distant planets, and, suddenly, fire.[21] When the dream ends, reality doesn't look or feel any better, just routine. The stillness of an early morning commute. A bad headache. Silence. A few pages later, while covering a protest at a nuclear power plant, he accidentally recalls his magic word, but his joy is fleeting.[22] Over the next several issues, he discovers that his past was a fantasy created for him by the ruthless Dr. Gargunza. Although Beck would no doubt have winced at the comparison, Moore's *Miracleman*, of the many variations on the character that have appeared since the 1960s, is closest in spirit to Parker, Beck, and Binder's original hero. While *Miracleman*, of course, is a series intended for older readers, at its core it addresses the same themes and concerns Binder and Beck explored in their best work, especially the Mr. Tawny series: the limits of fantasy, the flaws of memory, the inevitable but often fruitless search for an ideal past. Moran, like Billy, gets what he's always wanted, but in the process he loses the life he'd struggled so long to build. In the end, unable to function in the new world that Miracleman has created, he decides to let it all go, to bid farewell to his double identity. In issue no. 14, just before Moran transforms for the last time, he writes a note asking that Miracleman never speak the magic word again.[23] With all his questions about the past answered, Moran has no role to play in Miracleman's utopia. Maybe, as Beck suggested, it's sometimes best to leave the past alone. Then again, without nostalgia, we'd have no stories to tell, no means of measuring certain distances, not only between one point on a map and another—the drugstore in Venice, that statue in Painesville—but also between what is certain and what must remain unknown.

COMIC BOOKS, ARCHIVES, AND THE ART OF NOSTALGIA

I think I remember their names. We were classmates at St. John the Evangelist School in Watertown, Connecticut. One of them, I recall, once convinced me that he'd found a green meteorite, like a fragment from Superman's planet, in his backyard (it looked real enough, but later I learned it was just a rock). It's a birthday party, late November 1981 (fig. 5.2). The boys are holding toy pistols, dart guns, *Star Wars* blasters. One carries a glow-in-the-dark lightsaber, a knock-off from the discount bin at Kresge's or Kmart. At the rear of the photo, on a door leading to the kitchen and its tin ceiling, is a cutout of Charles Schulz's Snoopy dressed as a Pilgrim for Thanksgiving. In the lower right-hand corner, a *Superman II* board game sits on a rocking chair next to a white couch. On the other side of the photograph, just visible, is the leg of a Baldwin upright piano. I'm the kid wearing a *Shazam!* shirt with the ¾-length Crayola yellow sleeves.

After studying the nostalgia of others—Richard Lupoff, Harlan Ellison, Trina Robbins, Beck and Binder—I felt an obligation to write about my memories of Captain Marvel, but I quickly realized I had no origin story to share. I dimly recall the Saturday morning live-action series, a couple of Mego action figures, a 1977 Little Golden Book titled *Shazam! A Circus Adventure*, written by Bob Ottum and illustrated by Fawcett veteran Kurt Schaffenberger, who, like Beck, also worked on DC's revival of the hero in the 1970s.[24] Then,

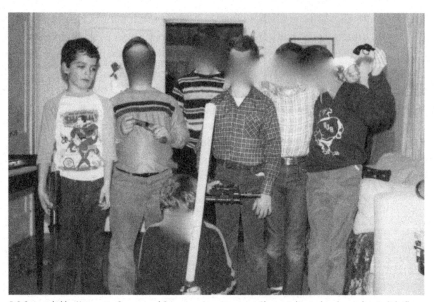

5.2 Surrounded by Micronauts, Snoopy, and Superman, I am wearing a *Shazam!* shirt in this photo taken in Oakville, Connecticut, in November 1981. From the author's collection.

looking through family photos, I found this record of my eighth birthday. Most of us in the photograph—a group of white, middle-class boys living just outside of Waterbury—are the grandkids of immigrants who arrived in the Naugatuck River Valley in the early twentieth century to work at the brass mills that, by 1981, had begun to close their doors. My mom has other family photos like this one of holidays and birthday parties, taken in the same living room thirty years earlier: my great aunts and uncles, my grandmother, my grandfather, my great-grandmother. I want to ask their forgiveness for, a couple of decades later, cluttering the room—*their* room—with plastic rifles, board games, and dolls. I have the sudden urge to tidy up, to ask the other kids to go home. But most of these boys, now adults, have children of their own, and today that room belongs to someone else. The toys? Long gone. Online I search for a shirt like the one my eight-year-old self is wearing, but I have no luck. What would I do with it, anyway? Would it help me remember anything not already on display here? Could it take me back to that room, to that space, over thirty years ago?

In *The Decoration of Houses*, Edith Wharton and architect Ogden Codman, Jr., caution against spending too much time in spaces designed for our ancestors. Each of us, they argue, "is unconsciously tyrannized over by the wants of others,—the wants of the dead and gone predecessors, who have an inconvenient way of thrusting their different habits and tastes across the current

5.3 A flying Captain Marvel toy from the 1940s. Captain Marvel and related characters © 2016 DC Comics.

of later existences" (Wharton and Codman 19). As a child, I had no idea of Captain Marvel's long and complex history. Maybe the shirt I'm wearing, like the lightsaber, was on sale at Kresge's or at the Marshalls on Main Street in Watertown, next to the pharmacy and the Friendly's. Just as I am standing in a room designed for those who came before me, I am wearing a shirt with a character created for children in the 1940s. In this photograph, the weight of nostalgia is literal, as the other boys and I, surrounded by products featuring Snoopy, Superman, and Captain Marvel, pose for the camera. Even *Star Wars*, which inspired the toy my friend is holding, began with George Lucas's affection for the Flash Gordon serials. We didn't know it, but it's true: we'd inherited a nostalgia for the popular heroes of the generations that preceded us.[25]

In the final pages of "The Big Red Cheese," Lupoff takes an inventory of what remains from a childhood spent reading comic books. He and other fans, he writes, "still have our ancient Captain Marvel paraphernalia" including "comix cards or stationery or statuettes, or our official Captain Marvel Club membership documents" (Lupoff, "Big Red" 92) (fig. 5.3). Ellison also has a collection of Captain Marvel memorabilia, from "the speedo planes" and "the pinbacks" to "the tattoos, the decals," and "the glow-in-the-dark sew-on patches," the kinds of merchandise that Beck found so distasteful ("Nay, Never Will I"; Beck, "What Really"). Long before eBay made finding childhood relics an easy and addictive hobby, collectors, with the help of advertisements in fanzines, bought, sold, and traded all sorts of toys, games, and other products produced in the 1940s and 1950s. Chip Kidd and Geoff Spear devote most of *Shazam! The Golden Age of the World's Mightiest Mortal* (2010) to lush photographs of these collectibles, from close-up photos of Marvel Family figures to puzzles, badges, and paper dolls, most of them courtesy of collector Harry Matetsky.

Of all the items on display in Kidd and Spear's book, the ones filled with the most "poignance," to borrow Alan Moore's word, are three faded color photographs of a little boy wearing a Captain Marvel costume, one based on the 1970s Saturday morning TV show. In the first, standing in a wood-paneled room, he lifts an ottoman over his head. In the next, he strikes another dramatic pose, this time leading with his right fist. In the last photo, the largest of the three, he holds some sort of post over his head, a suburban landscape behind him. At the bottom of the page, author, designer, and Captain Marvel fan Chip Kidd thanks his mother, Ann, for creating this Halloween costume, one "based on little more than existing comics drawings" (Kidd and Spear).[26] In the book, Kidd and Spear include other black-and-white photographs of children dressed in Captain Marvel and Mary Marvel costumes, much like the ones Richard and Pat Lupoff wore at the World Science Fiction Convention in 1960, where they debuted the first issue of *Xero* (Schelly, *Golden Age* 23–24). By dressing as the Marvels, the Lupoffs not only attracted some attention for their fanzine, but they also helped to bring Captain Marvel and Mary Marvel back to life.

In an editorial that introduces the first issue of *The Golden Age of Comics*, a 1982 magazine which includes an article about Captain Marvel by John G. Pierce and a generous selection of obscure Walt Kelly comics, Don and Maggie Thompson describe a comic book dreamscape that anticipates the final issue of Alan Moore's *Miracleman*:

> It is our belief that in an ideal world, nothing would ever go out of print. It should be possible for fans and casual readers alike to obtain the complete *Action Comics*, the complete works of Milton Caniff, and the entire run of any comic book, comic strip, or magazine at libraries. (Thompson and Thompson 4)

The writers admit that this is a "Utopian dream," but express the hope that this "untold wealth" of material will one day be accessible to everyone, not just "to a handful of long-time or wealthy (or both) collectors" (4). Thirty years later, this dream is slowly becoming a reality in the academic archives at Michigan State and Columbia University and at the Billy Ireland Cartoon Library & Museum at Ohio State. Meanwhile, schools devoted to the theory and practice of comics, including the Center for Cartoon Studies in White River Junction, Vermont, provide students with the training, and the community, necessary to continue a conversation about comics that echoes those late-night debates at Otto Binder's Englewood, New Jersey, home, or at Beck and Costanza's studio. As publishers such as Fantagraphics, Hermes, and IDW release beautifully designed, often lavish collections of long out-of-print comic strips and comic books, the Grand Comics Database offers up-to-date credits and publication information for several decades' worth of titles. Some of these comics, including all of Fawcett's books from the 1940s and 1950s, are also readily available at The Digital Comic Museum, where readers will find scans of all the Captain Marvel stories discussed in this book. The role of an archive is to make nostalgia obsolete. In the ideal space imagined by the Thompsons, no comic book hero ever disappears, and no one is ever very far from home.

That the Comic Art Collection at Michigan State, curated for years by Randall W. Scott, and the Billy Ireland are institutions built on this longing for what has vanished should come as no surprise. Every comic book page is, like a work of scholarship, an act of recovery, or at times a dream in which nothing is ever lost, as past, present, and future make room for each other and exist in harmony.[27] Studied carefully, a fanzine or a comic book, like Billy's Historama, might reveal several lifetimes to us, one generation after another of names, faces, and stories. The art of nostalgia is figuring out which one to tell next.

EPILOGUE

It's 8 p.m. on Friday, November 8, 1985, and I'm watching *The Twilight Zone* on WFSB Channel 3, the CBS affiliate in Hartford, Connecticut. Harlan Ellison's "Paladin of the Lost Hour," starring Danny Kaye and Glynn Turman, is on the air. Ellison will win both a Writers Guild of America award for his teleplay and a Hugo for the story itself, first published in 1985 and included in his 1988 collection *Angry Candy*.[1] It's a simple, familiar narrative about time, memory, and friendship. In the TV episode, Danny Kaye's character, Gaspar, is an old man looking for a successor. He carries a beautiful pocket watch with a terrible secret. He has no children, so he must leave the watch, and the memories of his late wife, Minna, to someone honest, kind, and humble. After Vietnam veteran Billy Kinetta (Turman's character) saves the old man from a violent mugging, the two share their stories. Slowly, they come to depend on each other, and Gaspar realizes that he's found the one he can trust with his legacy.

A courageous old man with a secret. A young man named Billy suffering from loneliness and trauma. A magical reality just below the surface of the one we think we know. Although Ellison's unproduced teleplay *The Dark Forces* is a more direct tribute to Billy and to Captain Marvel,[2] "Paladin of the Lost Hour," with its allusions to Frank Capra's 1937 film version of James Hilton's 1933 novel *Lost Horizon*, shares with Billy's origin story a fascination with time and mortality. Early in the published version of the narrative, not long after Gaspar has moved in with Billy—there's no secret subway tunnel in Ellison's story, just that chance meeting at a cemetery—the old man brings home a bag filled with toys, "tiny cars that turned into robots when the sections were unfolded" (Ellison, "Paladin" 13). Soon, Gaspar and Billy are sharing stories with each other. Although, for the sake of the universe, he must give Billy the magical watch, Gaspar possesses something far more precious: the memory of his wife. "He had gathered her together," Ellison writes, "all her dowry of love and taking care of him, her clothes and the way she wore them, her favorite knickknacks, a few clever remarks: and he packed it all up and delivered it to a new repository" ("Paladin" 16). Those "knickknacks," like the fragments of culture that Jack Smith once imagined sitting at the heart of his ideal city, are all that Gaspar can offer the man he calls his "last, best friend" (24).

Gaspar wonders if Billy remembers *Lost Horizon*, both the novel and Capra's film, which stars Ronald Colman. Before he dies, the ancient Father Perrault must find a new leader for the lost, utopian world of Shangri-La ("Paladin" 20). After explaining the nature and purpose of the watch, Gaspar asks, "Are you Ronald Colman?" (21). In the prologue of Hilton's novel, a writer named Rutherford warns the book's narrator that the fantastic story of Hugh Conway, the man who takes Father Perrault's place, is true. "Well, here it is, anyhow, and you can make what you like of it," Rutherford says, passing along his manuscript. Rutherford suggests that the narrator keep in mind Tertullian's phrase *quia impossibile est* as he reads it (Hilton 19). That paradoxical statement of faith, "it is certain, though it is impossible,"[3] might describe nostalgia itself—we believe in what we can no longer see. If it existed once, maybe it can live again, just like a hero in a comic book.

What else can be said about "impossible stories" like the ones C. C. Beck once described ("What Kind")? Some begin in the pages of a book, especially the magical ones from childhood. What did we first see in those books, and in the lives of those who created them? If we ask the right questions, maybe they'll answer. Writing about Captain Marvel has enabled me to touch on a range of topics, from Beck and Binder's legacy and the history of nostalgia to the promise of comics studies in the US. As I mention in the introduction, this book contains only one of the many possible stories that might be told about Captain Marvel, and about the comics that appealed to readers in Billy's America in the 1940s and 1950s. As I studied Beck and Binder's hero, I felt inspired and compelled to tell stories that might, like the Historama, bring the past into dialogue with the present and with the future. Often, like Billy, I found myself standing outside of that "weird underground cavern," wondering where it would take me (fig. 6.1). Billy, selling his newspapers, wonders if his meeting with Shazam was "a dream." It's still raining. According to the clock tower in the distance, it's been an hour since he first met the stranger. The light shining behind him, Billy is alone, but he remembers everything that just happened, from the train and the statues to the throne room and the granite block. And, dreaming or otherwise, when he speaks—when he says his magic word or tells one of his stories—he finds it again, almost as real and true as when he saw it all for the first time.[4]

I remember the room, the Curtis Mathes television set, the brown carpet, the black rotary phone hardwired to the wall. Don't sit too close to the screen, I hear someone say. Four years earlier, I am wearing a *Shazam!* shirt with ¾-length sleeves in the living room adjacent to this one, where I will watch "Paladin of the Lost Hour" in 1985. In 1981, my mother or my father takes a

6.1 Billy stands outside the subway tunnel after meeting Shazam for the first time in *Whiz Comics* no. 2. Script by Bill Parker and art by C. C. Beck. Reprinted in *The Shazam! Archives* vol. 1 (25). Captain Marvel and related characters © 2016 DC Comics.

picture. Danny Kaye, who starred as a pulp-fiction writer in the 1947 film version of *The Secret Life of Walter Mitty*, dies in 1987, just over a year after CBS broadcasts "Paladin of the Lost Hour." A year later, in March of 1988, C. C. Beck has an idea. He writes to his friend Trina Robbins. Would she like to read his "unpublished articles every so often?"[5] A few decades earlier, in the spring of 1945, Sabra Holbrook gives lectures in Chicago and in Garden City[6] as the kids at Junior High School 120 prepare to speak with Will Lieberson. The students, already fans, challenge Fawcett and its writers and artists to tell better stories. Roy Thomas, in an essay published in DC's *Secret Origins* no. 3 in 1986,[7] admits that "the full, true story of the circuitous route of Captain Marvel to fame and fortune and immortality in the fabled Golden Age of Comic-Books may never be told," especially in the absence of so many of "the original participants," those who worked for Fawcett in the 1940s (Thomas, "With One"). In 1964, Otto Binder writes Thomas a letter and warns scholars about the challenges they will face in studying the history of these "picture-story heroes" (Binder, "Special!" 112). Binder dies in 1974. In January 2014, I am on the phone in my Chicago apartment talking about Beck, Binder, Captain Marvel, and General Edward Paine with Harlan Ellison, who lived on Dempster in the early 1960s before he left for New York and then Los Angeles.[8] A few miles south is Soldier Field where, on the evening of September 2, 1942, my grandfather and the other members of his battalion inform, entertain, and comfort a crowd of spectators eager to know what the war will bring. In 1936, Earl Binder, also in Chicago, mails a letter that urges his brother, Otto, to keep writing, to imagine what he could be if he just keeps it up. After all, he's got plenty of stories to tell. Then, in New York in 1948, Wallace H. Martin hands Bill Parker a book. Does he recognize it? Yes, of course, it belongs to him. What does it say? Be careful. "Writing is far more abstract and unrealistic than art," Beck reminds the members of the Critical Circle in January 1989 ("What Kind"). Billy Batson, who was never real in the first place, watches his greedy uncle on a TV screen that isn't real, either, just a figment of Parker's imagination, brought to life by a few strokes of Beck's pencil. It's endless, really, one scene after the other, like panels in a comic book, each one like the one that came before it. Meanwhile, my mom remembers that birthday party in 1981. The other boys, she tells me, were misbehaving.[9] She has the pictures to prove it.

NOTES

1. There are numerous accounts of the National and Fawcett lawsuit in the comic book fan press dating back to the 1960s. As I mention in the introduction, Bob Ingersoll provides a detailed, concise, and accessible overview of the case in "The Cheese Stands Accused: A Look at the Superman/Captain Marvel Litigation," which is a revised version of his column "The Law Is a Ass" [*sic*] from the *Comics Buyer's Guide* no. 602 (May 31, 1985). Ingersoll also includes a version of the article at the *World Famous Comics* website, which houses an archive of his *CBG* columns (see the October 24, 2000, entry). Ingersoll bases his article in part on Michael Uslan's "When Titans Clash . . . in Court!" Gerard Jones briefly discusses the case in *Men of Tomorrow* (165–66) as does Larry Tye in *Superman: The High-Flying History of America's Most Enduring Hero* (54–55). Jim Steranko includes selections from the court decisions in the first chapter of *The Steranko History of Comics 2*, 17–21. Another useful summary appears in Les Daniels's *Comix: A History of Comic Books in America*, 13–14. To read some of the trial transcripts, refer to Kidd and Spear's *Shazam! The Golden Age of the World's Mightiest Mortal* (which does not include page numbers) and to my article "'A Leader of Men': Bill Parker on King Arthur & the Origin of Captain Marvel."

2. Quotations from Parker's testimony come from the case files stored at the National Archives in New York City. The page numbers come from the trial transcripts for *Detective Comics, Inc. and Superman, Inc. v. Fawcett Publications, Inc., Republic Pictures Corporation and Republic Pictures Corporation and Republic Productions, Inc.* To read his testimony, refer to the portion of the transcripts for New York, March 18 and 19, 1948.

3. It is not entirely clear from Parker's testimony which version of the King Arthur story he is holding. Sidney Lanier's popular *The Boy's King Arthur* first appeared in 1880, while Howard Pyle's *The Story of King Arthur and His Knights* dates from 1903. William Henry Frost's *The Knights of the Round Table* also appeared in 1898. Alan Lupack and Barbara Tepa Lupack provide an overview of Lanier's and Pyle's versions of the myth in *King Arthur in America* (75–92). The collection *The Fortunes of King Arthur* also includes brief mentions of Lanier and Pyle on 206–207 and 218–19. Thanks to Brannon Costello and to Katharine Burnett for suggesting these references to me as I was reading about King Arthur's popularity in the US.

4. Many of the histories of Captain Marvel are no longer in print but easily found through used bookstores or at various online retailers. Jim Steranko's history of Fawcett in *The Steranko History of Comics 2* draws on first-person accounts from C. C. Beck and Otto Binder and

remains an invaluable resource (6–37). P. C. Hamerlinck's *Fawcett Collectors of America*, now published as part of Roy Thomas's *Alter Ego*, continues to feature interviews, articles, and studies of the character. Hamerlinck's *Fawcett Companion: The Best of FCA*, which reprints *FCA* articles dating back four decades, is an essential handbook for any study of the character and of Fawcett's editors, writers, and artists. The Comic Art Collection at Michigan State University in East Lansing, Michigan, houses a significant number of the *FCA* newsletters, from its earliest days with Bernie McCarthy as its editor to Beck's *SOB* issues from the early 1980s. Bill Schelly's biography of Otto Binder, *Words of Wonder*, includes detailed accounts of Binder's time at Fawcett; consult Chapters 8, 9, 10, and 11. Schelly published a new, expanded edition of the biography in the spring of 2016. Most general histories of comic books in the United States include accounts of Captain Marvel and his popularity in the 1940s, including Wright's *Comic Book Nation* (18–19) and older histories such as Daniels's *Comix* (13–14) and Goulart's *Great History of Comic Books* (Chapter 12, 159–71). For an overview of the character from the 1940s to the present, also read Zack Smith's "An Oral History of Captain Marvel," posted online at *Newsarama* from December 24, 2010, to February 2011.

5. Superman appears with Billy and Captain Marvel on the cover of DC's *Shazam!* no. 1 (dated February 1973). The Fawcett heroes meet DC's Justice League in *Justice League of America* nos. 135, 136, and 137 in 1976. E. Nelson Bridwell discusses his work on these stories in his introduction to *Shazam! from the Forties to the Seventies*, 8. See also page 351 of that collection for other details on Bridwell's work on these *JLA* comics.

6. The quotations from Coxe's decision in the case are from *National Comics Publications, Inc. v. Fawcett Publications, Inc., et al.*, 93 F.Supp.349 (April 10, 1950). For more information on Coxe's ruling, as well as Judge Learned Hand's appellate decision, refer to the Works Cited section at the end of the book.

7. See *National Comics Publications, Inc. v. Fawcett Publications, Inc., et al.*, 93 F.Supp.349 (April 10, 1950).

8. *National Comics Publications, Inc. v. Fawcett Publications, Inc., et al.*, 93 F.Supp.349 (April 10, 1950).

9. These quotations are from Judge Learned Hand's ruling for the United States Second Circuit Court of Appeals in *National Comics Publications, Inc. v. Fawcett Publications, Inc.*, 191 F.2d 594 (August 30, 1951).

10. See *National Comics Publications, Inc. v. Fawcett Publications, Inc.*, 191 F.2d 594.

11. Consult 198 F.2d 927 for Hand's clarification, issued on September 5, 1952.

12. Binder and Beck's hero, of course, would return in the 1970s in the form of reprints published by DC, Fawcett's old nemesis. P. C. Hamerlinck provides a detailed account of National's decision to revive the character in the early 1970s. In "Can Lightning Strike Twice?" Hamerlinck cites an *Advertising Age* article from 1973 in which Carmine Infantino, DC's publisher, explained that he hoped "that Captain Marvel might help create a 'resurgence of the comics industry' by generating 'big enthusiasm in the trade and at the consumer level'" (61). Zack Smith discusses DC's *Shazam!* revival in "An Oral History of Captain Marvel: The Shazam Years, Pt. 1" on *Newsarama* (see the entry posted on December 31, 2010). Will Jacobs and Gerard Jones also discuss DC's *Shazam!* in Chapter 29 of *The Comic Book Heroes from the Silver Age to the Present*, 204–205.

13. All great comic book heroes, of course, eventually return. I discuss DC's revival of Billy and Captain Marvel—and Beck's short-lived involvement with the series *Shazam!*—in Chapter 1.

14. There's also an argument to be made that the era begins with the publication of Eastern Color Printing's *Famous Funnies* in 1934, but, for superhero comics, of course, the appearance of *Action Comics* no. 1 in 1938 is a watershed moment. For more on the "Golden Age" of comic books in the US, see, among others, Wright's *Comic Book Nation*, Gabilliet's *Of Comics and Men*, and Jones's *Men of Tomorrow*.

15. I discuss the introduction to *All in Color for a Dime* in more detail in the short essay "Nostalgia and *Strange Tales* #180."

16. For details on Parker's background, refer to pages 681–86 of his trial testimony from March 18, 1948.

17. That ashcan edition, now available in the first volume of DC's *The Shazam! Archives* (9–18), also helps to explain the numbering of what was in fact the first issue of *Whiz Comics* from Fawcett. See Bridwell, *Shazam! from the Forties to the Seventies*, 9, for more details. On pages 715–16 of his testimony Parker explains the purpose of the ashcan edition: "It is my understanding they were simply sent in interstate commerce to establish copyrights, and were never placed on sale, as I understand it" (Parker 716).

18. Harlan Ellison has drawn the connection between Billy's origin and *Lost Horizon* several times in his work, notably in his unproduced teleplay *The Dark Forces*, published in *Brain Movies: The Original Teleplays of Harlan Ellison* vol. 5. As I mention in the epilogue, his short story "Paladin of the Lost Hour," which appeared as an episode of *The Twilight Zone* in 1985, is also a variation on both *Lost Horizon* and Captain Marvel.

19. *Whiz Comics* no. 2 is cover-dated February 1940. The *Catalog of Copyright Entries* for 1940 lists *Whiz* no. 3 as having been submitted on January 12, 1940, so it's likely that Fawcett sought copyright for no. 2 in December 1939 or in early January of 1940. See entry 9746 of the 1940 *Catalog* for the entry. Billy's first appearance from *Whiz Comics* no. 2 has appeared in multiple collections from DC Comics and is also available online in the Fawcett section of the Digital Comics Museum. For print copies of the story, see vol. 1 of *The Shazam Archives!* (19–32), *Shazam! The Greatest Stories Ever Told* (8–20), and the more recent *Shazam! A Celebration of 75 Years* (8–21). For this book, I have used as my reference DC's *Famous First Edition* oversized facsimile edition of *Whiz Comics* no. 2, published in 1974, but have taken my image scans from *The Shazam! Archives* vol. 1 (an edition credited to C. C. Beck).

20. Binder provides a detailed account of his early work for Fawcett in his 1964 letter to *Alter Ego*. See Binder, "Special!" 111.

21. In the 1981 BBC documentary *The Comic Strip Hero*, Trina Robbins notes that her attempt to use *Shazam* as her magic word also failed. During a panel about C. C. Beck at Project: Comic Con in St. Louis on October 17, 2015, I asked Robbins about Billy's transformation into Captain Marvel. She responded that it should come as no surprise that Billy's word would work only for him. Each of us, she said, must discover our own magic word.

22. For more about the origin of Moore's *Miracleman*, consult my essay "Quotations from the Future." George Khoury's *Kimota! The Miracleman Companion* is an essential introduction to the character's long history, as is Pádraig Ó Méalóid's "Poisoned Chalice: The Extremely Long and Incredibly Complex Story of Marvelman," which began appearing at *The Beat: The News Blog of Comics Culture* on February 10, 2013, and ran until June of 2013. Ó Méalóid also interviewed Moore about the series for *The Beat* in three installments, posted on October 21, 23, and 25, 2013. Derek Wilson's "From Shazam! to Kimota!: The Sensational Story of England's Marvelman—The Hero Who Would Become Miracleman" is also a good introduction to the character.

After years of legal battles that dwarf the *National v. Fawcett* case in their complexity, Marvel began reprinting the series. Those reprints, which, at Moore's request, refer to him only as "The Original Writer," include summaries of the character's history. In the lead-up to the release of Moore's *Miracleman*, Marvel also reprinted a sampling of 1950s-era *Marvelman* comics.

23. The Street & Smith publication *How to Draw for the Comics* includes a short bio of Marcoux and a sample *Supersnipe* comic. It also includes a profile of Binder's brother Jack, who, like Marcoux, produced comics for Street & Smith.

24. In his memoir *The Comic Book Makers*, 60–61, Joe Simon discusses his and Jack Kirby's involvement in the first issue from 1941. He also discusses the lawsuit (64–65).

25. Recently there have been questions as to whether or not Joe Shuster drew the cover for *Action Comics* no. 1. While, for example, collections like *The Superman Chronicle*s attribute the cover to Shuster (see page 1 of vol. 1), other sources have questioned the authorship of the image. See, for example, Mark Seifert's article "Now You Know: The Car on the Cover of *Action Comics* #1 Is a 1937 DeSoto (But That's Just Part of the Story)" from *Bleeding Cool*, May 24, 2013. See also Seifert's link to Daniel Best's blog post "DC vs. Siegel: DC's Appeal Brief & Who DID Draw the *Action Comics* #1 Cover?" from *20th Century Danny Boy*, March 29, 2012.

26. Beck's testimony follows Parker's in the trial records. My copy of those records does not include the exact date of Beck's direct examination, but it appears to have taken place after Parker's second day of testimony on March 19, 1948.

27. Joseph Witek also discusses the "precivilized innocence" on display in funny animal comics in his chapter on Art Spiegelman's *Maus* in *Comic Books as History* (111).

28. For more on the significance of automobiles in US literature, see Cynthia Golomb Dettelbach's *In the Driver's Seat: The Automobile in American Literature and Popular Culture*, especially her discussion of Fitzgerald in Chapter 3. More general studies of the automobile in the cultural history of the United States include John B. Rae's *The American Automobile Industry* and Tom McCarthy's *Auto Mania: Cars, Consumers, and the Environment*. Shelby Smoak's 2007 dissertation *Framing the Automobile in 20th Century American Literature* includes a discussion of Tarkington and Fitzgerald. For more about automobiles and *The Great Gatsby*, consult John J. McNally's "Boats and Automobiles in *The Great Gatsby*: Symbols of Drift and Death"; Laurence E. MacPhee's "*The Great Gatsby*'s 'Romance of Motoring': Nick Carraway and Jordan Baker"; R. A. Corrigan's "Somewhere West of Laramie, on the Road to West Egg: Automobiles, Fillies, and the West in *The Great Gatsby*"; and Jacqueline Lance's more recent "*The Great Gatsby*: Driving to Destruction with the Rich and Careless at the Wheel."

29. Chris Gavaler describes Gatsby as a kind of superhero in his short online essay "Time-Traveling Supervillain Gatsby the Great."

30. Fragments of Andy Warhol's unfinished *Batman/Dracula* can be found online. A clip of the film, with Smith standing in a black cape, appears in Mary Jordan's 2007 documentary *Jack Smith and the Destruction of Atlantis*. For more about Smith's films, read J. Hoberman's *On Jack Smith's* Flaming Creatures *(and Other Secret-Flix of Cinemaroc)* as well as Hoberman and Jonathan Rosenbaum's *Midnight Movies* (especially Chapter 3).

31. Benjamin's discussion of the "secret affinities" of items found in the Paris arcades appears in *The Arcades Project* (540–41).

32. In her essay on Smith's best-known film, Susan Sontag writes that "*Flaming Creatures* is that rare modern work of art: it is about joy and innocence" (Sontag, *Against Interpretation* 229).

Her essay on "camp" has its roots in her fascination with Smith's film (see *Against Interpretation* 275).

CHAPTER 1

1. Letter to Trina Robbins, March 7, 1988.

2. P. C. Hamerlinck has edited and published some of Beck's Critical Circle essays in the pages of *Fawcett Collectors of America*. For this chapter, and for my other references to these articles, I refer to Beck's original typescripts mailed to the Circle in 1988 and 1989. Thanks again to Trina Robbins for sharing her copies of these letters and essays with me.

3. Letter to Trina Robbins, May 23, 1988.

4. P. C. Hamerlinck is currently at work on a full biography of Beck. Other biographical sources are also available. Hamerlinck compiled material from Beck's unpublished essays with Beck's drawings in "Preacher's Son," included in Jon B. Cooke and John Morrow's anthology *Streetwise: Autobiographical Stories by Comic Book Professionals* (59–67). Ron Goulart's *The Great Comic Book Artists* includes a short biography on Beck (10–11). To read more about Beck's life and times, refer to Jim Steranko's *The Steranko History of Comics* 2 (10–11); Jerry De Fuccio's "Charles Clarence Beck: The World's Second Mightiest Mortal"; Gary Groth's extensive interview with Beck in *The Comics Journal* no. 95 (February 1985): 57–77; and Beck's discussion with Eisner in *Will Eisner's Spirit Magazine* no. 41 (June 1983): 18–23, 42–43, reprinted in *Will Eisner's Shop Talk* (52–75) (my in-text citations refer to the *Shop Talk* collection and not to the page numbers in *Will Eisner's Spirit Magazine*). Other good resources on his life and times include his interview with Bruce Hamilton in *Special Edition Series 1*; Gary Brown's profile in *The Monster Times* ("C. C. Beck"); and Chris Padovano's interview in *Fan*.

5. Letter to Trina Robbins, January 5, 1989.

6. Beck's novella *The World's Mightiest Fat Head* appears in issues no. 226 and 227 of *The Comics Journal*.

7. For more on Swayze's memories of the musicians in the Fawcett offices, see his article in *Alter Ego* no. 98: 76.

8. For more on Binder's time at National, see Schelly's *Words of Wonder*, Chapters 12 and 13.

9. After Fawcett's settlement, Beck worked briefly with Joe Simon to develop The Silver Spider, an early version of the Archie Comics hero called The Fly. Simon discusses his work with Beck, and the significant changes Jack Kirby made to Beck's designs, in *The Comic Book Makers* (191–200). Simon's book includes samples of Beck's original pencils for the character; see 192, 197, and 200.

10. For more on Beck's relationship with Newton, see Barry Keller, "Don Newton: 'He Showed Us How to Do It Right.'" See also Don Newton's homepage for an account of editor Julius Schwartz's response to Beck's idea of working with an assistant. That page, dedicated to Newton's memory, also includes a detailed account of the Batman artist's sometimes contentious relationship with Beck. Beck describes his dissatisfaction with many of these new Captain Marvel stories in his later essays, notably "May We Have the Next Slide Please?"; "What Really Killed Captain Marvel?"; and "Are We Living in the Golden Age and Don't Know It?" P. C. Hamerlinck provides details on the DC revival of the hero in "Can Lightning Strike Twice?" as does Zack Smith in "An Oral History of Captain Marvel: The Shazam Years, Pt. 1" on *Newsarama* (see the entry posted on December 31, 2010). For more details on Captain Marvel's return, also read E. Nelson Bridwell's introduction to *Shazam! from the Forties to the Seventies* (15–16) and Will Jacobs and Gerard Jones's *The Comic Book Heroes from the Silver Age to the Present* (204–205).

11. DC continued to include reprints of Fawcett stories written by Binder and drawn by Beck and Costanza in *Shazam!* after Beck's departure.

12. In the short essay and slide show "Captain Marvel, C. C. Beck, and the Comics-Fan Subculture," Jaime Wolf includes images of some of Beck's Captain Marvel paintings. Wolf also discusses Beck's significance in the fanzine culture of the 1960s.

13. Letter to Trina Robbins, August 25, 1989.

14. Gary Groth explains the publishing arrangement for the collection in a letter to Beck, June 30, 1989. Beck shared Groth's letter and the news with the Critical Circle on July 28, 1989.

15. See, for example, Beck's essays "Comic Books for Grown-Ups" (December 1986) and "Sex and Violence in Comics" (September 1987).

16. The Pinis included a May 1980 letter from Beck in *Elfquest* no. 7. In the letter, Beck mentions how much both his daughter and his granddaughter enjoy the series. "Don't bother to answer this letter—you are far too busy. Just file it under 'fantastic praise' from a fellow who's known mostly as an old curmudgeon from the past who sees nothing good in today's world. There isn't much hope for the human race but we elves have been around a long time and are doing all right" (34). Beck also created a sword based on one from the series. The Pinis include a photo of the weapon—"Made from paper, f'r gosh sake!"—with other examples of *Elfquest* fan art in the same issue (page 37).

17. In a letter to Trina Robbins, dated June 19, 1989, Beck assured his friend and colleague, "Don't worry about our different views of things—that's what makes life interesting. Nothing bores me more than being in a group of people who agree on everything."

18. At the time of this undated letter, probably from 1988, Robbins and Beck were discussing the possibility that she might finish the work he had begun on *Malcolm Mugge*, a humorous science fiction Western Beck had created.

19. "Beck had a style that was firm," Harlan Ellison has observed. "It was implanted. You could see into that panel as if you were looking through a leaded glass window and you could see everything you needed to see, and anything that was extraneous your imagination could add to the picture" (Ellison, "Nay, Never Will I").

20. Beck was proud of the brevity of Billy's origin story. In "The Man of Steel," he compares the *Whiz Comics* no. 2 version of the story to the one written by Roy Thomas and drawn by Jerry Bingham and Steve Mitchell. That adaptation, published in DC's *Secret Origins* in 1986, Beck writes, "takes 125 panels to retell a story that Parker and I told in just 73. How's that for padding and embellishing and blowing all out of proportion a simple little children's story?" (Beck, "The Man of Steel" 7). For other readings of Billy's first appearance, see Colin Smith's analysis of the story posted on his website *Too Busy Thinking About My Comics* (June 12, 2010) and Christopher Knowles's *Our Gods Wear Spandex* (p. 124).

21. From the undated letter to Robbins, probably from 1988. I list the letter in the Works Cited under the name "Never draw any more than necessary."

22. From "Never draw any more than necessary."

23. These quotations come from the first issue of *Fatman*, which does not include page numbers.

24. From "Never draw any more than necessary."

25. What role does an artist play in society? "Each artist has a responsibility to keep from creating something which will add to the unhappiness of the world," Beck argued in a letter to the Critical Circle, dated February 20, 1989.

26. DC Comics includes reprints of this story in *Shazam! The Greatest Stories Ever Told* (80–96); *Showcase Presents Shazam!* (9–24; this collection also features black-and-white reprints of Beck's other Captain Marvel stories for the company); and *Shazam! A Celebration of 75 Years* (147–63).

CHAPTER 2

1. These quotations are from *Captain Marvel Adventures* no. 100, which does not include page numbers. Barrier and Williams include a reprint of the story in *A Smithsonian Book of Comic-Book Comics* (81–113).

2. I discuss Tawny's literary precedents in "The Secret Life of Mr. Tawny: *Captain Marvel Adventures* #102 & James Thurber's Walter Mitty."

3. In *The Rocket's Blast Special* no. 8, an issue dedicated to Captain Marvel and the Marvel Family, Gene Arnold notes that Tawny, although popular, was a character he "did not care for." When I mentioned to Harlan Ellison that I would be devoting a chapter to the talking tiger, he asked why I'd decided to spend so much time on the "worst" of all the Captain Marvel serials, then changed the subject.

4. For the allegorical qualities in Kelly's work, read Edward Mendelson's "Possum Pastoral."

5. Roy Thomas printed the six sample strips in *Alter Ego* in 1965. See Thomas and Schelly (144–46) to read the strips. Schelly also includes them in *Words of Wonder* (101).

6. The Catalog of Copyright Entries for 1951 lists September 5, 1951, as the copyright date for *CMA* no. 126, which is cover-dated November 1951.

7. *CMA* no. 126 does not include page numbers.

8. I discuss the history of these sorts of characters in more detail in my essay "Funny Animals" in *The Routledge Companion to Comics*, edited by Frank Bramlett, Roy T. Cook, and Aaron Meskin.

9. Tawny first appears in "Captain Marvel and the Talking Tiger" in *Captain Marvel Adventures* no. 79 (December 1947). The title page lists Beck as the "Chief Artist" of the issue. The copyright date for *CMA* no. 82 is December 31, 1947, according to the *Catalog of Copyright Entries* for 1948. For a list of Mr. Tawny's adventures, refer to the "Tawky Tawny Chronology" on the *Unofficial Guide to the DC Universe* website.

10. Spiegelman and other other members of the group, including Heer, discuss Beck and Captain Marvel in "Colloquy" (240–46). Later, Spiegelman also discusses "Captain Marvel in the Land of Surrealism," the story he and Françoise Mouly eventually selected for inclusion in *The TOON Treasury of Classic Children's Comics*. See "Colloquy" (335–36) and *The TOON Treasury* (274–81).

11. For more on Kafka's animal fables, read Abigail E. Gillman's "In Kafka's Synagogue"; Beatrice Hanssen's *Walter Benjamin's Other History: Of Stones, Animals, Human Beings, and Angels*; and Matthew T. Powell's "Bestial Representations of Otherness: Kafka's Animal Stories."

12. For a discussion of the relationship between memory and imagination, see Edward Casey's "The World of Nostalgia" (366–68). I also discuss Casey's essay, and its analysis of Hofer's dissertation, in Chapter 5.

13. Schwartz's "The Heavy Bear Who Goes With Me" appears in his *Selected Poems* (74–75).

14. On the Radiator Comics website, Sharpe's co-publisher, Neil Brideau, writes that Sharpe's "choice to draw everyone as anthropomorphic animals actually humanizes the story more." This

is so, he argues, because realism might "have created a barrier between the reader and the subjects" (Brideau).

15. For a detailed account of Binder's life and times, read Schelly's definitive biography, *Words of Wonder*. Hamerlinck's *Fawcett Companion* includes Matt Lage's interview with Binder. Recently, Hamerlinck has also been serializing portions of Binder's "Memoirs of a Nobody" in *Fawcett Collectors of America*. That manuscript, along with all of the material Binder left to Sam Moskowitz, is housed at the Cushing Memorial Library at Texas A&M University.

16. For more on Binder's *Jon Jarl* series, see Schelly, *Words of Wonder* (102).

17. Binder includes this reference to Lovecraft in a letter to Earl dated January 20, 1936. He refers to Howard in another letter to Earl dated June 7, 1936. Cushing Memorial Library and Archives, Texas A&M University.

18. Earl Binder letter to Otto Binder, April 6, 1936. Cushing Memorial Library and Archives, Texas A&M University.

19. For details on Binder's work at National, refer to Chapters 12 and 13 of Schelly's *Words of Wonder*.

20. From Ellison, interview with the author, January 2014. As this book was about to go to press, Roy Thomas and P. C. Hamerlinck published this interview as "'Nay, Never Will I Serve Thee, Mr. Mind!' Or, 'I Think I was Always a Fawcett Kid'" in *Alter Ego* no. 138/*Fawcett Collectors of America* no. 197 (March 2016), 4–16. Any citations from the interview that appear in this book are from the original manuscript of the interview, which Ellison edited and revised in the summer of 2014.

21. Asimov writes about Binder's influence in the introduction to the paperback edition of *The Caves of Steel* (vii–xi).

22. Otto Binder letter to Sam Moskowitz, October 4, 1952. Cushing Memorial Library and Archives, Texas A&M University.

23. H. L. Gold letter to Otto Binder, February 17, 1953. Binder's response to Gold is dated February 21, 1953. Cushing Memorial Library and Archives, Texas A&M University.

24. Otto Binder letter to Sam Moskowitz, October 4, 1952. Cushing Memorial Library and Archives, Texas A&M University.

25. In researching Binder, I asked science fiction historian Betty Hull if her husband, Frederik Pohl, had any memories of the writer. Pohl began his career in the late 1930s and was a prolific writer and editor until his death in 2013. Through Hull, Pohl responded that Binder was "before his time." As Hull pointed out to me, this was quite a statement, given that Pohl, although a decade younger than Binder, began his career in the 1930s.

26. Oscar J. Friend letter to Otto Binder, dated July 6, 1953. Cushing Memorial Library and Archives, Texas A&M University. For more about Binder's struggle to return to science fiction, see also *Words of Wonder* (119–22).

27. Oscar J. Friend letter to Otto Binder, dated August 8, 1953. Cushing Memorial Library and Archives, Texas A&M University. Friend and his co-editor Leo Margulies included Binder's "The Teacher from Mars" in the collection *My Best Science Fiction Story*, first published in 1949 and reissued in paperback by Pocket Books early in 1954. Some of the writers Friend praises in this 1953 letter are included in the book, notably Henry Kuttner and Murray Leinster. Manly Wade Wellman, a friend from Binder's pulp days and another writer who made the transition from science fiction to comics, also makes an appearance.

28. *Argosy* serialized *Lords of Creation* in 1939.

29. Binder's "Testing, Testing" appears in *Universe Science Fiction* no. 5 (May 1954): 114–24.

30. Otto Binder letter to Oswald Train, dated November 7, 1953. Cushing Memorial Library and Archives, Texas A&M University.

31. Otto Binder letter to Sam Moskowitz, dated October 15, 1952. Cushing Memorial Library and Archives, Texas A&M University.

32. John W. Campbell, Jr., letter to Otto Binder, dated February 15, 1938. Cushing Memorial Library and Archives, Texas A&M University.

33. Binder adapted "The Teacher from Mars" for EC Comics. Drawn by Joe Orlando with colors by Marie Severin, it appeared in *Weird Science-Fantasy* no. 24 (June 1954). I write briefly about this adaptation in "Is Otto Binder and Joe Orlando's 'I, Robot' a Protest Novel?" For more about Binder's work for EC, refer to Chapter 11 of *Words of Wonder*.

34. The *Catalog of Copyright Entries* for 1952 lists February 6 as the copyright date for *CMA* no. 131.

35. *CMA* no. 131 does not include page numbers.

36. I discuss Binder's memo in more detail in "Otto Binder's Magic Words: The Writer's Plan to Save *Captain Marvel Adventures*." This article includes the full text of Binder's notes. Although it does not include a date, the note probably dates from 1952, as it appears in the same portion of the Binder archive as his two letters to Sam Moskowitz from the fall of that year.

37. Otto Binder letter to Sam Moskowitz, dated October 4, 1952. Cushing Memorial Library and Archives, Texas A&M University.

38. The *Catalog of Copyright Entries* for 1953 lists July 10, 1953, as the copyright date for *CMA* no. 149.

39. *CMA* no. 149 does not include page numbers.

40. Most notable of these appearances is "The Troubles of the Talking Tiger," written by Denny O'Neil and drawn by C. C. Beck, in *Shazam!* no. 7 (cover-dated November 1973). Mr. Tawny even appears on the cover.

41. Kerry Soper discusses Walt Kelly's affection for Bridgeport, Connecticut, in *We Go Pogo* (20–21). I also discuss Kelly's Connecticut background in "Bumbazine, Blackness, and the Myth of the Redemptive South in *Pogo*" (33–34). For more about Kelly's hometown and its impact on his work, read Eric Jarvis's "The Comic Strip *Pogo* and the Issue of Race."

42. Read Chapter 14 of Schelly's *Words of Wonder* for more about Binder's relationship to comic book fandom in the United States in the 1960s.

CHAPTER 3

1. Don Maris includes a copy of this Captain Marvel Club letter in his 1975 reprint collection *The Best of*. Maris's collection also includes black-and-white reprints of four World War II-era Captain Marvel stories as well as advertising materials from Fawcett. Like other early fan magazines, Maris's does not have page numbers. Maris's collection has long been out of print, but copies do sometimes appear on eBay and other online comics websites.

2. For these advertisements, see Maris's "best of" collection.

3. See the introduction to Maris's "best of" collection for his memories of the character. "Captain Marvel in the World of If" first appeared in *Captain Marvel Adventures* no. 42 (January 1945).

4. For Wright's description of Captain Marvel's personality traits, see Chapter 1 of *Comic Book Nation*: "Whereas Superman evinced self-assuredness and control, Captain Marvel seemed more like a bumbling overgrown child, and his adventures had a distinctively whimsical quality about them" (18–19). In *Champions of the Oppressed* (28, 155–56), Murray also discusses the character and his impact on young children.

5. See the introduction to Maris's "best of" collection.

6. For other discussions of American soldiers' appetite for comic book heroes, see Schelly's discussion of Otto Binder's success at Fawcett Publications. Binder, Schelly points out, "found himself writing for a vast audience: millions of children and teenagers, as well as large numbers of servicemen who were within reach of a PX" (Schelly, *Words* 87). Michael C. C. Adams describes "a media generation" that "had come of age with talking pictures and radio." Adams also points out that "[b]y 1942, twelve million comic books a month were sold, one-third to people over eighteen. They were the favorite reading of the private soldier" (Adams 10–11). For more details on the soldiers who read these comics, also refer to Robert G. Weiner's "'Okay, Axis, Here We Come!' Captain America and the Superhero Teams from World War II and the Cold War" in B. J. Oropeza's *The Gospel According to Superheroes: Religion and Popular Culture* (83–101). In addition to Susan J. Matt's work, for more about the training of US soldiers during the war, consult August B. Hollingshead's "Adjustment to Military Life" and Thomas E. Rodgers's "Billy Yank and G. I. Joe." For more about the Marvel Family and masculinity in the 1950s, as well as about superheroes and postwar consumer culture, read Mark Best's "Domesticity, Homosociality, and Male Power in Superhero Comics of the 1950s."

7. In his essay on the air campaign over Nazi Germany, W. G. Sebald describes "the rather unreal effect of the eyewitness reports," a consequence of "the clichés" that are inevitable in the face of "total destruction, incomprehensible in its extremity," as writers attempt to describe the devastating effects of combat on both soldiers and civilians (24–25). These phrases, he writes, serve "to cover up and neutralize experiences beyond our ability to comprehend" (25).

8. For a more detailed discussion of World War II as imagined and understood by popular culture, read Edward Wood, Jr., *Worshipping the Myths of World War II: Reflections on America's Dedication to War*; Michael C. C. Adams's *The Best War Ever: America and World War II*; and Paul Fussell's work, especially *Wartime: Understanding and Behavior in World War II*. In *Up Front* (1944), a collection of World War II cartoons featuring the iconic characters Willie and Joe, cartoonist Bill Mauldin describes the social and psychological impact of the myth of the ideal soldier (8).

9. In his discussion of the futility of trying to document that "real war" in books, movies, or other forms of media, Fussell cites another American writer who found it impossible to convey the scope and the aftermath of modern warfare: "After scrutinizing closely the facts of the American Civil War, after seeing and listening to hundreds of the wounded, Walt Whitman declared: 'The real war will never get in the books.' Nor will the Second World War, and 'books' includes this one" (Fussell 290).

10. I first wrote about comic books and the Army War Show in my article "'Join the Parade to Victory!' Captain Marvel and the Army War Show—June 1942." Thanks again to P. C. Hamerlinck for giving me the opportunity to write about those performances, Swayze's cover, and Captain Marvel. Very little has been written about the War Show itself. My quotations from the War Department memos come from the National Archives in Washington, DC, which houses several months' worth of planning memos and correspondence related to these exhibitions. Newspaper accounts about the shows are also very common, especially for performances in major cities like Chicago. For other details, read Kimberly Guise's short post about the Show at the National

WWII Museum website. See also Gary Banas's article "Army War Show—Provisional Task Force 1942." I have drawn on the *Army War Show 1942 Provisional Task Force* yearbook for more information about these performances. Copy of the yearbook courtesy of the late Nunzio and Patricia Stango.

11. The *Catalog of Copyright Entries* for 1942 lists May 29 as the copyright date for *CMA* no. 12.

12. Text from "Here's YOUR Army!" from *Attack: The Story of the United States Army*, a souvenir program sold at the War Show performances in the summer and fall of 1942. Like the shows themselves, profits for this booklet benefited Army Emergency Relief.

13. The *Chicago Daily Tribune* for Wednesday, September 2, 1942, includes a preview of the War Show's first performance in the city: "City Gets Taste of War in Army Show's Preview" (2, 10).

14. See Swayze's "We Didn't Know . . . It Was the Golden Age!" (74–76).

15. The Grand Comics Database speculates that C. C. Beck drew the story with assistance from Pete Costanza, but its entry for this issue does not list a writer.

16. In his discussion of comic books and the "mediated war" (100), Christopher Murray argues that "the mass media offered fantasies that responded to and negotiated anxieties created by the war" (101). As a result, he writes, "these narratives moved the war into the realm of myth, a battle against evil" (101).

17. Like other early issues of *Captain Marvel Adventures*, no. 12 has page numbers. I have included these page references after my citations. The title page of this issue does not list the names of Fawcett's editors but does mention the members of Fawcett's Editorial Advisory Board along with the company's president, W. H. Fawcett, Jr.

18. Portions of this section of the chapter about "Capt. Marvel and the Mark of the Black Swastika" first appeared in an earlier form as "'What Manner of Man Is He?': Humor and Masculine Identity in Captain Marvel's World War II Adventures" in *Studies in American Humor*, new series 3, no. 27 (2013): 33–62. Thanks to editor Ed Piacentino and to the anonymous peer reviewers for their guidance and suggestions on that article.

19. Like *Captain Marvel Adventures* no. 12, *CMA* no. 20 includes page numbers.

20. Kidd and Spear's photographic history of Captain Marvel does not include page numbers. A copy of this "Code of Ethics" appears later in the book. Kidd and Spear note that this memo details "the 1942 writing guidelines for all of the Fawcett titles." Amy Kiste Nyberg briefly discusses Fawcett's "Code" in *Seal of Approval: The History of the Comics Code* (107).

21. The *Catalog of Copyright Entries* for 1943 lists January 1 as the copyright date for *CMA* no. 20.

22. In his description of "the everyman hero" during World War II, Murray notes that, "According to this rhetoric, unlike the brainwashed masses of the enemy, the average American soldier fought for his family or for apple pie and Hollywood movies—in short, for home and a simple love of life and liberty, not a specific ideology" (Murray 111–12).

23. Captain Marvel's reference to the Devil as "Old Scratch" suggests links to Benét's popular short story "The Devil and Daniel Webster," which was first published in 1937. The film version, directed by William Dieterle from a screenplay co-written by Benét himself (Singer 265; Cooksey 20), was released in the autumn of 1941. When asked his name, the Devil replies, "'I've gone by a good many,' said the stranger carelessly. 'Perhaps Scratch will do for the evening. I'm often called that in these regions'" (Benét 37). See Robert Singer's "One Against All: The New England Past and Present Responsibilities in *The Devil and Daniel Webster*" and Thomas L. Cooksey's "*The Devil and Daniel Webster, Cabin in the Sky*, and *Damn Yankees*—American Contributions to the Faust Legend" for discussions of the cultural significance of the film as the US entered

World War II. As Cooksey argues, "Webster and Scratch embody two conflicting interpretations of America and American history, a dichotomy that took on special significance when the movie appeared in 1941, during the dark days of the Second World War" (21).

24. During coverage of the 2014 San Diego Comic-Con, Brandon Schatz at Heidi MacDonald's website *The Beat* posted a story about Dwayne Johnson's involvement with the project. Schatz includes a link to a video from the website *Total Film* in which Johnson discusses possible roles in an upcoming summer blockbuster: "There's a character out there that we're going to announce very soon that I'm going to play." He then pauses before he explains that this character has "the power of Superman" and "can throw down." After another brief pause, Johnson looks again at the interviewer: "Just say the word. That's all I'm going to say." In subsequent discussions of the film, now slated for release in 2019, Johnson confirmed that he would play Black Adam, but as of this writing there has been no further discussion of who will play the film's title role.

25. In a criticism of Roy Thomas and Jerry Bingham's adaptation of Billy's origin story in *Secret Origins* no. 3 (June 1986), Beck argues that DC revived the character once again to "recoup the money they've been losing by aiming their comic books at nostalgia-haunted adults instead of at children" (Beck, "The Man of Steel" 7).

26. Steranko points out, for example, that the "folksy, low-key" quality of Binder's scripts might be "contrasted" with the atmosphere in the comics published by Fawcett's competitors, notably "Timely's pervasive climate of fear or National's focus on ultimate power" (Steranko 15).

27. The *Catalog of Copyright Entries* for 1945 lists November 24, 1944, as the copyright date for *CMA* no. 42.

28. The Grand Comics Database attributes the story's script to Binder. For more information, see the entry for *Captain Marvel Adventures* no. 42.

29. Unlike the other issues I discuss in this chapter, *Captain Marvel Adventures* no. 42 does not include page numbers.

30. For more on comic books, wartime propaganda, and "ideology," see Murray 100–103.

31. Writing in 1989, Fussell argues that "[t]he postwar power of 'the media'" and its ability "to determine what shall be embraced as reality is in large part due to the success of the morale culture in wartime. It represents, indeed, its continuation" (164).

32. For more about how writers attempt to address and to narrate these tragedies, read Sebald's essay "Air War and Literature" from *On the Natural History of Destruction*.

33. In the last year of the war, Fussell writes, when "almost everyone had had a relative killed or wounded or knew someone who had," most Americans understood too well "that the war had something very gruesome about it" (Fussell 143).

34. In his discussion of the history of Coney Island in the book *Delirious New York*, architect and theorist Rem Koolhaas argues that "entertainment," especially under industrial capitalism, "can only skirt the surface of myth, only hint at the anxieties accumulated in the collective unconscious" (Koolhaas 42).

35. Is World War II as distant from us as we'd like to believe? Writing about history, of course, always poses challenges, and often calls for the kind of imaginative thinking that Beck so often celebrated. "For a historian of Middle Kingdom Egypt," Edward Said writes in *Orientalism*, "'long ago' will have a very clear sort of meaning, but even this meaning does not totally dissipate the imaginative, quasi-fictional quality one senses lurking in a time very different and distant from our own" (55).

CHAPTER 4

1. The *Catalog of Copyright Entries* for 1945 lists August 1 as the copyright date for *CMA* no. 48.

2. *Captain Marvel Adventures* no. 48 does not include page numbers.

3. It is important to note here that the depiction of African Americans in the pulp fictions of the 1930s and 1940s has a long and complex history, one that requires more analysis and historical detective work. While many readers will be familiar, for example, with the racial stereotypes in narratives such as H. P. Lovecraft's "The Call of Cthulhu" (1928), there are depictions of African Americans in the pulps that might at first appear to be more forward-looking and progressive. For example, as Erika Frensley points out in her essay "Pulps—Television of the 1930s," characters like The Shadow and The Avenger worked with agents whose performance of a stereotypical blackness proved essential to these white heroes in their mission to fight crime; see Frensley 6–7. The Avenger is also engaged in a masquerade, as, following the murder of his wife and his son, the skin of his face becomes white and paralyzed—so much so, in fact, that he can reshape and disguise himself at will. Denny O'Neil and Jack Kirby explored some of these ideas on race and identity in *Justice, Inc.* no. 2, which features their adaptation of "The Sky Walker," the 1939 adventure which first introduced Josh and Rosabel Newton to The Avenger's cast of characters (see the 1972 Warner Paperback Library Reprint of "The Sky Walker," especially Chapter III, and DC Comics' *Justice, Inc.* no. 2). Andrew Helfer and Kyle Baker also created a two-issue *Justice, Inc.* series for DC Comics in 1989. For a discussion of pulp fiction of the 1930s and 1940s and its audience, see Erin A. Smith's *Hard-Boiled: Working Class Readers and Pulp Magazines*.

4. In one of the comments on Brian Cronin's post about Steamboat at *Comic Book Resources*, a writer going by the name "Hoosier X" makes the important point that "[t]he existence of the Youth Builders [*sic*] in 1945 also pretty effectively demolishes the rationalization that everybody was just racist in olden times so we should just excuse it or ignore it" (posted April 18, 2014, at 10:02 a.m.). Micheaux's 1945 novel *The Case of Mrs. Wingate*, as its jacket copy explains, tells the story of "Nazi activity inside black America," and the heroic Sidney Wyeth's attempts to stop it. For more on Micheaux's novels and films, read Pearl Bowser and Louise Spence's *Writing Himself into History*.

5. Brian Cronin includes an image from Steamboat's final scene in his brief article on the character. See "Comic Book Legends Revealed," installment no. 467, at *Comic Book Resources* for April 18, 2014. In his column, Cronin also includes sample pages from "Capt. Marvel and the Voodoo Showboat."

6. See "Captain Marvel and Mr. Tawny's New Home" from *Captain Marvel Adventures* no. 90 (November 1948).

7. In the last two decades, scholars have written extensively on minstrelsy and its impact on popular culture in the United States. Read, for example, Chapter 6 of Charles Hamm's *Yesterdays*, a history of popular music in the US, for the origin of "Zip Coon." David Roediger's *The Wages of Whiteness* and Eric Lott's *Love and Theft* are two now-classic texts on the subject. For a more recent study of minstrelsy's persistent role in music, television, and film, read Yuval Taylor and Jake Austen's *Darkest America*.

8. Beck also discusses the character in his autobiographical essay in *Streetwise* (62).

9. In "Mr. Mind and the Monster Society of Evil," Beck, writing in the mid-1980s, indirectly alludes to Steamboat when he writes about the racial and cultural stereotypes that filled the comic books of the 1940s: "It is true that much of the male chauvinism, the super-patriotic

Americanism, and the degrading treatment of minorities that was displayed in the comics of nearly a half-century ago would not be acceptable today." Those images, he argues, might "be too tame" in comparison to the "horrible things" on display "in our comics and on our television screens" (Beck, "Mr. Mind" A–93).

10. The Grand Comics Database entry for *America's Greatest Comics* no. 2 attributes the splash page of the issue to Beck and to Mac Raboy.

11. The story in which Steamboat first appears does not include a title. I have followed the example of *The Shazam! Archives* vol. 4 in referring to it as "The Park Robberies."

12. *America's Greatest Comics* no. 2 includes page numbers, which I have cited here for the convenience of the reader.

13. The *Catalog of Copyright Entries* for 1942 lists February 11 as the copyright date for *America's Greatest Comics* no. 2.

14. Following the conclusion is a full-page announcement about the Club itself, suggesting that the entire story is an advertisement designed to attract new members. Perks of that membership included a badge and a Captain Marvel Club Card, all for only 5 cents to cover shipping and handling.

15. *Captain Marvel Adventures* no. 10 includes page numbers.

16. For the "existential" ramifications of these static images, especially as related to superhero comic books, see Marc Singer, "'Black Skins' and White Masks: Comic Books and the Secret of Race" (108).

17. The *Rocket's Blast Special* no. 8, which also features Don Newton's atmospheric retelling of Billy's origin story, as well as art from Beck, does not include page numbers. An advertisement for the *Special* in *The Rocket's Blast/Comicollector* no. 91 urges fans to pick up a copy: "Even if you're not a Capt[.] Marvel fan, if you appreciate fine comic art, you must have this issue."

18. The *Catalog of Copyright Entries* for 1943 lists February 26 as the copyright date for *CMA* no. 22.

19. *Captain Marvel Adventures* no. 22 includes page numbers. The issue also features the first installment of the popular Monster Society of Evil serial (33–44), which introduced Captain Marvel's other great nemesis, Mr. Mind. For Binder's comments on the serial, see "Special!" (110). For comments on the countless racial stereotypes in those stories, see part 3 of Zack Smith's "An Oral History of Captain Marvel" online at *Newsarama*. In 2007, Jeff Smith wrote and drew *Shazam! The Monster Society of Evil* for DC Comics in 2007. Aside from its name, his book shares little in common with the original series from the 1940s, although it does remain close in spirit to Binder and Beck's later work.

20. See the *Chicago Sunday Tribune* article "World We Want to Live In Topic at Bateman PTA," March 18, 1945.

21. See "Sabra Holbrook to Direct Panel" from the *Nassau Daily Review-Star*, March 23, 1945. Also refer to the Works Cited section at the end of this book for information on the Youthbuilders material located in the NAACP microfilm archives.

22. See the *Thirty-Third Annual Report of the Board of Gas and Electric Light Commissioners of the Commonwealth of Massachusetts* (33a) for a listing that includes Robert W. Rollins, Holbrook's father, as one of the company's directors.

23. For more about Moore's involvement with the character, read Pádraig Ó Méalóid's series of articles for *The Beat*. For a discussion of Cream's role in *Miracleman*, read Julian Darius's posts at *Sequart*, notably the two-part installment on "Evelyn Cream and Race in *Miracleman*, Chapter

9." George Khoury's *The Miracleman Companion* provides an essential overview of Marvelman and the character's long and complex history, as does Derek Wilson's "From Shazam! to Kimota!: The Sensational Story of England's Marvelman—The Hero Who Would Become Miracleman." In my essay "Quotations from the Future: Harvey Kurtzman's 'Superduperman,' Nostalgia, and Alan Moore's *Miracleman*," I provide a brief summary of that history as well as a discussion of the influence of Harvey Kurtzman and Brian Eno on Moore's work. In 2014, Marvel Comics began reprinting Moore's *Miracleman* stories. Those reprints, at Moore's insistence, do not include his name. Moore talks about his involvement with the character and the property's legal history in the third part of Ó Méalóid's "The Alan Moore/Marvelman Interview: Part III" from *The Beat* (October 25, 2013).

24. In my discussion of Moore and Cream, I refer to the full-color Eclipse versions of *Miracleman* published in the 1980s. Because of possible legal problems with Marvel, the character's name was changed when these stories appeared in the US. Moore discusses the name change in "M*****man: Full Story and Pics" (31).

25. For this sequence, read *Miracleman* no. 2 (October 1985): 11, 14.

26. See *Miracleman* no. 3 (November 1985), which does not include page numbers.

27. Adilifu Nama discusses the relationship between Captain America and the Falcon in Chapter 3 of *Super Black: American Pop Culture and Black Superheroes*.

28. Alan Moore, letter to the author, early 2013.

29. *Miracleman* no. 5 does not include page numbers.

30. *Miracleman* no. 6 includes page numbers, but they begin on the comic's title page following an introductory sequence.

31. Kempner reports that after this debate these students met with Judge Hubert Delany. As they spoke with him, and after he encouraged them to "fight for justice for all human beings because it is the right thing to do," they abandoned some of their questions in part because "what they hadn't been prepared for was Judge Delany himself. With a newfound respect," she continues, "John said, 'Why, he was a Negro'" (Kempner n.p.).

CHAPTER 5

1. In Chapter 29 of *The Comic Book Heroes from the Silver Age to the Present*, Will Jacobs and Gerard Jones discuss DC's attempt to appeal to fandom's nostalgia for the comic books of the 1940s by bringing back Captain Marvel in the early 1970s. "While the Golden Age seemed intensely interesting when written about glowingly by Jim Steranko," they point out, "the return of Captain Marvel brought home the fact that most of the old comics were light costumed-hero fare of the type that fandom had wanted to leave behind at the end of the Silver Age" (Jacobs and Jones 205). Beck echoes these sentiments about reader responses to DC's *Shazam!* series in "The Man of Steel" and "Are We Living in a Golden Age and Don't Know It?" In the second of those two essays, Beck writes, "Several years ago Sol Harrison, then president of DC, told me at a convention in Philadelphia, 'We proved that the Golden Age can't be brought back, didn't we?'" (Beck, "Are We" 118). DC's *Shazam!* title lasted for thirty-five issues, from late 1972/early 1973 until 1978. The character and the rest of the Marvel Family then appeared, with art by Beck's protégé, Don Newton, as a backup feature in *World's Finest Comics* beginning with issue no. 253 (Oct./Nov. 1978). Since the late 1970s, DC has featured the character in a number of titles, from Jerry Ordway's *The Power of Shazam!* in the 1990s to Grant Morrison's recent and well-received

"Captain Marvel and The Day That Never Was!" in *The Multiversity: Thunderworld Adventures* no. 1 (February 2015).

2. A history of the other Captain Marvels, as well as DC's various revivals of the hero, requires a book all its own. To read more about DC's *Shazam!* from the 1970s, and Beck's involvement with the title, read P. C. Hamerlinck's "Can Lightning Strike Twice? C. C. Beck & the Return of the Big Red Cheese." Aside from Parker and Beck's hero, Captain Mar-Vell, created by Stan Lee and Gene Colan in the late 1960s, is perhaps the best-known character bearing the name. When Roy Thomas took over writing duties on the Marvel Comics title, he and Gil Kane included several direct allusions to the original Fawcett Captain Marvel, not only his costume but also the hero's relationship with Rick Jones, who serves as a kind of alter ago. For more on Captain Mar-vell, read Jacobs and Jones, *The Comic Book Heroes from the Silver Age to the Present* (148, 165–66). Jim Starlin is the writer and artist most closely associated with Captain Mar-Vell because of a popular and innovative run on the character in the early 1970s. For more on Starlin's work, see Jacobs and Jones, Chapter 33 (226–29). Also read Starlin's *The Life and Death of Captain Marvel*, which includes *The Death of Captain Marvel*, the first in Marvel's graphic novel series published in 1982. Other Marvel heroes with the name include Monica Rambeau, a team member of The Avengers in the 1980s, and most recently, Carol Danvers, in Kelly Sue DeConnick's popular *Captain Marvel* series.

3. For more details on Wertham and his impact on comic book history and scholarship, consult Bart Beaty's *Fredric Wertham and the Critique of Mass Culture*. For a more general overview of Wertham's impact on comics in the 1950s, read Bradford W. Wright's *Comic Book Nation*, especially Chapter 6, and David Hadju's *The Ten-Cent Plague: The Great Comic-Book Scare and How It Changed America*. For an assessment of Wertham based on a careful examination of his papers, read Carol L. Tilley's essay "Seducing the Innocent: Fredric Wertham and the Falsifications That Helped Condemn Comics." Tilley's essay also appears with full illustrations in *Alter Ego* vol. 3, no. 128 (September 2014).

4. Beck's drawing of Billy and Captain Marvel appears on the inside back cover of *The Rocket's Blast Special* no. 8, published in the early 1970s.

5. The literature on nostalgia has grown exponentially in the last decade. Aside from the texts I cite in this chapter, there are a number of other resources available. For recent articles on the psychology of nostalgia, read W. Richard Walker and John J. Skowronski's "Autobiographical Memory and the Creation of Meaning from Personally Experienced Events"; Clay Routledge and others' "The Past Makes the Present Meaningful: Nostalgia as an Existential Resource"; Jana Rutherford and Eric H. Shaw's "What Was Old Is New Again: The History of Nostalgia as a Buying Motive in Consumer Behavior"; Rutherford's dissertation "What Is Old Is New Again: The Role of Discontinuity in Nostalgia-Related Consumption"; and Constantine Sedikides and others' "Nostalgia: Past, Present, and Future." For discussions of nostalgia in relation to literature, history, and philosophy, refer to Sinead McDermott's "Future-Perfect: Gender, Nostalgia, and the Not Yet Presented in Marilynne Robinson's *Housekeeping*"; Svetlana Boym's "Nostalgia and Its Discontents," which summarizes some of the key points of her book *The Future of Nostalgia*; Susan J. Matt's "You Can't Go Home Again: Homesickness and Nostalgia in U.S. History" (*Journal of American History* vol. 94, no. 2, September 2007, 469–97); and Leswin Laubscher's "Of Odysseus and Abraham: Nostalgia, *heimweë*, and the Ways (of) Home." Osvaldo Oyola refers to McDermott in his blog post "On Collecting Comics & Critical Nostalgia." For more details on nostalgia and 20th century American culture, read Stephanie Coontz, *The Way We Never Were: American Families and the Nostalgia Trap*. Willis H. McCann provides an overview of

older studies on nostalgia in the article "Nostalgia: A Review of the Literature." George Steiner's *Nostalgia for the Absolute*, broadcast as a series of lectures on the CBC in 1974, foreshadows the concerns of his 1991 book *Real Presences* in his attempt to study the vacuum left behind in Western culture by the gradual erosion of religion: "That nostalgia—so profound, I think, in most of us—was directly provoked by the decline of Western man and society, of the ancient and magnificent architecture of religious certitude" (Steiner 5).

6. James Agee's reviews and discussion of *Let There Be Light* appear in *Agee on Film* (228–29). For a good overview of the history of the film, read Scott Simmon's "*Let There Be Light* (1946) and Its Restoration." I discuss *Let There Be Light* and "Captain Marvel Goes Crazy!" from *Captain Marvel Adventures* no. 56 (March 15, 1946) in "The World's Mightiest Mortal Gets Psychoanalyzed: 'Captain Marvel Goes Crazy!' & John Huston's *Let There Be Light*."

7. In Art Spiegelman's tribute to Kurtzman, first published in *The New Yorker* in 1993 and included in *MetaMaus*, his cartoon avatar notes that "*Mad* was an urban junk collage that said 'Pay attention! The mass media are *lying* to you . . . including this comic book!'" (Spiegelman 191).

8. I discuss Kurtzman, Moore, and Marcuse's "one-dimensional man" in my essay "Quotations from the Future."

9. For more details on these recent studies, read John Tierney's "What Is Nostalgia Good For? Quite a Bit, Research Shows." See also Xinyue Zhou, et al., "Heartwarming Memories: Nostalgia Maintains Physiological Comfort."

10. Ellison, interview with the author, January 2014.

11. Lecture on "The Secret History of Chicago Zines," presented at Powell's University Village store, Chicago, April 19, 2014. Text courtesy of Jake Austen.

12. For histories of fanzine culture in the United States, read Stephen Duncombe's *Notes from Underground: Zines and the Politics of Alternative Culture* (1997; reprinted 2008); Amy Spencer's *DIY: The Rise of Lo-Fi Culture* (2008); Janice Radway's "Zines, Half-Lives, and Afterlives: On the Temporalities of Social and Political Change"; and Anne Elizabeth Moore's "Be a Zinester: How and Why to Publish Your Own Periodical." For specifics on the history of American comic book fanzines in the 1960s, read Bill Schelly's *The Golden Age of Comic Fandom*, especially Chapters 1 and 2 (12–35).

13. In "The Secret History of Chicago Zines," Jake Austen mentions a few of the well-known figures who got their start in the pages of fanzines: "Other early fanzines were produced by devoted, knowledgeable science fiction and fantasy fans, and noted fanzine writers included Ray Bradbury, Harlan Ellison, and Gene Simmons of Kiss." For more on Simmons and his fanzines, see Russ Maheras, "Gene Simmons and KISS: Channeling One's Inner Superhero."

14. Michael E. Uslan explores Binder's relationship with comics fandom in Chapters 8 and 9 of *The Boy Who Loved Batman*.

15. After making this statement, Kerouac goes on to read a passage from *Visions of Cody* (295), a novel written in the early 1950s but not published until 1972, three years after his death. Kerouac also includes the final paragraph from *On the Road* in his performance. Thanks to Beat scholars Tony Trigilio and Kurt Hemmer for their assistance in tracking down this material from *Visions of Cody*.

16. In the typescript of Trina Robbins's "C. C. Beck; An Appreciation," she includes a handwritten note alluding to Beck's use of "open D tuning" when singing and performing.

17. Ellison, interview with the author, January 2014.

18. Moore discusses the influences on his idea for Marvelman/Miracleman in his interview with Khoury (11–12). Pádraig Ó Méalóid traces a few of these influences in his "Alan Moore and *Superfolks*" series of articles for *The Beat*, in which he writes about the possible impact of Robert

Mayer's novel *Superfolks* on Moore's superhero work in the 1980s. See pages 183-184 of Grant Morrison's *Supergods* for a discussion of Captain Marvel, Miracleman, and nostalgia. Morrison argues that Moore's version of Mike Moran "stood for comics' aging demographic," those readers "who'd grown up with these heroes and still found it hard or unreasonable to let go" (184).

19. In his interview with Chris Richards, Moore discusses the impact of New Wave science fiction on his work (Richards, "Alan Moore"). Moore also discusses the musical influences on his work in his *Chain Reaction* interview with Brian Eno and in the article "Indoor Thunder."

20. From Alan Moore, *Miracleman* no. 16 (1). This first page appears on the inside front cover of the issue.

21. See *Miracleman* no. 1 (Eclipse Comics, August 1985): 12–13.

22. For Moran's commute, read *Miracleman* no. 1 (14). He remembers his magic word on pages 16–17 of the same issue (Eclipse Comics, August 1985).

23. See *Miracleman* no. 14 (Eclipse Comics, April 1988): 10–12.

24. The title page of the book incorrectly lists his last name as *Shafenburger*.

25. In *On Photography*, the classic study that shaped Marianne Hirsch's thinking on Spiegelman's *Maus*, Susan Sontag argues that family photographs are filled with "ghostly traces" that "supply the token presence of the dispersed relatives" as they offer us the "imaginary possession of a past that is unreal" (Sontag, *On Photography* 9), perhaps like the one, as Boym and Edward Casey have argued, at the root of some nostalgic reflection.

26. Kidd and Spear's book does not include page numbers, but these photos appear very early in the text as an introduction.

27. In his discussion of the reader's experience of works that devote each page to only one image—wordless novels, for example, or narratives like Martin Vaughn-James's *The Cage*—Thierry Groensteen argues that, unlike a page filled with panels, "dialogue among the images depends on the persistence of the memory of pages already turned" (Groensteen, *Comics and Narration* 35). Hillary Chute, in a brief comparison of comics and film from the introduction to *Graphic Women*, writes that the medium enables "a reader to be in control of when she looks at what and how long she spends on each frame." As a result, she continues, "[o]ne of the important effects of the 'time' of comics, then, is slowed-down reading and looking" (9). In her essay, "'The Shadow of a Past Time': History and Graphic Representation in *Maus*," Chute notes that "[i]n the hybrid form of comics, two narrative tracks never exactly synthesize or fully explain each other" (201). She also cites a 1995 interview in which Art Spiegelman speaks about the "different chunks of time" in comics with "each box being a different moment of time—and you see them all at once. As a result you're always, in comics, being made aware of different times inhabiting the same space" (Chute, "'Shadow'" 201–202).

EPILOGUE

1. Ellison discusses the story's publication history in the liner notes from *Paladin of the Lost Hour*, a recording released in 1995.

2. The back cover of Ellison's 2013 collection *Harlan Ellison's Brain Movies* vol. 5 includes details on his pitch to NBC, in which he noted the various allusions to Hilton, Capra, "the marvelous works of H. P. Lovecraft," "the *Dr. Strange* comics," and "to Billy Batson, Captain Marvel,

and the old wizard Shazam" in *The Dark Forces*. Ellison includes two drafts of the teleplay in the collection on pages 194–356.

3. Thanks to my colleague Dr. Rich Johnson for this translation.

4. In "Theses on the Philosophy of History," Walter Benjamin cautions writers to mind what they say, since "every image of the past that is not recognized by the present as one of its own concerns threatens to disappear irretrievably. (The good tidings which the historian of the past brings with throbbing heart may be lost in a void the very moment he opens his mouth)" (Benjamin, *Illuminations* 255).

5. Beck, letter to Trina Robbins, March 7, 1988.

6. For more on her Garden City lecture, read "Sabra Holbrook to Direct Panel."

7. *Secret Origins* no. 3 features Thomas's adaptation of Billy's first appearance with art by Jerry Bingham and Steve Mitchell.

8. Ellison discusses his time in Chicago and in Evanston, including a reference to his "Dempster Street apartment," in the introduction to *Gentleman Junkie* (14).

9. Specifically, she says, we'd gotten into her rolls of wrapping paper and were "hitting each other" with them.

WORKS CITED

Adams, Michael C. C. *The Best War Ever: America and World War II*. Baltimore: Johns Hopkins University Press, 1994. Print.

Agee, James. *Agee on Film: Criticism and Comment on the Movies*. New York: Modern Library, 2000. Print.

Alleman, Alli. "Re: CM Question." Message to the author, October 12, 2015. E-mail.

"America's Greatest Comics #2." Entry from the *Grand Comics Database*, December 15, 2015. Web.

Arlen, Harold (music), and Johnny Mercer (lyrics). "Ac-Cent-Tchu-Ate the Positive." Bing Crosby and the Andrews Sisters. Decca Records, 1944.

Army War Show. Soldier Field, Chicago, September 2–12, 1942. Army Emergency Relief. Ticket for admission to the show.

Army War Show Provisional Task Force 1942. Atlanta: Albert Love Enterprises, n.d. (circa 1942/43). Print.

Arnold, Gene. *The Rocket's Blast Special* no. 8 (fanzine devoted to "Captain Marvel, World's Mightiest Mortal"). Miami: S. F. C. A./G. B. Love, 1970. Print.

Asimov, Isaac. *I, Robot*. Greenwich, CT: Fawcett Publications, 1970. Print.

———. Introduction to "I, Robot." By Otto Binder. *Isaac Asimov Presents: The Great SF Stories 1 (1939)*. Eds. Isaac Asimov and Martin H. Greenberg. New York: DAW Books, 1979: 11. Print.

———. "The Story Behind the Robot Novels." *The Caves of Steel*. New York: Bantam Books, 1991: vii–xvi. Print.

Atkinson, Rick. *An Army at Dawn: The War in North Africa, 1942–1943*. New York: Henry Holt, 2002. Print.

Attack: The Story of the United States Army. Army Emergency Relief booklet published to accompany the Army War Show, 1942. Print. Includes text piece "Here's YOUR Army!"

Austen, Jake, and James Porter. "The Secret History of Chicago Zines." Lecture presented at Powell's Books, Chicago, Illinois, April 19, 2014. Copy of the lecture courtesy of the authors.

Banas, Gary. "Army War Show—Provisional Task Force 1942." *Trading Post* (American Society of Military Insignia Collectors), April–June 2003: 31–33. Print.

Barrier, Michael, and Martin Williams, eds. *A Smithsonian Book of Comic-Book Comics*. New York: Smithsonian Institution Press and Harry N. Abrams, 1981. Print.

Beaty, Bart. *Comics Versus Art*. Toronto: University of Toronto Press, 2012. Print.

———. *Fredric Wertham and the Critique of Mass Culture*. Jackson: University Press of Mississippi, 2005. Print.

Beck, C. C. "Apples and Oranges." *FCA (Fawcett Collectors of America)/SOB* no. 14/3 (August 1980): N.p. Courtesy of the Comic Art Collection, Michigan State University.

———. "Are Some of the Problems of Comic Illustration Insoluble?" 1988. TS. Collection of Trina Robbins, San Francisco.

———. "Are We Living in the Golden Age and Don't Know It?" *The Comics Journal* no. 135 (April 1990): 117–18. Print.

———., ed. "Autobiographies of Critical Circle Members 1989," July 28, 1989. TS. Collection of Trina Robbins, San Francisco.

———. "Childhood Habits," 1988. TS. Collection of Trina Robbins, San Francisco.

———. "Comic Books for Grown-Ups." *The Comics Journal* no. 113 (December 1986): 7. Print.

———. Deposition of C. Clarence Beck. *Detective Comics, Inc. and Superman, Inc. vs. Fawcett Publications, Inc., et al.,* United States District Court S.D. New York. April 12–18, May 2, 1944. National Archives, New York City.

———. "Golden Ages," July 28, 1989. TS. Collection of Trina Robbins, San Francisco.

———. "Good Art." *The Comics Journal* no. 106 (March 1986): 7–9. Print.

———. "Good Taste in Comic Art," 1988. TS. Collection of Trina Robbins, San Francisco.

———. "The Human Quality of the Captain Marvel Characters." *Fawcett Companion: The Best of FCA (Fawcett Collectors of America).* Ed. P. C. Hamerlinck. Raleigh: TwoMorrows Publishing, 2001: 28–29. Print.

———. Interview with Bruce Hamilton. "Introduction . . . Bruce Hamilton Talks to C. C. Beck." *Special Edition Series 1: A Complete Collection of Captain Marvel Adventures from* Whiz Comics 7–28. By Alan Light, Bruce Hamilton, and Murray Bishoff. East Moline, IL: Special Edition Reprints, 1974: N.p. Print.

———. Interview with Chris Padovano. *Fan* (1977): N.p. Print.

———. "Is the Wagon Coming to Take Me Away to the Lard Factory?" April 17, 1989. TS. Collection of Trina Robbins, San Francisco.

———. Letter to the Critical Circle, February 20, 1989. TS. Collection of Trina Robbins, San Francisco.

———. Letter to the Critical Circle, July 28, 1989. TS. Collection of Trina Robbins, San Francisco.

———. Letter to Critical Circle Members about his stroke, September 25, 1989. TS. Collection of Trina Robbins, San Francisco.

———. Letter to Trina Robbins, March 7, 1988. TS. Collection of Trina Robbins, San Francisco.

———. Letter to Trina Robbins, January 5, 1989. TS. Collection of Trina Robbins, San Francisco.

———. Letter to Trina Robbins, June 19, 1989. Collection of Trina Robbins, San Francisco.

———. "The Man of Steel." *The Comics Journal* no. 112 (October 1986): 6–7. Print.

———. "May We Have the Next Slide Please?" *Inside Comics* vol. 1, no. 4 (Winter 1974–75): 24–26. Print.

———. "Mr. Mind and the Monster Society of Evil." *The Comic Book Price Guide* no. 15 (1985–86). By Robert M. Overstreet. New York: Harmony Books, 1985: A–89–A–93. Print.

———. "Name Calling and Verbal Abuse in the Comic World," March 15, 1989. TS. Collection of Trina Robbins, San Francisco.

———. "Name Calling and Verbal Abuse in the Comics [*sic*] World." *Comics Journal* no. 131 (September 1989): 109. Print. (I cite from Beck's original manuscript in my references to this essay.)

———. "Never draw any more than necessary." Letter to Trina Robbins, n.d. (probably 1988). TS. Collection of Trina Robbins, San Francisco.

———. "Preacher's Son." Edited and designed by P. C. Hamerlinck. *Streetwise: Autobiographical Stories by Comic Book Professionals*. Eds. Jon B. Cooke and John Morrow. Raleigh: TwoMorrows Publishing, 2000: 59–67. Print.

———. "Racial Inheritance in Story and Art," May 26, 1989. TS. Collection of Trina Robbins, San Francisco.

———. "Real Facts About an Unreal Character," July 14, 1988. TS. Collection of Trina Robbins, San Francisco.

———. "Sex and Violence in Comics." *The Comics Journal* no. 117 (September 1987): 128. Print.

———. *The Shazam! Archives* vol. 1. New York: DC Comics, 1992. Print.

———. "Some Basic Principles of Comic Art," June 4, 1988. TS. Collection of Trina Robbins, San Francisco.

———. Trial tr. *Detective Comics, Inc. and Superman, Inc. vs. Fawcett Publications, Inc., Republic Pictures Corporation, and Republic Productions, Inc.* New York, March 1948. United States District Court S.D. New York. National Archives, New York City.

———. Untitled cartoon of Billy and Captain Marvel from the inside back cover of *The Rocket's Blast Special* no. 8 (N.d., early 1970s). Print.

———. "Vanishing Point." *Astounding Science Fiction* vol. LXIII, no. 5 (July 1959): 135–39. Print.

———. "What Kind of Writing and Art Do You Prefer?" January 19, 1989. TS. Collection of Trina Robbins, San Francisco.

———. "What Really Killed Captain Marvel?" 1988. TS. Collection of Trina Robbins, San Francisco.

———. "The World's Mightiest Fat Head." *The Comics Journal* no. 226 (August 2000): part 1, 36–61. Print.

———. "The World's Mightiest Fat Head." *The Comics Journal* no. 227 (September 2000): part 2, 83–104. Print.

Benesch, Otto. *Rembrandt as a Draughtsman: An Essay with 115 Illustrations*. London: Phaidon Press, 1960. Print.

Benét, Stephen Vincent. *The Devil and Daniel Webster*. New York: Farrar & Rinehart, 1937. Print.

Benjamin, Walter. *The Arcades Project*. Trans. Howard Eiland and Kevin McLaughlin. Cambridge: Belknap Press, 1999. Print.

———. *Illuminations: Essays and Reflections*. Trans. Harry Zohn. New York: Schocken Books, 1968. Print.

Berger, John. "Why Look at Animals?" *About Looking*. New York: Pantheon Books, 1980: 1–26. Print.

Best, Daniel. "DC vs. Siegel: DC's Appeal Brief & Who DID Draw the *Action Comics* #1 Cover?" *20th Century Danny Boy*, March 29, 2012. Web. December 9, 2015.

Best, Mark. "Domesticity, Homosociality, and Male Power in Superhero Comics of the 1950s." *Iowa Journal of Cultural Studies* no. 6 (Spring 2005): 80–99. Print.

Binder, Eando. *Adam Link—Robot*. New York: Paperback Library, 1965. Print.

———. *Lords of Creation*. Philadelphia: Prime Press, 1949. Print.

———. "Testing, Testing." *Universe Science Fiction* no. 5 (May 1954): 114–24. Print.

Binder, Earl. Letter to Otto Binder, April 6, 1936. TS. Cushing Memorial Library and Archives, Texas A&M University.

Binder, Otto. Letter to Earl Binder, January 20, 1936. TS. Cushing Memorial Library and Archives, Texas A&M University.

———. Letter to Earl Binder, June 7, 1936. TS. Cushing Memorial Library and Archives, Texas A&M University.

———. Letter to Sol Cohen, March 12, 1953. TS. Cushing Memorial Library and Archives, Texas A&M University.

———. Letter to Horace Gold, February 21, 1953. TS. Cushing Memorial Library and Archives, Texas A&M University.

———. Letter to Sam Moskowitz, October 4, 1952. TS. Cushing Memorial Library and Archives, Texas A&M University.

———. Letter to Sam Moskowitz, October 15, 1952. TS. Cushing Memorial Library and Archives, Texas A&M University.

———. Letter to "Shazamail!" *Shazam!* vol. 1, no. 4. New York: National Periodical Publications, Inc. (July 1973): N.p. Print.

———. Letter to Oswald ("Ozzie") Train, November 7, 1953. TS. Cushing Memorial Library and Archives, Texas A&M University.

———. "Memoirs of a Nobody," n.d. TS. Cushing Memorial Library and Archives, Texas A&M University. In *Words*, Schelly dates the manuscript to 1948. See pp. 114-116.

———. "Otto in Binderland." *Alter Ego: The Best of the Legendary Comics Fanzine.* Eds. Roy Thomas and Bill Schelly. Raleigh: TwoMorrows Publishing, 2008: 142–43. Print.

———. "*Questions—on what to do about CMA from now on. . . .,*" n.d. (probably 1952). Cushing Memorial Library and Archives, Texas A&M University.

———. "Special!—A Long, Long Letter from Mr. Marvel Family Himself—Otto Binder!" *Alter Ego: The Best of the Legendary Comics Fanzine.* Eds. Roy Thomas and Bill Schelly. Raleigh: TwoMorrows Publishing, 2008: 110–12. Print.

———. "The Teacher from Mars." *My Best Science Fiction Story.* Eds. Leo Margulies and Oscar J. Friend. New York: Pocket Books, 1954: 18–19. Print. The editors include Binder's preface to the story.

———. "'We Were More or Less Inspired.'" Interview with Matt Lage. *Fawcett Companion: The Best of FCA (Fawcett Collectors of America).* Ed. P. C. Hamerlinck. Raleigh: TwoMorrows Publishing, 2001: 59–64. Print.

———. *What We Really Know About Flying Saucers.* Greenwich, CT: Fawcett Publications, 1967. Print.

Binder, Otto, writer. C. C. Beck, artist. *Fatman, the Human Flying Saucer* no. 2. St. Louis: Milson Publishing Co., Inc., June 1969. Print.

———. "Fatman Meets Tinman!" *Fatman, the Human Flying Saucer* no. 1. St. Louis: Milson Publishing Publishing Co., Inc., April 1967: N.p. Print.

Bogle, Donald. *Toms, Coons, Mulattoes, Mammies, & Bucks: An Interpretive History of Blacks in American Films.* New York: Continuum, 1993. Print.

Bowser, Pearl, and Louise Spence. *Writing Himself into History: Oscar Micheaux, His Films, and His Audiences.* New Brunswick, NJ: Rutgers University Press, 2000. Print.

Boyd, Robert. "Captain Marvel Artist, C. C. Beck, Dead at 79." *The Comics Journal* no. 134 (February 1990): 14. Print.

Boym, Svetlana. *Architecture of the Off-Modern.* New York: Temple Hoyne Buell Center for the Study of American Architecture and Princeton Architectural Press, 2008. Print.

———. *The Future of Nostalgia.* New York: Basic Books, 2001. Print.

———. "Nostalgia and Its Discontents." *Hedgehog Review* (Summer 2007): 7–18. Print.

Brideau, Neil. "Product Description" for Sam Sharpe's *Viewotron* no. 2. *Radiator Comics*, n.d. Web. December 9, 2015.

Bridwell, E. Nelson. Introduction. *Shazam! from the Forties to the Seventies*. New York: Harmony Books, 1977: 7–16. Print.

Bridwell, E. Nelson, plot. Martin Pasko, script. Dick Dillin and Frank McLaughlin, artists. Julius Schwartz, editor. "Crisis in Eternity." *Justice League of America* vol. 17, no. 135 (October 1976). New York. DC/National Periodical Publications, Inc. Print.

———, plot. Martin Pasko, script. Dick Dillin and Frank McLaughlin, artists. Julius Schwartz, editor. "Crisis on Earth-S!" *Justice League of America* vol. 17, no. 136 (November 1976). New York: DC/National Periodical Publications, Inc. Print.

———, plot. Martin Pasko, script. Dick Dillin and Frank McLaughlin, artists. Julius Schwartz, editor. "Crisis in Tomorrow!" *Justice League of America* vol. 17, no. 137 (December 1976). New York: DC/National Periodical Publications, Inc. Print.

Broadfoot, Barry. *Six War Years, 1939–1945: Memories of Canadians at Home and Abroad*. Toronto: Doubleday Canada, 1974. Print.

Brown, Gary. "C. C. Beck." *Monster Times* no. 25 (August 1973): 6–7. Print.

Brown, Gary, and Wayne DeWald. "Captain Marvel Is No Superman, But . . ." *Comixscene* no. 2 (January–February 1973): 6–8. Print.

"C. C. Beck." *The Art of Don Newton*, n.d. Web. December 19, 2015.

Camelon, David. "Parade U.S. Might in Rain at War Show." *Chicago Herald-American*, September 3, 1942: 6. Print. Clipping courtesy of the Harold Washington Library, Chicago.

Campbell, John W., Jr. Letter to Otto O. Binder, February 15, 1938. TS. Cushing Memorial Library and Archives, Texas A&M University.

Campiti, David. "When lightning struck the final time." *Comics Buyer's Guide* no. 840 (December 22, 1989): 27. Print.

"Captain Marvel Adventures #12." Entry from the *Grand Comics Database*, n.d. Web. December 15, 2015.

"Captain Marvel Adventures #42." Entry from the *Grand Comics Database*, n.d. Web. December 15, 2015.

"Captain Marvel and the Adventure Within an Adventure." *Captain Marvel Adventures* vol. 17, no. 102. Greenwich, CT: Fawcett Publications, Inc. (November 1949): N.p. Print.

"Captain Marvel and His Feud with Mr. Tawny." *Captain Marvel Adventures* vol. 19, no. 113. Greenwich, CT: Fawcett Publications, Inc. (October 1950): N.p. Print.

"Capt. Marvel and the Mark of the Black Swastika." *Captain Marvel Adventures* vol. 4, no. 20. Louisville, KY: Fawcett Publications, Inc. (January 22, 1943): 4–19. Print.

"Captain Marvel and Mr. Tawny's New Home!" *Captain Marvel Adventures* vol. 15, no. 90. Greenwich, CT: Fawcett Publications, Inc. (November 1948): N.p. Print. (Beck receives credit as "Chief Artist" on the first page of this issue.)

"Captain Marvel and Mr. Tawny's Quest for Youth." *Captain Marvel Adventures* vol. 22, no. 131. Greenwich, CT: Fawcett Publications, Inc. (April 1952): N.p. Print.

"Captain Marvel and the Return of Mr. Tawny." *Captain Marvel Adventures* vol. 14, no. 82. Greenwich, CT: Fawcett Publications, Inc. (March 1948): N.p. Print. (The title page lists Beck as the "Chief Artist" of this issue.)

"Captain Marvel and the Talking Tiger." *Captain Marvel Adventures* vol. 14, no. 79. Greenwich, CT: Fawcett Publications, Inc. (December 1947). Print.

"Capt. Marvel and the Voodoo Showboat." *Captain Marvel Adventures* vol. 4, no. 22. Louisville, KY: Fawcett Publications, Inc. (March 26, 1943): 20–31. Print. (Don Maris includes a black-and-white reprint of this story in his 1975 "best of" collection. I have scanned images from Maris's collection for inclusion in Chapter 4.)

"Captain Marvel and the Warrior of Wai." *Captain Marvel Adventures* vol. 2, no. 10. Louisville, KY: Fawcett Publications, Inc. (May 1, 1942): 44–52. Print.

"Captain Marvel and the World's Mightiest Dream!" *Captain Marvel Adventures* vol. 8, no. 48. Greenwich, CT: Fawcett Publications, Inc. (Aug.–Sept. 1945): N.p. Print. (The tile page lists Beck as the "Chief Artist" for this issue.)

"Captain Marvel Battles the Plot Against the Universe." *Captain Marvel Adventures* vol. 17, no. 100. Greenwich, CT: Fawcett Publications, Inc. (September 1949): N.p. Print. (Barrier and Williams include this story in *A Smithsonian Book of Comic-Book Comics* 81–113.)

"Captain Marvel in Mr. Tawny . . . Hermit." *Captain Marvel Adventures* vol. 25, no. 149. Greenwich, CT: Fawcett Publications, Inc. (October 1953): N.p. Print.

"Captain Marvel in the World of If." *Captain Marvel Adventures* vol. 7. no. 42. Greenwich, CT: Fawcett Publications, Inc. (January 1945): N.p. Print. (Don Maris includes a black-and-white reprint of this story in his 1975 "best of" collection. In the original issue, the title page lists Beck as the "Chief Artist.")

"Captain Marvel Joins the Army." *Captain Marvel Adventures* vol. 2, no. 12. Louisville, KY: Fawcett Publication, Inc. (June 26, 1942): 4–19. Print.

"Captain Marvel: Mr. Tawny's Fight for Fame." *Captain Marvel Adventures* vol. 21, no. 126. Greenwich, CT: Fawcett Publications, Inc. (November 1951): N.p. Print. For scans, I have used the reprint of this story that appears in *Shazam!* vol. 2, no. 14. New York: National Periodical Publications (September–October 1974): 53–58. Print. The reprint credits the art to Beck.

Casey, Edward S. "The World of Nostalgia." *Man and World* 20 (1987): 361–84. Print.

Catalog of Copyright Entries (Periodicals). Part 2, new series, vol. 35, no. 1 (January–December 1940). Washington, DC: United States Government Printing Office, 1941. Print.

———. New series, vol. 37, nos. 1–4 (January–December 1942). Washington, DC: United States Government Printing Office, 1943. Print.

———. New series, vol. 38, nos. 1–4 (January–December 1943). Washington, DC: Library of Congress Copyright Office, 1943. Print.

———. Part 2, new series, vol. 40, nos. 1–4 (January–December 1945). Washington, DC: United States Government Printing Office, 1946. Print.

———. Third series, vol. 2, part 2, no. 1 (January–June 1948). Washington, DC: Library of Congress Copyright Office, 1948. Print.

———. Third series, vol. 5, part 2, no. 1 (January–June 1951). Washington, DC: Library of Congress Copyright Office, 1951. Print.

———. Third series, vol. 6, part 2, nos. 1–2 (January–December 1952). Washington, DC: Library of Congress Copyright Office, 1952. Print.

———. Third series, vol. 7, part 2, no. 1 (January–June 1953). Washington, DC: Library of Congress Copyright Office, 1954. Print.

"City Gets Taste of War in Army Show's Preview." *Chicago Daily Tribune*, September 2, 1942: 12. Print. Clipping courtesy of the Harold Washington Library, Chicago.

Chaney, Michael. "Animal Subjects of the Graphic Novel." *College Literature* vol. 38, no. 3 (Summer 2011): 129–49. Print.

Chute, Hillary L. *Graphic Women: Life Narrative & Contemporary Comics*. New York: Columbia University Press, 2010. Print.

———. "'The Shadow of a Past Time': History and Graphic Representation in *Maus*." *Twentieth Century Literature: A Scholarly and Critical Journal* 52.2 (2006): 199–230. Print.

Cooksey, Thomas L. "*The Devil and Daniel Webster, Cabin in the Sky*, and *Damn Yankees*—American Contributions to the Faust Legend." *Journal of Popular Film and Television* vol. 27, no. 3 (Fall 1999): 18–27. Print.

Coontz, Stephanie. *The Way We Never Were: American Families and the Nostalgia Trap*. New York: Basic Books, 1992. Print.

Corrigan, R. A. "Somewhere West of Laramie, on the Road to West Egg: Automobiles, Fillies, and the West in *The Great Gatsby*." *Journal of Popular Culture* vol. 7, no. 1 (Summer 1973): 152–58. Print.

Costello, Brannon. "Fascism and Mass Culture in Howard Chaykin's *Blackhawk*." *ImageText* vol. 7, no. 2: N.p. Web. December 9, 2015.

Costello, Brannon, and Qiana Whitted, eds. *Comics and the U.S. South*. Jackson: University Press of Mississippi, 2012. Print.

Crabb, Cindy. "Cape Cod." *Doris* no. 31 (2014): N.p. Print.

———. "i believe." *The Encyclopedia of Doris*. Athens, OH: Doris Press, 2011: 18–19. Print.

Cremins, Brian. "Bumbazine, Blackness, and the Myth of the Redemptive South in Walt Kelly's *Pogo*." *Comics and the U.S. South*. Eds. Brannon Costello and Qiana J. Whitted. Jackson: University Press of Mississippi, 2012: 29–61. Print.

———. "Captain Marvel, *The Master*, and the Feminine Embrace." *The Comics Grid* (December 6, 2012). Web. December 9, 2015.

———. "Is Otto Binder and Joe Orlando's 'I, Robot' a Protest Novel?" *The Hooded Utilitarian*, January 2, 2014. Web. December 9, 2015.

———. "'Join the Parade to Victory!': Captain Marvel and the Army War Show—June 1942." Ed. P. C. Hamerlinck. *Alter Ego* vol. 2, no. 121 (November 2013)/*P. C. Hamerlinck's Fawcett Collectors of America* no. 172 (October 2012): 76–80. Print.

———. "'A Leader of Men': Bill Parker on King Arthur & the Origin of Captain Marvel (excerpts from Parker's 1948 Testimony)." Ed. P. C. Hamerlinck. *Alter Ego* vol. 3, no. 131 (March 2015)/*P. C. Hamerlinck's Fawcett Collectors of America* no. 190 (March 2015): 76–80. Print.

———. "Nostalgia and *Strange Tales* #180." *The Comics Grid* vol. 3 (January 24, 2013). Web. December 9, 2015.

———. "Otto Binder's Magic Words: The Writer's Plan to Save *Captain Marvel Adventures*." Ed. P. C. Hamerlinck. *Alter Ego* vol. 3, no. 123 (March 2014)/*P. C. Hamerlinck's Fawcett Collectors of America* no. 182 (March 2014): 77–80. Print.

———. "Quotations from the Future: Harvey Kurtzman's 'Superduperman,' Nostalgia, and Alan Moore's *Miracleman*." *Studies in American Humor*, new series 3, no. 30 (2014): 169–89. Print.

———. "The Secret Life of Mr. Tawny: *Captain Marvel Adventures* #102 & James Thurber's Walter Mitty." Ed. P. C. Hamerlinck. *Alter Ego* vol. 3, no. 125 (June 2014)/*P. C. Hamerlinck's Fawcett Collectors of America* no. 184 (June 2014): 77–80. Print.

———. "'What Manner of Man Is He?': Humor and Masculine Identity in Captain Marvel's World War II Adventures." *Studies in American Humor* new series 3, no. 27 (2013): 33–62. Print.

———. "The World's Mightiest Mortal Gets Psychoanalyzed: 'Captain Marvel Goes Crazy!' & John Huston's *Let There Be Light.*" Ed. P. C. Hamerlinck. *Alter Ego* vol. 3, no. 127 (August 2014)/*P. C. Hamerlinck's Fawcett Collectors of America* no. 187 (August 2014): 77–80. Print.

Cronin, Brian. "Comic Book Legends Revealed #467." *Comic Book Resources*, April 18, 2014. Web. December 9, 2015.

Daniels, Les. *Comix: A History of Comic Books in America.* New York: Bonanza Books, 1971. Print.

Darius, Julian. "Evelyn Cream and Race in *Miracleman*, Chapter 9." *Sequart Organization*, March 4, 2013. Web. December 9, 2015.

Daston, Lorraine, and Gregg Mitman, eds. *Thinking with Animals: New Perspectives on Anthropomorphism.* New York: Columbia University Press, 2005. Print.

Davis, Fred. *Yearning for Yesterday: A Sociology of Nostalgia.* New York: Free Press, 1979. Print.

Debord, Guy. *The Society of the Spectacle.* No translator listed. Detroit: Black & Red, 1983. Print.

Decker, Dwight R. "Some Opinionated Bastards." *The Comics Journal* no. 64 (July 1981): 107. Print.

DeConnick, Kelly Sue, writer. David Lopez, artist. *Captain Marvel, Vol. 1: Higher, Further, Faster, More.* New York: Marvel Comics, 2014. Print.

De Fuccio, Jerry. "Charles Clarence Beck: The World's Second Mightiest Mortal." *The Comic Book Price Guide* no. 15 (1985–86). By Robert M. Overstreet. New York: Harmony Books, 1985: A-78–A-88. Print.

Delany, Samuel R. *Times Square Red, Times Square Blue.* New York: New York University Press, 1999. Print.

De La Ree, Gerry. "Captain Marvel's Mouthpiece: Poor Boy's Superman Has a Ghost Writer Living in Englewood." *Bergen Evening Record Week-end Magazine*, February 7, 1953: 2–3. Print. Scan courtesy of the George T. Potter Library, Ramapo College of New Jersey.

Dettelbach, Cynthia Golomb. *In the Driver's Seat: The Automobile in American Literature and Popular Culture.* Westport, CT: Greenwood Press, 1976. Print.

Dorfman, Ariel. *The Empire's Old Clothes: What the Lone Ranger, Babar, and Other Innocent Heroes Do to Our Minds.* Durham: Duke University Press, 2010. Print.

Dos Passos, John. *U.S.A. (The 42nd Parallel, 1919, The Big Money).* New York: Library of America, 1996. Print.

Du Bois, W. E. B. *The Souls of Black Folk.* New York: Bantam, 2005. Print.

Duck, Leigh Anne. *The Nation's Region: Southern Modernism, Segregation, and U.S. Nationalism.* Athens: University of Georgia Press, 2006. Print.

Duncombe, Stephen. *Notes from Underground: Zines and the Politics of Alternative Culture.* Bloomington: Microcosm Publishing, 2008. Print.

"Dwayne Johnson reveals Shazam DC movie role?" *Total Film.* YouTube, July 21, 2014. Web. December 9, 2015.

Ebert, Roger. "Introduction: How Propellor-Heads, BNFs, Sercon Geeks, Newbies, Recovering GAFIAtors and Kids in Basements Invented the World Wide Web, All Except for the Delivery System." *The Best of Xero.* Eds. Pat Lupoff and Dick Lupoff. San Francisco: Tachyon Publications, 2004: 1–11. Print.

Ehrenbard, Bob. "Youthbuilders 'Outlaw' Intolerance: Their Business Is Practicing Democracy." *New York Amsterdam News*, February 7, 1948. The Papers of the NAACP, Richard J. Daley Library, University of Illinois Chicago.

Eisner, Will. "C. C. Beck." *Will Eisner's Shop Talk.* Milwaukie, OR: Dark Horse Comics: 52–75. Print.

————. *Comics & Sequential Art*. Tamarac, FL: Poorhouse Press, 2001. Print.

————. *Graphic Storytelling*. Tamarac, FL: Poorhouse Press, 1996. Print.

Ellison, Harlan. "The Children of Nights." *Gentleman Junkie and Other Stories of the Hung-Up Generation*. New York: Pyramid Books, 1975: 11–22. Print.

————. *Harlan Ellison's Brain Movies* vol. 5. Los Angeles: An Edgeworks Abbey Offering, 2013. Print.

————. "Harlan Talks About Writing 'Paladin.'" *Harlan Ellison Reads Paladin of the Lost Hour*. Sherman Oaks, CA: Harlan Ellison Recording Collection, 1995. CD.

————. "'Nay, Never Will I Serve Thee, Mr. Mind!' Or, 'I Think I Was Always a Fawcett Kid.'" Phone interview with the author, January 20, 2014. Edited and expanded for publication by Ellison in the summer of 2014.

————. "Paladin of the Lost Hour." *Angry Candy*. Boston: Houghton Mifflin, 1988. 3–25. Print.

Ellison, Ralph. "Twentieth-Century Fiction and the Black Mask of Humanity." *Shadow & Act*. New York: Signet, 1964: 42–60. Print.

Famous First Edition no. C-26 (reprint of *Action Comics* no. 1). New York: National Periodical Publications, Inc., 1974. Print.

Famous First Edition vol. 1, no. F-4 (reprint of *Whiz Comics* no. 2). New York: National Periodical Publications, Inc., Oct.–Nov. 1974. Print.

"Fan-Man Feedback." *Fatman, the Human Flying Saucer* no. 1. St. Louis: Milson Publishing, April 1967: N.p. Print.

Fanon, Frantz. *Black Skin, White Masks*. Trans. Richard Philcox. New York: Grove Press, 2008. Print.

Feiffer, Jules. *The Great Comic Book Heroes*. New York: Bonanaza Books, 1965. Print.

Fitzgerald, F. Scott. *The Great Gatsby*. New York: Scribner, 1925. Print.

Frensley, Erika. "Pulps—Television of the 1930s." *Pulp Masters*. Ed. James Van Hise. Self-published (revised edition, February 2002): 4–10. Print.

Freud, Sigmund. *The Uncanny*. Trans. David McClintock. New York: Penguin Books, 2003. Print.

Friend, Oscar J. Letter to Otto Binder, July 6, 1953. TS. Cushing Memorial Library and Archives, Texas A&M University.

————. Letter to Otto Binder, August 8, 1953. TS. Cushing Memorial Library and Archives, Texas A&M University.

Frost, William Henry. *The Knights of the Round Table: Stories of King Arthur and the Holy Grail*. New York: Charles Scribner's Sons, 1898. Print.

Fussell, Paul. *Wartime: Understanding and Behavior in the Second World War*. New York: Oxford University Press, 1989. Print.

Gabilliet, Jean-Paul. *Of Comics and Men: A Cultural History of American Comic Books*. Trans. Bart Beaty and Nick Nguyen. Jackson: University Press of Mississippi, 2010. Print.

Gavaler, Chris. "Time-Traveling Supervillain Gatsby the Great." *The Hooded Utilitarian*, May 30, 2012. Web. December 9, 2015.

Gillman, Abigail E. "In Kafka's Synagogue." *Journal of the Kafka Society of America* vol. 26, nos. 1–2 (June 2002): 11–17. Print.

Gilroy, Paul. *Darker Than Blue: On the Moral Economies of Black Atlantic Culture*. Cambridge: Belknap Press, 2010. Print.

Gold, Horace L. Letter to Otto Binder, February 17, 1953. TS. Cushing Memorial Library and Archives, Texas A&M University.

Goulart, Ron. *The Great Comic Book Artists*. New York: St. Martin's Press, 1986. Print.

———. *Ron Goulart's Great History of Comic Books*. New York: Contemporary Books, 1986. Print.

Green, Justin. *Binky Brown Meets the Holy Virgin Mary*. Berkeley, CA: Last Gasp, 1972. Print.

Groensteen, Thierry. *Comics and Narration*. Trans. Ann Miller. Jackson: University Press of Mississippi, 2013. Print.

———. *The System of Comics*. Trans. Bart Beaty and Nick Nguyen. Jackson: University Press of Mississippi, 2007. Print.

———. "Why Are Comics Still in Search of Cultural Legitimization?" Trans. Shirley Smolderen. *A Comics Studies Reader*. Eds. Jeet Heer and Kent Worcester. Jackson: University Press of Mississippi, 2009: 3–11. Print.

Groth, Gary. Letter to C. C. Beck, July 28, 1989. TS. Collection of Trina Robbins, San Francisco.

———. "'With One Magic Word . . .': An Interview with C. C. Beck." *The Comics Journal* no. 95 (February 1985): 57–77. Print.

Guise, Kimberly. "The Army War Show." *See & Hear: Museum Blog*, the National WWII Museum. June 12, 2012. Web. December 9, 2015.

Hadju, David. *The Ten-Cent Plague: The Great Comic-Book Scare and How It Changed America*. New York: Picador, 2009. Print.

Hamerlinck, P. C. "Introduction." *Fawcett Companion: The Best of FCA (Fawcett Collectors of America)*. Ed. P. C. Hamerlinck. Raleigh: TwoMorrows Publishing, 2001: 6–7. Print.

———, ed. *Fawcett Companion: The Best of FCA (Fawcett Collectors of America)*. Raleigh: TwoMorrows Publishing, 2001. Print.

Hamerlinck, Paul. "Speak My Name! The Origin of Captain Marvel (Bill Parker's Story Adapted by Original Artist C. C. Beck)." Afterword by Paul Hamerlinck. *Alter Ego* no. 110 (June 2012): 65–70. Print.

Hamerlinck, Paul Charles. "Can Lightning Strike Twice? C. C. Beck & the Return of the Big Red Cheese." *Comic Book Artist* vol. 1, no. 1 (Spring 1998): 61–63. Print.

Hamilton, Bruce. "Introduction . . . Bruce Hamilton Talks to C. C. Beck." *Special Edition Series 1: A Complete Collection of Captain Marvel Adventures from* Whiz Comics 7–28. By Alan Light, Bruce Hamilton, and Murray Bishoff. East Moline, IL: Special Edition Reprints, 1974: N.p. Print.

Hamm, Charles. *Yesterdays: Popular Song in America*. New York: W. W. Norton, 1979. Print.

Hanssen, Beatrice. *Walter Benjamin's Other History: Of Stones, Animals, Human Beings, and Angels*. Berkeley: University of California Press, 1998. Print.

Hatfield, Charles. *Alternative Comics: An Emerging Literature*. Jackson: University Press of Mississippi, 2005. Print.

Heer, Jeet. From "A Colloquy on Classic Kids' Comics Moderated by Art Spiegelman with Paul Karasik, Jeff Smith, Seth, Paul Levitz, Monte Wolverton, Michael Barrier, Jeet Heer, Frank Young, Chris Duffy, Bob Heer and Others." *The Comics Journal* no. 302 (January 2013): 236–360. Print.

Heintjes, Tom. "An Interview with C. C. Beck." *Hogan's Alley*, May 4, 2012. Web. December 1, 2015.

Helfer, Andrew, writer. Kyle Baker, artist. Bob Lappan, letters. *Justice, Inc.* (Books One and Two). New York: DC Comics, 1989. Print.

"Here's YOUR Army!" *Attack: The Story of the United States Army*. Washington, DC: Army Emergency Relief, 1942: N.p. Print.

Hilton, James. *Lost Horizon*. New York: Harper Perennial, 2012. Print.

Hirsch, Marianne. *Family Frames: Photography, Narrative, and Postmemory*. Cambridge: Harvard University Press, 1997. Print.

———. *The Generation of Postmemory: Writing and Visual Culture After the Holocaust*. New York: Columbia University Press, 2012. Print.

Hoberman, J. *On Jack Smith's* Flaming Creatures *(and Other Secret-Flix of Cinemaroc)*. New York: Granary Books/Hips Road, 2001. Print.

Hoberman, J., and Jonathan Rosenbaum. *Midnight Movies*. New York: Da Capo Press, 1991. Print.

Hofer, Johannes. "Medical Dissertation on Nostalgia by Johannes Hofer." Trans. Carolyn Kiser Anspach. *Bulletin of the Institute of the History of Medicine* vol. 2 (August 1934): 376–91. Print.

Holbrook, Sabra. *Children Object*. New York: Viking Press, 1943. Print.

———. Letter to Ruby Hurley, 1948. TS. From the Papers of the NAACP, Richard J. Daley Library, University of Illinois Chicago.

Hollingshead, August B. "Adjustment to Military Life." *American Journal of Psychology* vol. 51, no. 5 (March 1946): 439–47. Print.

How to Draw for the Comics. New York: Street & Smith, n.d. Print. (Includes short biographies of George Marcoux and Jack Binder.)

Ingersoll, Bob. "The Cheese Stands Accused! A Look at the Superman/Captain Marvel Litigation." *Alter Ego* vol. 3, no. 3 (Winter 2000): 20–23. Print.

Ivie, Larry. "The Original Captain Marvel." *Larry Ivie's Monsters and Heroes: The Magazine of Pictorial Imagination* no. 4 (March 1969): 18–28. Print.

Jack Smith and the Destruction of Atlantis. Dir. Mary Jordan. Tongue Press/Monk Media, 2006. Film.

Jacobs, Will, and Gerard Jones. *The Comic Book Heroes from the Silver Age to the Present*. New York: Crown Publishers, 1985. Print.

Jameson, Fredric. *The Cultural Turn: Selected Writings on the Postmodern, 1983–1998*. London: Verso, 1998. Print.

Jarvis, Eric. "The Comic Strip *Pogo* and the Issue of Race." *Studies in American Culture* vol. 21, no. 2 (1998): 85–94. Print.

Johnson, Charles. Foreword. *Black Images in the Comics: A Visual History*. By Fredrik Strömberg. Seattle: Fantagraphics Books, 2003: 5–19. Print.

Johnson, Richard. "Re: Help on Tertullian." Message to the author, August 21, 2014. E-mail.

Jones, Gerard. *Men of Tomorrow: Geeks, Gangsters, and the Birth of the Comic Book*. New York: Basic Books, 2004. Print.

Kafka, Franz. *The Complete Stories*. New York: Schocken Books, 1971. Print.

Keller, Barry. "Don Newton: 'He Showed Us How to Do It Right.'" *Back Issue* vol. 1, no. 19 (December 2006): 50–66. Print.

Keller, David H. "The Revolt of the Pedestrians." *Amazing Stories: 60 Years of the Best Science Fiction*. Eds. Isaac Asimov and Martin H. Greenberg. Lake Geneva, WI: TSR, 1985: 9–27. Print.

Kempner, Mary Jean. "'Not a cynic in the class': Youthbuilders, Inc., a Children's Forum Which Allows Action to Speak as Loudly as Words." *Vogue* (incorporating *Vanity Fair*), March 1, 1946. From the Papers of the NAACP, Richard J. Daley Library, University of Illinois Chicago.

Kerouac, Jack. "Jack Kerouac on *The Steve Allen Show* with Steve Allen 1959." *Historic Films Stock Archive Footage.* YouTube, January 12, 2015. Web. December 2, 2015.

——. *Visions of Cody.* New York: McGraw-Hill Book Company, 1972. Print.

Kerr, Adelaide. "Youth Builders Organize to Work for Better World." *Spokane Daily Chronicle,* September 3, 1947: 13. Print.

Khoury, George, ed. *Kimota! The Miracleman Companion.* Raleigh: TwoMorrows Publishing, 2001. Print.

Kidd, Chip, and Geoff Spear. *Shazam! The Golden Age of the World's Mightiest Mortal.* New York: Abrams Comicarts, 2010. Print.

Kimmel, Michael. *Manhood in America: A Cultural History.* New York: Free Press, 1996.

Koolhaas, Rem. *Delirious New York.* New York: Monacelli Press, 1994. Print.

Kurtzman, Harvey, with Michael Barrier. *From Aargh! to Zap!: Harvey Kurtzman's Visual History of the Comics.* New York: Prentice Hall, 1991. Print.

Kurtzman, Harvey, and Wally Wood. "Superduperman." *Mad* no. 4 (April–May 1953): 1–8. Reprinted in Kurtzman and Barrier 48–49. Print.

Lacy, Norris J., ed. *The Fortunes of King Arthur.* Cambridge: D. S. Brewer, 2005. Print.

Lage, Matt. "'Visual Expression': Will Lieberson—Fawcett Comics Executive Editor." *Fawcett Companion: The Best of FCA.* Ed. P. C. Hamerlinck. Raleigh: TwoMorrows Publishing, 2001: 92–97. Print.

——. "'We Were More or Less Inspired': Otto Binder: An Interview with Captain Marvel's Mightiest Writer." *Fawcett Companion: The Best of FCA.* Ed. P. C. Hamerlinck. Raleigh: TwoMorrows Publishing, 2001: 59–64. Print.

Lance, Jacqueline. "*The Great Gatsby*: Driving to Destruction with the Rich and Careless at the Wheel." *Studies in American Culture* vol. 23, no. 2 (October 2000): 25–35. Print.

Lanier, Sidney. *The Boy's King Arthur: Sir Thomas Malory's History of King Arthur and His Knights of the Round Table.* Illustrated by N. C. Wyeth. New York: Charles Scribner's Sons, 1950. Print.

Laubscher, Leswin. "Of Odysseus and Abraham: Nostalgia, *heimweë*, and the Ways (of) Home." *Peace and Conflict: Journal of Peace Psychology* vol. 18, no. 3 (August 2012): 214–24. Print.

Let There Be Light. Dir. John Huston. US Army, 1946 (released 1981). Film.

Lieberson, Will. Interview with Matt Lage. "'Visual Expression': Will Lieberson—Fawcett Comics Executive Editor." *Fawcett Companion: The Best of FCA (Fawcett Collectors of America).* Ed. P. C. Hamerlinck. Raleigh: TwoMorrows Publishing, 2001: 92–97. Print.

Light, Alan, Bruce Hamilton, and Murray Bishoff. *Special Edition Series 1: A Complete Collection of Captain Marvel Adventures from* Whiz Comics *7–28.* East Moline, IL: Special Edition Reprints, 1974. Print.

Lott, Eric. *Love and Theft: Blackface Minstrelsy and the American Working Class.* New York: Oxford University Press, 2013. Print.

Lupack, Alan, and Barbara Tepa Lupack. *King Arthur in America.* Cambridge: D. S. Brewer, 1999. Print.

Lupoff, Pat. "Those Were the Good Old Days." *The Best of Xero.* Eds. Pat Lupoff and Dick Lupoff. San Francisco: Tachyon Publications, 2004: 33–35. Print.

Lupoff, Pat, and Dick Lupoff, eds. *The Best of Xero.* San Francisco: Tachyon Publications, 2004. Print.

Lupoff, Richard. "The Big Red Cheese." *All in Color for a Dime.* Eds. Dick Lupoff and Don Thompson. New Rochelle, NY: Arlington House, 1970. 66–95. Print.

Lupoff, Richard and Don Thompson (Eds). *All in Color for a Dime.* New Rochelle, NY: 1970. Print.

Lupoff, Richard A. "Introduction: Binder, Rhymes with Tinder." *Words of Wonder: The Life and Times of Otto Binder*. By Bill Schelly. Seattle: Hamster Press, 2003: 7–14. Print.

———. "We Didn't Know What We Were Doing." *The Best of Xero*. Eds. Pat Lupoff and Dick Lupoff. San Francisco: Tachyon Publications, 2004: 12–32. Print.

MacPhee, Laurence E. "*The Great Gatsby*'s 'Romance of Motoring': Nick Carraway and Jordan Baker." *Modern Fiction Studies* no. 18 (Summer 1972): 207–212. Print.

Maheras, Russ. "Gene Simmons and KISS: Channeling One's Inner Superhero." *The Hooded Utilitarian*, April 29, 2013 (5:17 a.m.). Web. December 15, 2015.

Maris, Don. "Notes from a Comic Book Freak." *The Best of Captain Marvel*. Norman, OK: Self-published, 1975: inside front cover. Print. (Note: The cover of this collection includes the title *The Best of*, then a caption that reads *Captain Marvel Rides the Engine of Doom*. I have listed its title as *The Best of Captain Marvel* to assist those looking for copies. In the text itself, I often refer to the collection as Maris's "best of.")

Marcuse, Herbert. *One-Dimensional Man*. Boston: Beacon Press, 1964. Print.

Marja, Fern. "Youthbuilders' Lounge Aids Fight Against Delinquency." *New York Post*, Home News, July 28, 1948. From the Papers of the NAACP, Richard J. Daley Library, University of Illinois Chicago.

———. "Youthbuilders Teach Kids to Use Tools of Democracy." *New York Post*, Home News, July 27, 1948. From the Papers of the NAACP, Richard J. Daley Library, University of Illinois Chicago.

———. "Youthbuilders Units Study, Then Act on Civic Issues." *New York Post*, Home News, July 27, 1948. From the Papers of the NAACP, Richard J. Daley Library, University of Illinois Chicago.

The Master. Dir. Paul Thomas Anderson. The Weinstein Company/Annapurna Pictures/Ghoulardi Film Company, 2012. Film.

Matt, Susan J. *Homesickness: An American History*. New York: Oxford University Press, 2011. Print.

Mauldin, Bill. *Back Home*. New York: William Sloane Associates, 1947.

———. *Up Front*. New York: Henry Holt, 1945. Print.

McCann, Willis H. "Nostalgia: A Review of the Literature." *Psychological Bulletin* vol. 38, no. 3 (March 1941): 165–82. Print.

McCarthy, Tom. *Auto Mania: Cars, Consumers, and the Environment*. New Haven: Yale University Press, 2007. Print.

McCloud, Scott. *Understanding Comics: The Invisible Art*. New York: Harper Perennial, 1993. Print.

McComas, J. Francis. Letter to Otto Binder, April 24, 1953. TS. Cushing Memorial Library and Archives, Texas A&M University.

———. Letter to Otto Binder, July 30, 1953. TS. Cushing Memorial Library and Archives, Texas A&M University.

McDermott, Sinead. "Future-Perfect: Gender, Nostalgia, and the Not Yet Presented in Marilynne Robinson's *Housekeeping*." *Journal of Gender Studies* vol. 13, no. 3 (November 2004): 259–70. Print.

McNally, John J. "Boats and Automobiles in *The Great Gatsby*: Symbols of Drift and Death." *Husson Review: A Journal of Business and the Liberal Arts* vol. 5, no. 1 (January 1971): 11–17. Print.

Mendelson, Edward. "Possum Pastoral." *Phi Beta Pogo*. Eds. Mrs. Walt Kelly and Bill Crouch, Jr. New York: Fireside, 1989: 15–20. Print.

Micheaux, Oscar. *The Case of Mrs. Wingate*. New York: Book Supply Company, 1945. Print.

Miller, Arthur. *Death of a Salesman*. New York: Viking Press, 1981. Print.

Mills, Charles W. *Blackness Visible: Essays on Philosophy and Race*. Ithaca: Cornell University Press, 1998. Print.

Mom, Gijs. *The Electric Vehicle: Technology and Expectations in the Automobile Age*. Baltimore: Johns Hopkins University Press, 2004. Print.

Moskowitz, Sam. *Seekers of Tomorrow: Masters of Modern Science Fiction*. New York: Ballantine Books, 1967. Print.

———, ed. *The Coming of the Robots*. New York: Collier Books, 1963.

Moore, Anne Elizabeth. "Be a Zinester: How and Why to Publish Your Own Periodical." *Fall of Autumn*. N.d. Web. December 1, 2015.

Moore, Alan. "Alan Moore's Original Proposal." *Kimota! The Miracleman Companion*. Ed. George Khoury. Raleigh: TwoMorrows Publishing, 2001: 24–29. Print.

———. *Chain Reaction: Alan Moore Interviews Brian Eno*. *Chain Reaction*, episode 6, series 5 (2011). Interview recorded for BBC Radio 4, December 14, 2004. MP3.

———. "Indoor Thunder: Landscaping the Future with Brian Eno." *Arthur* (July 2005): 29, 34. Print.

———. Letter to the author, 2013. MS.

———. "M*****man: Full Story and Pics." *Miracleman* no. 2. Guerneville, CA: Eclipse Comics (October 1985): 15, 31. Print.

———, writer. Garry Leach, artist. G. George, letters. Dez Skinn, editor. *Miracleman* no. 1. Guerneville, CA: Eclipse Comics (August 1985). Print.

———, writer. Garry Leach, artist. *Miracleman* no. 2. Guerneville, CA: Eclipse Comics (October 1985). Print.

———, writer. Alan Davis, artist. Ron Courtney, colors. Dez Skinn, editor. *Miracleman* no. 3. Guerneville, CA: Eclipse Comics (November) 1985. Print.

———, writer. Alan Davis, artist. *Miracleman* no. 5. Guerneville, CA: Eclipse Comics (January 1986). Print.

———, writer. Chuck Beckum, artist. Wayne Truman, letters. Ron Courtney, colors. *Miracleman* no. 6. Guerneville, CA: Eclipse Comics (February 1986). Print.

———, writer. John Totleben, artist. Sam Parsons, colors. Wayne Truman, letters. Letitia Glozer, editor. *Miracleman* no. 14. Forestville, CA: Eclipse Comics (April 1988). Print.

———, writer. John Totleben, artist. Sam Parsons, colors. Wayne Truman, letters. Letitia Glozer, editor. *Miracleman* no. 16. Forestville, CA: Eclipse Comics (December 1989). Print.

Morrison, Grant. *Supergods: What Masked Vigilantes, Miraculous Mutants, and a Sun God from Smallville Can Teach Us About Being Human*. New York: Spiegel & Grau, 2012. Print.

———, writer. Cameron Stewart, artist. Nathan Fairbairn, colors. Steve Wands, letters. Rickey Purdin, editor. Eddie Berganza, group editor. "Captain Marvel and The Day That Never Was!" *The Multiversity: New Thunderworld Adventures* no. 1. New York: DC Comics, February 2015. Print.

Morrison, Toni. *Playing in the Dark: Whiteness and the Literary Imagination*. New York: Vintage Books, 1992. Print.

Murray, Christopher. *Champions of the Oppressed: Superhero Comics, Popular Culture, and Propaganda in America During World War II*. Cresskill: Hampton Press, 2011. Print.

Nama, Adilifu. *Super Black: American Pop Culture and Black Superheroes*. Austin: University of Texas Press, 2011. Print.

"Negro Villain in Comic Book Killed by Youngsters." Credited to the Associated Negro Press (ANP). *Chicago Defender*, National Edition, May 5, 1945: 11. ProQuest Historical Newspapers. Clipping courtesy of Qiana Whitted.

Nelson, Scott Reynolds. *Steel Drivin' Man: John Henry, the Untold Story of An American Legend*. New York: Oxford University Press, 2006. Print.

Newton, Don. "The 'New' Captain Marvel." *FCA (Fawcett Collectors of America)/SOB* vol. 14, no. 3 (August 1980): N.p. Courtesy of the Comic Art Collection, Michigan State University.

Nyberg, Amy Kiste. *Seal of Approval: The History of the Comics Code*. Jackson: University Press of Mississippi, 1998. Print.

Ó Méalóid, Pádraig. "Alan Moore Speaks about Marvelman." Posted in three installments on *The Beat: The News Blog of Comics Culture*, October 21, 23, and 25, 2013. Web. December 9, 2015.

———. "Alan Moore and Superfolks." Posted in three installments on *The Beat: The News Blog of Comics Culture*, October 25 and November 11 and 18, 2012. Web. December 9, 2015.

———. "Poisoned Chalice: The Extremely Long and Incredibly Complex Story of Marvelman." *The Beat: The News Blog of Comics Culture*. The series began on February 10 and continued until June 9, 2013. Web. December 9, 2015.

O'Neil, Denny. *The Super Comics: From Popeye to the Incredible Hulk*. New York: Scholastic Books Services, 1980. Print.

———, writer. C. C. Beck, artist. *Shazam!* vol. 1, no. 1. Edited by Julius Schwartz. New York: National Periodical Publications, Inc. (February 1973). Print.

———. "The Troubles of the Talking Tiger." *Shazam!* vol. 1, no. 7. New York: National Periodical Publications, Inc. (November 1973): 1–8. Print.

———, writer. Jack Kirby, penciller. Mike Royer, letters and ink. "The Skywalker." *Justice, Inc.* vol. 1, no. 2. New York: National Periodical Publications, Inc. (July–Aug. 1975). Print.

Ordway, Jerry, writer and artist. John Costanza, letters. *The Power of Shazam!* New York: DC Comics, 1994. Print.

Ottum, Bob, and Kurt Schaffenberger (misidentified on the title page as *Shafenburger*), *Shazam! A Circus Adventure*. Racine, WI: Golden Press/Western Publishing Company, 1977. Print.

"Oust 'Steamboat' from Comic Strip." Credited to the Associated Negro Press (ANP). *Atlanta Daily World* vol. 17, no. 237 (May 4, 1945): 1. Print.

Overstreet, Robert M. *The Comic Book Price Guide* no. 15 (1985–86). New York: Harmony Books, 1985. Print.

Oyola, Osvaldo. "On Collecting Comics & Critical Nostalgia." *The Middle Spaces*, July 8, 2014. Web. December 9, 2015.

Padovano, Chris. Interview with C. C. Beck. *Fan* (1977): N.p. Print.

"The Park Robberies." *The Shazam Archives* vol. 4. New York: DC Comics, 2003: 174–94. Print.

Parker, Bill. Trial tr. *Detective Comics, Inc. and Superman, Inc. vs. Fawcett Publications, Inc., Republic Pictures Corporation, and Republic Productions, Inc.* New York, March 18 and 19. United States District Court S.D. New York. National Archives, New York City.

Parker, Bill, and C. C. Beck. "Introducing Captain Marvel." *Shazam! The Greatest Stories Ever Told*. New York: DC Comics, 2008. 8–20. Print.

Parker, Elsie S., ed. "Youthbuilders' Experiment." *National Municipal Review* vol. 37, no. 7 (July 1948): 391–92. Print.

Pierce, John G. "C. C. Beck: An American Original." *Comics Buyer's Guide* no. 840 (December 22, 1989): 27–28, 30, 32. Print.

———. "Levity, Learning, and Lightning Bolts." *The Golden Age of Comics* no. 1 (1982): 71–78. Print.

———. "'One of the Most Real Characters Ever to Appear': An Analysis of Mr. Tawny." *Fawcett Companion: The Best of FCA (Fawcett Collectors of America)*. Ed. P. C. Hamerlinck. Raleigh: TwoMorrows Publishing, 2001. 31. Print.

Pini, Wendy, writer and artist. Richard Pini, writer and letters. *Elfquest* vol. 1, no. 7 (May 1980). Print.

Pollard, Tomas Glover. "Playing a Terrible Game of Pretend: Masculine Performance and Gender Humor in the World War II Novels of Heller, Vonnegut, Pynchon, and Weaver." Ph.D. dissertation, Texas A&M University, 2003. Print.

Powell, Matthew T. "Bestial Representations of Otherness: Kafka's Animal Stories." *Journal of Modern Literature* vol. 32, no. 1 (Fall 2008): 129–42. Print.

Pyle, Howard. *The Story of King Arthur and His Knights*. New York: Signet/New American Library, 1986. Print.

Radway, Janice. "Zines, Half-Lives, and Afterlives: On the Temporalities of Social and Political Change." *PMLA* vol. 126, no. 1 (January 2011): 140–150. Print.

Rae, John B. *The American Automobile Industry*. Boston: Twayne Publishers, 1984. Print.

Richards, Chris. "Alan Moore." *The Art of Dismantling: A Radical Artisan Collective and Ongoing Interview Series*. March 17, 2011. Web. June 22, 2014.

Ritivoi, Andreea Deciu. *Yesterday's Self: Nostalgia and the Immigrant Identity*. Lanham, Maryland: Rowman & Littlefield, 2002. Print.

Robeson, Kenneth (pseudonym for Paul Ernst). *The Avenger #3: The Sky Walker*. New York: Warner Paperback Library, 1967. Print.

Robbins, Trina. "C. C. Beck; An Appreciation." (N.d., probably late 1989). TS. Collection of Trina Robbins, San Francisco.

———. Interview in the BBC documentary *The Comic Strip Hero*. Batmite's Superhero Channel. YouTube, February 5, 2009. Web. December 9, 2015.

The Rocket's Blast/Comicollector no. 91 (N.d., early 1970s.) Print.

Rodgers, Thomas E. "Billy Yank and G.I. Joe: An Exploratory Essay on the Sociopolitical Dimensions of Soldier Motivation." *Journal of Military History* vol. 69, no. 1 (January 2005): 93–121. Print.

Roediger, David R. *The Wages of Whiteness: Race and the Making of the American Working Class*. London: Verso, 1991. Print.

Routledge, Clay, Constantine Sedikides, Tim Wildschut, and Jacob Juhl. "Finding Meaning in One's Past: Nostalgia as an Existential Resource." *The Psychology of Meaning*. Eds. Keith D. Markman, Travis Proulx, and Matthew J. Lindberg. Washington, DC: American Psychological Association, 2013: 297–316. Print.

Routledge, Clay, et al. "The Past Makes the Present Meaningful: Nostalgia as an Existential Resource." *Journal of Personality and Social Psychology* vol. 101, no. 3 (September 2011): 638–52. Print.

Rutherford, Jana. "What Is Old Is New Again: The Role of Discontinuity in Nostalgia-Related Consumption." Dissertation, Florida Atlantic University, 2011. Print.

Rutherford, Jana, and Eric H. Shaw. "What Was Old Is New Again: The History of Nostalgia as a Buying Motive in Consumer Behavior." Presentation at the 15th Annual Biennial Conference on Historical Analysis and Research in Marketing (CHARM), May 19–22, 2011.

"Sabra Holbrook to Direct Panel." *Nassau Daily Review-Star*, March 23, 1945: 17. Print.

Said, Edward. *Orientalism*. New York: Vintage Books, 1994. Print.

Saunders, Ben. *Do the Gods Wear Capes?: Spirituality, Fantasy, and Superheroes*. New York: Continuum, 2011. Print.

Schatz, Brandon. "DC Movie Casting: Dwayne 'The Rock' Johnson Says Something About Something." *The Beat: The News Blog of Comics Culture*, July 22, 2014. Web. December 9, 2015.

Schelly, Bill. *The Golden Age of Comic Fandom*. Seattle: Hamster Press, 2003. Print.

———. *Words of Wonder: The Life and Times of Otto Binder*. Seattle: Hamster Press, 2003. Print.

Schwartz, Delmore. *In Dreams Begin Responsibilities and Other Stories*. New York: New Directions, 1978. Print.

———. *Selected Poems, 1938–1958: Summer Knowledge*. New York: New Directions, 1959. Print.

Sebald, W. G. *On the Natural History of Destruction*. Trans. Anthea Bell. New York: Modern Library, 2003. Print.

Sedikides, Constantine, et al. "Nostalgia: Past, Present, and Future." *Current Directions in Psychological Science* vol. 17, no. 5 (October 2008): 304–307. Print.

Seifert, Mark. "Now You Know: The Car on the Cover of *Action Comics* #1 Is a 1937 DeSoto (But That's Just Part of the Story)." *Bleeding Cool*, May 24, 2013. Web. 9 December 2015.

Sharpe, Sam. "Mom" in *Viewotron* no. 2. Chicago: Radiator Comics and Viewotron Press, Spring 2015 (second printing). Print.

Shaw, Bruce. *The Animal Fable in Science Fiction and Fantasy*. Jefferson: McFarland, 2010. Print.

The Shazam Archives vol. 4. New York: DC Comics, 2003. Print.

"Shazam Captain Marvel Club." November 1945. Included in Don Maris, *The Best of Captain Marvel*. Norman, OK: Self-published, 1975: N.p. Print.

Shazam! A Celebration of 75 Years. New York: DC Comics, 2015. Print.

Shazam! The Greatest Stories Ever Told. New York: DC Comics, 2008. Print.

Shklovsky, Victor. "Art as Technique." Trans. Lee T. Lemon and Marion Reis. *The Critical Tradition: Classic Texts and Contemporary Trends*. Ed. David H. Richter. New York: Bedford Books, 1989: 738–48. Print.

Showcase Presents Shazam! vol. 1. New York: DC Comics, 2006. Print.

Shukert, Elfrieda Berthiaume, and Barbara Smith Scibetta. *War Brides of World War II*. Novato, CA: Presidio Press, 1988. Print.

Siegel, Jerry, and Joe Shuster. *The Superman Chronicles* vol. 1. New York: DC Comics, 2006. Print.

Simmel, Georg. *On Individuality and Social Forms: Selected Writings*. Chicago: University of Chicago Press, 1971. Print.

Simmon, Scott. "*Let There Be Light* (1946) and Its Restoration." *National Film Preservation Foundation*, 2012. Web. December 9, 2015.

Simon, Joe, with Jim Simon. *The Comic Book Makers*. New York: Crestwood/II Publications, 1990. Print.

Singer, Marc. "'Black Skins' and White Masks: Comic Books and the Secret of Race." *African American Review* vol. 36, no. 1 (2002): 107–119. Print.

Singer, Robert. "One Against All: The New England Past and Present Responsibilities in *The Devil and Daniel Webster*." *Literature Film Quarterly* vol. 22, no. 4 (1994): 265–71. Print.

Smith, Erin A. *Hard-Boiled: Working Class Readers and Pulp Magazines*. Philadelphia: Temple University Press, 2000. Print.

Smith, Jack. *Wait for Me at the Bottom of the Pool: The Writings of Jack Smith*. Eds. J. Hoberman and Edward Leffingwell. New York: High Risk Books, 1997. Print.

Smith, Jeff, writer and artist. Steve Hamaker, colors. *Shazam! The Monster Society of Evil*. New York: DC Comics, 2009. Print.

Smith, Zack. "An Oral History of Captain Marvel." Posted in a series of installments on *Newsarama*, December 24, 2010, to February 25, 2011. Web. December 9, 2015.

Smoak, Shelby. "Framing the Automobile in 20th Century American Literature: A Spatial Approach." Dissertation, University of North Carolina, Greensboro, 2007. Print.

Sontag, Susan. *Against Interpretation and Other Essays*. New York: Picador, 1966. Print.

———. *On Photography*. New York: Picador, 1977. Print.

Soper, Kerry D. *We Go Pogo: Walt Kelly, Politics, and American Satire*. Jackson: University Press of Mississippi, 2012. Print.

Spencer, Amy. *DIY: The Rise of Lo-Fi Culture*. London: Marion Boyars, 2008. Print.

Spiegelman, Art. *MetaMaus*. New York: Pantheon, 2011. Print.

Spiegelman, Art, and Françoise Mouly, eds. *The TOON Treasury of Classic Children's Comics*. New York: Abrams Comicarts, 2009. Print.

Starlin, Jim. *The Life and Death of Captain Marvel*. New York: Marvel Comics, 2002. Print.

Steiner, George. *Nostalgia for the Absolute*. Toronto: House of Anansi Press, 1997. Print.

———. *Real Presences*. Chicago: University of Chicago Press, 1991. Print.

Steranko, Jim. *The Steranko History of Comics 2*. Reading: Supergraphics, 1972. Print.

Strömberg, Fredrik. *Black Images in the Comics: A Visual History*. Seattle: Fantagraphics Books, 2003. Print.

Surles, A. D. Memo to Commanding General, Army Ground Forces, War Department. "Subject: Assistance for Army Emergency Relief Campaign," April 22, 1942. TS. National Archives and Records Administration, Washington, DC.

Swayze, Marc. "We Didn't Know . . . It Was the Golden Age!" *Alter Ego* no. 98/*P. C. Hamerlinck's Fawcett Collectors of America* no. 157 (December 2010): 74–76. Print.

Taylor, Yuval, and Jake Austen. *Darkest America: Black Minstrelsy from Slavery to Hip-Hop*. New York: W. W. Norton, 2012. Print.

Tarkington, Booth. *The Magnificent Ambersons*. New York: Charles Scribner's Sons, 1920. Print.

"Tawky Tawny Chronology." *Unofficial Guide to the DC Universe*, n.d. Web. December 15, 2015.

Thirty-Third Annual Report of the Board of Gas and Electric Light Commissioners of the Commonwealth of Massachusetts. Boston: Wright & Potter, 1918. Web. December 2, 2015.

Thomas, Roy, writer. Barry Smith, artist. Dan Adkins, inks. Sam Rosen, letters. Stan Lee, editor. "The Coming of Conan!" *Conan the Barbarian* vol. 1, no. 1. New York: Marvel Comics (October 1970). Print.

Thomas, Roy. "One Man's Family: The Saga of the Mighty Marvels." *Alter Ego: The Best of the Legendary Comics Fanzine*. Eds. Roy Thomas and Bill Schelly. Raleigh: TwoMorrows Publishing, 2008: 102–109. Print.

———. "Tawny Tiger, Burning Bright . . ." *Alter Ego: The Best of the Legendary Comics Fanzine*. Eds. Roy Thomas and Bill Schelly. Raleigh: TwoMorrows Publishing, 2008: 144-46. Print.

———. "With One Magic Word . . ." *Secret Origins* no. 3. New York: DC Comics (June 1986): n.p. Print.

Thomas, Roy, and Bill Schelly, eds. *Alter Ego: The Best of the Legendary Comics Fanzine*. Raleigh: TwoMorrows Publishing, 2008. Print.

Thompson, Don, and Maggie Thompson. "All in Color for a Dime." Editorial. *The Golden Age of Comics* no. 1 (1982): 4. Print.

Thompson, Kim. "The Golden Thread." *Critters* no. 1 (June 1986). Fantagraphics Books. Inner front cover and 32–33. Print.

Thompson, Maggie. "C. C. Beck Dies: Famed as 'Captain Marvel' artist." *Comics Buyer's Guide* no. 839 (December 15, 1989): 1, 3. Print.

Thompson, Terry W. "'He Sprang the Machine': 'The Secret [Technological] Life of Walter Mitty.'" *South Carolina Review* vol. 41, no. 1 (Fall 2008): 110–15. Print.

Thurber, James. *The Thurber Carnival*. New York: Modern Library, 1957. Print.

Tierney, John. "What Is Nostalgia Good For? Quite a Bit, Research Shows." *New York Times*, July 8, 2013. Web. October 14, 2013.

Tilley, Carol L. "Seducing the Innocent: Fredric Wertham and the Falsifications That Helped Condemn Comics." *Information & Culture* vol. 47, no. 4 (2012): 383–413. Print.

Tye, Larry. *Superman: The High-Flying History of America's Most Enduring Hero*. New York: Random House, 2012. Print.

Uslan, Michael E. *The Boy Who Loved Batman*. San Francisco: Chronicle Books, 2011. Print.

———. "When Titans Clash . . . in Court!" *The Amazing World of DC Comics* vol. 5, no. 16 (April 1978): 6–10. Print.

Van Hise, James, ed. *Pulp Masters*. Self-published (revised edition, February 2002). Print.

Walker, Richard W., and John J. Skowronski. "Autobiographical Memory and the Creation of Meaning from Personally Experienced Events." *The Psychology of Meaning*. Eds. Keith D. Markman, Travis Proulx, and Matthew J. Lindberg. Washington, DC: American Psychological Association, 2013: 149–170. Print.

Weiner, Robert G. "'Okay, Axis, Here We Come!' Captain America and the Superhero Teams From World War II and the Cold War." *The Gospel According to Superheroes: Religion and Popular Culture*. Ed. B. J. Oropeza. New York: Peter Lang, 2008: 83–101. Print.

Wertham, Fredric. *The World of Fanzines: A Special Form of Communication*. Carbondale, IL: Southern Illinois University Press, 1973.

Wharton, Edith, and Ogden Codman, Jr. *The Decoration of Houses*. New York: W. W. Norton, 1998. Print.

Whitted, Qiana. "'And the Negro thinks in hieroglyphics': Comics, Visual Metonymy, and the Spectacle of Blackness." *Journal of Graphic Novels and Comics* vol. 5, no. 1 (2014): 79–100. Print.

Williams, Martin. "About 'Captain Marvel' and C. C. Beck." *A Smithsonian Book of Comic-Book Comics*. Eds. Michael Barrier and Martin Williams. New York: Smithsonian Institution Press and Harry N. Abrams, 1981: 79–80. Print.

Wilson, Derek. "From Shazam! to Kimota!: The Sensational Story of England's Marvelman—The Hero Who Would Become Miracleman." *Alter Ego* vol. 3, no. 87 (July 2009): 4–15. Print.

Witek, Joseph. *Comic Books as History: The Narrative Art of Jack Jackson, Art Spiegelman, and Harvey Pekar*. Jackson: University Press of Mississippi, 1989. Print.

Wolf, Jaime. "Captain Marvel, C. C. Beck, and the Comics-Fan Subculture." *The New Yorker*, March 28, 2011. Web. December 9, 2015.

Wood, Edward W., Jr. *Worshipping the Myths of World War II: Reflections on America's Dedication to War.* Washington, DC: Potomac Books, 2006. Print.

"World We Want to Live In Topic at Bateman PTA." *Chicago Sunday Tribune,* March 18, 1945: part 3, 3. Print.

World's Finest Comics no. 253 (October–November 1978). New York: DC Comics. Print.

Wright, Bradford W. *Comic Book Nation: The Transformation of Youth Culture in America.* Baltimore: Johns Hopkins University Press, 2001. Print.

Yancy, George. *Look, a White! Philosophical Essays on Whiteness.* Philadelphia: Temple University Press, 2012. Print.

"Youthbuilders, Inc." *Time* vol. 35, no. 21 (May 20, 1940): 60. Print.

Zhou, Xinyue, Tim Wildschut, Constantine Sedikides, Xiaoxi Chen, and Ad J. J. M. Vingerhoets. "Heartwarming Memories: Nostalgia Maintains Physiological Comfort." *Emotion* vol. 12, no. 4 (August 2012): 678–84. Print.

COURT DOCUMENTS

I have included Beck's deposition as well as his and Parker's 1948 courtroom testimony in the Works Cited. The following are the relevant rulings in the *National v. Fawcett* case:

Detective Comics, Inc., et al. v. Fawcett Publications, Inc., et al., 4 F.R.D. 237. District Court, S.D. New York. November 24, 1944. Westlaw. Web. June 2014.

National Comics Publications, Inc. v. Fawcett Publications, Inc., et al., 93 F.Supp. 349. United States District Court S.D. New York. April 10, 1950. On Motion for Retaxation June 23, 1950. Judge Alfred Conkling Coxe, Jr. Westlaw. Web. June 2014.

National Comics Publications, Inc. v. Fawcett Publications, Inc., et al., 191 F.2d 594. United States Second Circuit Court of Appeals. August 30, 1951. Judge Learned Hand (writing for Judges Hand, Chase, and Frank). Westlaw. Web. June 2014.

National Comics Publications, Inc. v. Fawcett Publications, Inc., 198 F.2d 927. United States Second Circuit Court of Appeals. September 5, 1952. Judge Learned Hand (writing for Judges Hand, Chase, and Frank). Westlaw. Web. June 2014.

The depositions and trial transcripts related to the case are housed at the National Archives in New York City. To access these materials, request the records for United States District Court Southern District of New York (SDNY) Docket No. Civ 15–383.

INDEX

CPSIA information can be obtained
at www.ICGtesting.com
Printed in the USA
BVOW04*0445231116
468671BV00002B/3/P